BETRAYED

CHILD SEX ABUSE IN THE HOLOCAUST

Beverley Chalmers (DSc (Med); PhD)

Grosvenor House
Publishing Limited

The right of Beverley Chalmers to be identified as the author of this
work has been asserted in accordance with Section 78
of the Copyright, Designs and Patents Act 1988

The book cover is copyright to Beverley Chalmers
The front cover image is credited to:
www.istockphoto.com/gb/portfolio/baona

This book is published by
Grosvenor House Publishing Ltd
Link House
140 The Broadway, Tolworth, Surrey, KT6 7HT.
www.grosvenorhousepublishing.co.uk

A CIP record for this book
is available from the British Library

ISBN 978-1-83975-021-2

DEDICATION

To the children who were sexually abused during the Nazi era

To the children who survived the Holocaust and those who did not

To my own children and to theirs

ACKNOWLEDGEMENTS

Multiple people have contributed to the writing of this book in both direct and indirect ways. My husband, Bernie, as always, has been steadfast in his support, astute in his critical reviews of multiple drafts, and endlessly patient in his willingness to accommodate my dedication to long hours of work at unpredictable and, often, inopportune times. For the past sixteen years, he has not only tolerated, but accepted and encouraged, my single-minded determination to immerse myself in the inestimable horror of children's (and women's) experiences of sexual abuse in the Holocaust. For the past fifty years he has been my best friend, my constant companion, my mentor, my support, and my inspiration. My sincerest thanks are an inadequate expression of my immense gratitude and love.

Our three daughters, and their children, are a constant reminder of just how precious children are. I have had to constantly ward off thoughts of them while writing about the sexual abuse of those children who lived through the Nazi era.

On an academic level I am indebted to the many who reviewed drafts of this manuscript, discussed issues related to the book endlessly with me, challenged me when developing the primary theses addressed in the text, assisted with structuring and restructuring the narrative, not once but through multiple drafts, and contributed detailed editorial comments. Noam Rachmilevitch of the Ghetto Fighters House Archives in Israel encouraged me, facilitated my research, provided incredibly valuable sources, gave generously of his time on a number of occasions, and carefully reviewed an early draft of the text. He restored my faith in, and appreciation of, the incredibly important role of archivists. I am grateful to Prof Dan Kaznelson, and Dr. Tessa Chelouche, both of Israel, whose interests lie primarily in Medicine and the Holocaust, who carefully reviewed penultimate drafts of the book, and gave me valuable leads to follow. Archivists Haim Cohen, Hani Gat and Margalit Shlain who did their best to assist me to access testimonies, and Ora Gluck, who helped me find sources and encouraged me when I encountered obstacles. My thanks also go to Shula and Abraham Werner, both survivors, who have always supported my work, facilitated valuable contacts for me, provided a second home for me and my family in Israel for some decades, and offered me invaluable and much appreciated acceptance, love and friendship.

My sincerest thanks go to Dr. Dana Solomon and Simon Solomon for their critical reviews of the multiple drafts of this book. As some of my fiercest critics – steeped in Holocaust and Genocidal studies – they challenged me to achieve new heights and to overcome what appeared to be insuperable obstacles at the time. In addition, I gratefully acknowledge the precise and critical editorial skills, as well as typesetting and publication preparations provided by D-Editions. I would be lost without them.

Last but not least, I acknowledge the children whose testimonies and memoirs are recounted in this book as well as the many who could not report on their experiences. Their bravery and courage in reporting on their experiences of sexual abuse is the foundation on which this book is based. It is written in their honour.

Contents

CHAPTER 1: A TABOO SUBJECT

Jewish children were sexually abused during the Nazi era, although acknowledging this is taboo. Nazi ideology, while advocating killing children, did not promote child sex abuse directly, but facilitated such abuse indirectly through its total destruction of Jewish family life with its normal safeguards for child safety. Antisemitic Nazi policy established Jews as legitimate targets for extermination, targeted children as primary subjects for eradication, and destroyed Jewish families. As a result, children were left vulnerable and unprotected from sexual abuse in homes, villages, ghettos, camps, and hiding places, while those in authority turned a blind eye when Jewish children were sexually assaulted or murdered. Their sexual abuse was then hidden by perpetrators, the children, survivors, rescuers, and Holocaust scholars. This book provides evidence of multiple acts of sexual abuse of Jewish children during all stages of the Holocaust, and shines a spotlight on the voices of these children that have, to date, been shrouded in silence. As Rosen says: "Given the standard of inhumanity set by the Third Reich, the sexual abuse of hidden children can surprise us only because it is the one atrocity that hasn't really come to light after all these years."[1]

Perpetrators were ordinary people who were also Nazis, members of the SS, *Einsatzgruppen* members, *Wehrmacht* soldiers, their allies in occupied countries, Russian soldiers at the end of the war, as well as rescuers of children who were hidden, in Europe, and those who offered homes to children who were sent to "safety" in countries beyond Europe's borders. The majority of abusers were Gentiles: a handful were Jewish. Few of the perpetrators reported in this book – unlike most of the perpetrators of child sex abuse of children today – followed the well acknowledged pedophilic pattern of grooming children for sexual abuse. For most perpetrators, sexual assault was a

1

crime of opportunity, authority and violence, often coupled with anti-semitic justification, and occasionally, religious vengeance.

Women and children were saved as a priority in both World War I and II. In contrast, children were specifically killed to prevent them growing up to avenge their parents' deaths in the Holocaust, as also occurred in the Armenian genocide perpetrated by the Turks,[2] and in the Rwandan genocide against Tutsis.[3] In almost all genocides and wars, however, children become the victims of terror, hardship, starvation and violence, such as in Cambodia[4] and during the Stalinist starvation of Ukraine[5]. Under the Nazis, Jewish children were primary targets for extinction from the earliest years of the Nazi regime and throughout the period of Nazi rule. While a third of Europe's Jews survived the Holocaust, only about 10% of Jewish children remained alive in 1945.[6] In our most recent genocides, children have been deliberately targeted for sexual abuse and rape, such as in Rwanda[7] and Darfur, Sudan,[8] unlike in the Holocaust where such abuse of Jewish youth was specifically forbidden under both German laws against child sexual abuse and Nazi prohibitions against *Rassenschande* (racial shame) and homosexuality. Although child sex abuse was illegal in Nazi Germany, and sexual abuse crimes perpetrated against German youth under 14 were prosecuted and reported, none of these trials include mention of Jewish child targets.[9] This is not surprising, as neither the Nazis themselves would admit to the crime of *Rassenschande* nor would Jewish children draw attention to themselves by reporting sexual assaults. Such crimes were likely always hidden by both prosecutor and victim thereby facilitating their occurrence. Without negative consequences for such crimes there was little to deter the perpetrators.

Nazi policies targeting Jews, from the earliest days of the Hitler regime, led many families to seek escape routes. Men left their families to flee to safer countries, while many were arrested and sent to camps for periods of time: their wives took on the management of their families, often resulting in them seeking work outside the home. Traditional familial controls, guidance and safety restrictions disintegrated. Ghettoization brought excessively difficult conditions leaving children to take on the roles of breadwinners and caregivers of sick parents and elderly grandparents: roles formerly occupied by their overwhelmed and emotionally, physically and economically battered parents. Hiding children, before or after ghettoization, became one of the few potentially feasible options parents faced to save them. Although many children were moved to family settings, they were surrounded by those who could, and sometimes did, abuse them, taking advantage of the opportunity provided by the isolation of the adoptive family unit and the secrecy required to hide the children in the midst of the Nazi perpetrated genocide. While many rescuers were honourable and deserving of the highest regard and appreciation, some were emotionally, physically and sexually abusive. They wielded enormous power over the hidden children by threatening their or their families' exposure to the Nazis and, likely, murder, if the children resisted their demands – although, possibly unknown to the children – they themselves could then also expect punishment if not death. Children had few, if any, choices or avenues of escape and frequently had no one – such as parents, siblings, friends, teachers, religious officials or adults – to turn to for help. Alternatively, children were left alone, or were sent to orphanages, both secular and religious, for care, where these were available, both inside and outside of ghettos. Such orphanages were not always immune from child sex abuse, as has become blatantly evident in the extensive abuse of young people in other educational, caregiving, and religious institutions during much of the twentieth century.[10]

The largest group of child survivors were those who were hidden. Most of those who were sexually assaulted in hiding were abused by Gentile members of their rescuing foster families, most often the foster father, or foster siblings. Sexual abuse by both Nazis and their collaborators as well as by rescuers took many forms, ranging from voyeurism to fondling and to penetrative sexual contact, often accompanied by physical violence, and almost always by emotional abuse.

Nazism and family disruption occurred over the dozen years of Nazi rule: a lengthy time during which antisemitic propaganda pervaded every aspect of life, from education, religion, art, music, theatre, film, newspapers, radio, books, magazines, politics, economics, justice, medicine and one's social life. None could escape Nazi antisemitism, least of all the children.

CHILDREN COULD NOT ESCAPE, BUT THEIR STORIES COULD

It does not seem to be acceptable for many Holocaust scholars today to talk or write about sexual abuse of Jewish children – or indeed of women or men – in the Holocaust. At a conference in Akko, Israel, on Medicine and the Holocaust, held in April 2017, at which I presented a paper based on my book *Birth, Sex and Abuse: Women's Voices under Nazi Rule* illustrating the role of the medical profession in manipulating women's reproductive lives to implement the genocide of Jews, audience members expressed disapproval of my discussing such topics as rape and sexual abuse of women during the Holocaust, saying it was not necessary to talk about such things, either in book form or at conferences. Likewise, in 2009, in Rochester, New York, Father Patrick Desbois, when giving a talk mentioning rape of Jewish girls, reports that someone in the audience got up and said "That's impossible. Never would a German, an SS soldier, touch a Jewish girl. It was forbidden."[11] Ka-Tzetnik[12] was condemned in the years after WWII for writing fictionalized accounts of child sexual abuse, apparently based on his siblings' experiences, but perceived as titillating and unnecessarily exposing this intimate and degrading subject.[13] Innumerable books, fictional and non-fictional, have reported on the most horrific atrocities of the Holocaust. Few, however, have addressed the issue of child sexual abuse although, notably, Elie Wiesel is acclaimed for – among a multitude of other things – exposing the rawest of emotions in response to the prolonged dying of a child *piepel* (male youth sexual slave) hanged on the gallows in a camp.[14] My attempts to explore this issue have been blocked, both explicitly and implicitly, seventy years later.

The stories of the girls and boys who were sexually abused and whose lives were largely destroyed by these experiences – over and above the horrors experienced by all during the Holocaust and World War II – are told here. Because we have been hesitant to confront their truths, we have condemned their stories to oblivion and in so doing have, albeit unintentionally, protected their perpetrators by not holding them to account. We have, in reality, become bystanders, if not accomplices, to multiple crimes against children.

This book challenges this silence. We owe it to the children whose lives were destroyed by sexual abuse to learn about it, to record it, and to expose it – and to hold the perpetrators to account, if only posthumously, for their actions. The children who had the courage to reveal their sexual abuse deserve to be heeded, even if this acknowledgement is long overdue.

SOURCES OF INFORMATION

As is the case with the majority of Holocaust literature documenting the experiences of victims, the vast majority of the experiences of children can never be known because most children were murdered before they could tell their stories. The Nazi eugenics and euthanasia programs killed approximately 5,000 -7,000 children – both Jewish and non-Jewish.[15] In ghettos, children died primarily from starvation and exposure. In extermination camps, the majority of children were murdered on arrival. Some adolescents were used for forced labour under brutal conditions that contributed to their demise. Hundreds, if not thousands, of children were used for medical experimentation, often in so-called terminal experiments in which they were destined to be killed as part of the research protocol. Hundreds of thousands were shot at the edge of mass graves by the *Einsatzgruppen*, the SS and *Wehrmacht* forces in German-occupied Poland and the Soviet Union. Many children were killed in reprisal actions for assaults on German officers, such as occurred at Lidice. In occupied countries, Aryan-looking children were kidnapped and transferred to the Reich for Germanization: if they later did not meet standards set for their appearance or behaviour, they were killed. Few of these were ever reunited with their families.[16]

In September 1939, when war began, there were 1.6 million Jewish children living in territories that Germany would occupy. When war ended in May 1945 as many as 1.1 million and perhaps 1.5 million of them were dead.[17] The survival rate of children was far lower than among the general adult population. Between 6 - 11% (estimates vary) of Europe's prewar population of Jewish children survived compared to 33% of adults.[18]

Only 3.1% of Jewish children sent to Auschwitz survived; 5% survived in Theresienstadt[19]; 3% of children in Poland, who mainly survived in hiding[20];10% in Holland; 2.1% in Belgium and 1.4 % – 4.3% in France.[21] In total, an estimated 60,000 to 165,000 children survived.[22]

A game played by children in Displaced Persons camps after the war expresses these losses well:

> A small child picks up a handful of sand and says: 'I had this many children'. He throws the sand in the air. Some of it falls on the ground. 'That many died', cries the child; he catches the rest: 'And this many lived.'[23]

Most children who survived were hidden. A few managed to resist or were rescued. In ghettos they were active in smuggling food; some joined partisan or resistance movements. Some were rescued by such actions as the *Kindertransport* and others were hidden.[24] In Lodz, for example, of the 1,246 surviving children who were registered in Jewish communities after the war, 59% survived by hiding on the Aryan side, 22% survived the camps, 10% lived in forests, 5% survived in the ghettos and 3% joined partisan groups and lived.[25]

If children were sexually abused by Nazis or their collaborators, it is likely that they were killed, at least in part, to prevent them from revealing their abuse, which was illegal in Germany. Some might have killed the children to prevent exposure of their crime of *Rassenschande* (racial shame) or, in the case of boys, of homosexuality. The voices of those who were murdered can never be heard and their experiences can seldom be shared.

Sources of information about children in general, and child sex abuse in particular, during the Holocaust are scarce. There are few records of children in the Holocaust, either from German or Nazi records,[26] or from rescuers or other people who may have encountered them. The Nazis killed Jews who did not have utilitarian value to them, for example, as workers or subjects of experiments. Children were no different; they were Jews with minimal value as labourers, and there was little reason to record anything more about them, from the Nazi perspective. In addition, children posed a threat to the future of Nazism if allowed to reach adulthood with intent to avenge their parents. As Heinrich Himmler articulated:

> We came to the question: what about the women and children? I have decided to find a clear solution here too. In fact, I did not regard myself as justified in exterminating men – let us say killing them or having them killed – while letting avengers in the shape of children grow up [...] The difficult decision had to be taken to make this people disappear from the face of the earth.[27]

Alternatively, those who hid children or attempted to rescue them had excellent reasons for not keeping any records – discovery of these by the Germans would have endangered the rescue organization, the rescuers, and the children.[28]

Young children lacked skills to record their own experiences, while older children faced shortages of materials and opportunities to write their records of their lives. A number of children's diaries were written in the war years, in addition to the widely known diary of Anne Frank.[29] Some were written in leather or clothbound books, or in gold embossed journals received as gifts, that were treasured and carried from homes to ghettos and to camps. Some smuggled or stole scraps of paper, pencil stubs or ink pens and wrote in school books, address books, on the backs of notices, on brown paper bags and in the margins of other published books. Many of the diaries survived only in fragments.[30] Writing such diaries was dangerous, and hiding these pages was imperative to protect the children and their families' safety. Hiding places were not easily come by. For example: Berthe Jeanne (Bertje) Bloch van Rhijn, a Dutch girl who hid with her family in a large house with a garden, kept a diary throughout the Nazi occupation period. Her parents recognized the potential danger that the diary posed and buried it in the garden for safekeeping. It was occasionally taken out for her to write her entries, and then was hidden again.[31] Zimra Harsanyi's diary, written in thick notebooks, was smuggled out of Auschwitz with the help of a *kapo*: additional notes that she wrote after that time were kept on scraps of paper hidden in her shoes until liberation.[32] Edith van Hessen, living in The Hague, entrusted her diaries to a friend shortly before going into hiding under an assumed identity: she recovered her writings from her friend after the war.[33] Janina Bauman hid her diary, written in the Warsaw ghetto, in a hole in the floor of a stranger's apartment where she found them, intact, after the war.[34] In 1943, part of Gertrude Schneider's diary was hidden in the Riga ghetto, wrapped in oilcloth, shortly before she and her family were deported to Kaiserwald concentration camp: she retrieved it in 1971.[35] More than fifty-five children's diaries, written during the war, have emerged from all corners of Europe.[36] In addition, there are memoirs from multiple survivors who were children during the war but who only chose to, or were able to, record their stories after the war ended and, particularly, as they aged. Some consider that, as their lives are drawing to a close, time is running out to record these experiences for posterity. The records of above-ground rescue and refugee organizations are also valuable sources as are the writings of adults who worked with children or wrote about them. In the immediate postwar years, testimonies from children in Displaced Persons camps and children's homes in Poland and Germany were collected and published by Benjamin Tenenbaum, the Jewish Historical Commission in Poland and the Central Historical Commission in Munich.[37] These were ultimately transferred to Yad Vashem in Israel. In addition, adult chronicles of life under Nazi occupation also included documentaries on children's lives such as the *Chronicle of the Lodz Ghetto*[38] and Emanuel Ringelblum's *Notes from the Warsaw Ghetto*.[39]

Many who were children during the Nazi era are still reluctant to reveal their stories at all, leading family and friends to wonder if this is indicative of possible sexual abuse at that time. For example, Ora*, a Dutch child, was hidden in eight different homes that were all good to her. But her sister was also hidden in a number of different homes. Her sister has never talked about these years and says she can't remember them. Ora* believes that her sister does not want to remember them, implying that abuse might have occurred, although there is no certainty that this is the reason.[40] Her story remains hidden.

DEFINING A CHILD

Defining who is a "child" is difficult. Dwork studied children aged between birth and sixteen years when Nazism affected their lives.[41] The Nazis themselves murdered most children under the age of thirteen on admission to the camps – although there were some exceptions to this. The age of children who were raped and/or murdered is not always clarified in testimonies: often those who were raped are described as "young girls" or a "young child" by witnesses to the events who may not have known the specific age of the girls or boys.[42] Heifetz defined a child survivor as "one under the age of thirteen between 1933 and 1945 who lived in Europe, who was an eyewitness to persecution, whose life was threatened directly or indirectly, and whose psychological, emotional and physical life was altered in an essential way by the Holocaust, both during and after these years."[43] Today, United Nations organizations study children under the age of eighteen in research into child abuse, child marriage and sexual trafficking of girls.[44] For the purposes of this book, I focused on children who were under the age of around fourteen at any time between 1930 and 1945 – although reports of "young girls" and some older teenagers were included especially when referring to rape. I sought out testimonies in archival sources from those who were born between 1930 and 1945 who were likely still children during the war years. Ages of the children mentioned in the book are included whenever known.

DEFINING CHILD SEX ABUSE

The *World Report on Violence and Health* defines sexual abuse as "any sexual act, attempt to obtain a sexual act, unwanted sexual comments or advances, or acts to traffic a person's sexuality, using coercion, threats of harm or physical force, by any person regardless of relationship to the victim, in any setting, including but not limited to home and work."[45]

This definition is, however, egregiously limited in that it excludes both the key concept of consent as well as ignoring the possibility of children's agreement to sexual acts following periods of grooming, or emotional or pharmacological manipulation. Sexual abuse usually involves oral, anal or genital penetration, but any range of behaviours including touching, fondling, or kissing can be included. In this text, a broad approach is used, with forced witnessing of sexual activity by a child being included as abuse in addition to groomed sexual consent, and child initiated sexual contact as a means of survival. The concept that there is no such thing as consensual sex with a child, because a child is too young developmentally, and/or too dependent on the perpetrator to give true consent[46] is accepted as central to this text. Most children who are sexually abused regard this as the most traumatic event of their lives.[47]

ACCESSING ARCHIVES

I found most of the testimonies included in this book in survivor memoirs and archival material. My search for these accounts brought considerable condemnation and exclusion from academic study of the subject from the most respected archives in Israel and elsewhere. My first meeting with an Israeli archivist, was met with the words, "You know this subject is taboo?" His actual assistance, and offer of further assistance with my research, was, one day later, totally blocked by his director: no information on this subject could or would be divulged. Similarly, my next approach to two other Israeli libraries were initially met with enthusiasm, encouragement and assistance, only for all doors to both these libraries being rapidly slammed shut as my subject matter became evident. A search of these libraries' records for the keywords "Sexual and Abuse and Children" revealed fifteen records: eight of these were from children born in 1930 or later and therefore no older than fifteen at the end of the war, and therefore of direct relevance to my research. Although I was told these existed, I was not allowed to access them. Numerous requests to obtain these testimonies, both from myself, my Israeli colleagues, and even other archivists who supported my endeavours, were stonewalled: I did not even receive replies – polite or impolite – to my, and my colleagues' multiple inquiries. I did, however, meet with more reasoned and ready assistance from the Ghetto Fighters House archivists in the Western Galilee, who assisted me enthusiastically and with significant academic expertise. This is the site of one of the most outstanding children's museums of the Holocaust in the world and an educational centre. My assurance – given to every archive I approached – that I would respect the confidentiality of testimonies was accepted as sufficient to facilitate my study in these archives. In this book, unless I refer to testimonies published by others, or freely available in online searches, I have removed information, including names and dates of birth, to avoid any identification of the testimony. Randomly assigned names, indicated by an asterisk* in the text, are used to provide an "identity" for these victims.

While ultimately successful, my archival searches in North American libraries were also difficult. While the vast majority of the over 52,000 testimonies held in the Visual History Archives of the Shoah Foundation can be viewed online, a number – more than 3,000 – have restricted access and can only be viewed in person at a library or resource centre that has full access to the Visual History Archive. Some of the testimonies that I needed to consult fell into this restricted access category. I explored eleven of the sites listed as having "full access" on the Visual History Archive website that were feasible for me to visit (in Ottawa, Montreal, Toronto, Winnipeg, and Vancouver in Canada, and Washington DC in the USA), with only one – the University of Toronto – being able to assist me. While these administrative hurdles make access to sensitive information difficult, the subject matter of my study may also play a part. The conservative Israeli society, coupled with its lasting image as a victim, and the formalities associated with North American society made access to the sensitive information I sought, challenging. Dwork's writings may be relevant: Historians have been able to deal with the history of adults, or of an entire people, but they have not been able to face the even more harrowing subject of the persecution of children.[48]

Survivors born after 1929 authored 429 (5.9%) of the 7,300 testimonies recorded by the Central Jewish Historical Commission in Poland between 1944 -1984.[49] Such reports were regarded as "powerful emotional communications of resistance and other heroic acts, demonstrating the young survivors' courage, practical survival skills, and the vigor of their resistance."[50] However, the inability of children to articulate an adult's understanding of the world led early interpreters of their reports to discount them as inaccurate and immature.[51]

Later, from 1981-1995, the Fortunoff Video Archive for Holocaust Testimonies at Yale University collected 34,000 testimonies while Steven Spielberg's Shoah Visual History Foundation has, since 1994, collected over 52,000 testimonies.[52] These developments were accompanied by an increasing value being placed on testimonies supported by such recognized historians as Omer Bartov,[53] Christopher Browning,[54] Lawrence Langer[55] and Jan T Gross.[56] In addition, a growing interest in the history of children in the Holocaust – as perceived and reported by the youth themselves – was stimulated by such writers as Deborah Dwork[57] and Nicholas Stargardt.[58] A number of collections of children's writings or stories exist including those published by Boas,[59] Holliday,[60] Marks,[61] Stein,[62] Woolf,[63] and Zapruder.[64] Many of these children, and testimonies of others, report sexual abuse during the Nazi era. Remarkably, neither Heberer's[65] extensive report on children's lives during the Holocaust (supported by the United States Holocaust Memorial Museum), nor Bogner's review of the lives of children who were hidden in Christian families and institutions, particularly in Poland, (published by Yad Vashem), report any instances of child sexual abuse.[66] Craig-Norton's in-depth analysis of some *Kindertransport* children does mention that sexual abuse occurred, but provides no details.[67]

TESTIMONIES REPORTING SEXUAL ASSAULT

The primary sources utilized in this text are English language memoirs, testimonies, books, and articles reporting on various forms of sexual assault. An online search of the Visual History Archive of the United States Holocaust Memorial Museum for the keywords "sexual assault" revealed 2,255 Jewish testimonies, 1,071 in English, 1,184 in nineteen other languages (primarily in Hebrew, French, Hungarian and Spanish), 827 of which were written by females and 244 males. When this search was limited to Jewish victims born between 1930-1945 and who therefore experienced the Nazi era and particularly the war years as children, 459 testimonies were listed, 285 of which are available in English and 164 in other languages. Of the English testimonies, 234 were provided by women and fifty-one by men. Further examination of these reports revealed that not all reflected personal experience, or witnessing, of sexual assault, but often reported generalizations such as "many women were raped." There is no way of ascertaining the exact number of reports of child sexual abuse that are held in archives. With over 52,000 testimonies now recorded by the Shoah Foundation alone, and with multiple variations in language that might indirectly refer to sexual abuse such as "he hurt me," or "he lay down with me" in addition to those explicitly noted with keywords such as "sexual abuse," it is virtually impossible to identify, listen to and record every instance that occurred. There is no logical reason to presume that sexual abuse experiences might have differed among children who all spoke European languages at the time of the Holocaust but who have now recorded their memoirs or testimonies in English or in another language. It is probable that had access to the reports in languages other than English been possible, then the number of incidents of child sexual abuse would simply be higher than that reported in this book.

In all, 160 individual accounts of sexual abuse of Jewish children are reported in this text, drawn from testimony and memoirs, as well as from scholarly books and journal articles. Sexual abuse of seventeen non-Jewish children is also reported: eight of these were German children and nine British children in the UK evacuated from potential war zones to the countryside, for safety. I obtained thirty reports of child sex abuse from restricted access testimonies in the Ghetto Fighters House and the Shoah Visual History Foundation archives and these have been assigned false names that are noted by an asterisk. Average age, when known, of the children who were sexually abused was eleven years with twenty-seven being nine years old or younger, twenty-one being ten or eleven, twenty-eight being twelve to fourteen years old and twenty-four being fifteen or older. The oldest abused hidden child was fourteen. The average age at which hidden children were abused was almost ten years (9.9). The average age at which girls in camps were raped was about ten years (10.3) with boys in camps reporting rape on

13

average at thirteen years (13.1). Most of the boys who were raped were used as *piepels* or sexual slaves in camps. These boys were generally older than thirteen, as most children under this age were killed on arrival at the camps. Only boys younger than fifteen or sixteen were included in this text, although youth who were far older than this were also used as sexual slaves in camps. For the sake of academic accuracy, I have included a full list of all accounts of sexual abuse reported in this book in tabular form in Appendices 1 and 2, although this "dry" listing denies the children their voices. I have, however, quoted extensively from children's own writings in the text of this book, to allow their voices to be heard.

THE VALIDITY OF CHILDREN'S REPORTS OF SEXUAL ABUSE

Today, child survivors' testimonies are an essential source in historical investigations concerning their lives, however, this was not always the case. Children's testimonies have, in the past, been dismissed based on the idea that children are too young to understand or accurately report these events.[68] Sexually abused child Holocaust survivors can, and do, remember their experiences with accuracy – when the abuse occurred, how old they were, the circumstances in which it occurred, who the perpetrator was, and their reactions to it.[69] Michlic clarifies that children are quite capable of differentiating between severe and less devastating experiences. They are capable of rating these experiences as "standard," "normal/boring," "horrible" and "the most horrible and embarrassing," such as sexual abuse, the latter only disclosed to closest friends.[70] Michlic's comparisons of early testimonies and those given later by the same children show constancy – and remain almost intact – despite the passage of time, confirming Dwork's earlier findings.[71] Dwork interviewed children two to three years after their first testimony had been recorded and found their two accounts to be consistent. Some of those whom she interviewed gave oral testimonies to archive collections many years later. When she compared her interviews with these later oral testimonies, they were again consistent with much the same language being used to describe similar events.[72]

Children's reports of the sexual abuse they experienced may also have been limited by their inadequate understanding of sex. As Stargardt reports: "Fourteen-year-old girls who have had no sex education let alone sexual experience, did not have words for describing what had happened, and neither the schools nor their families seemed to have helped girls or boys to talk about their experiences."[73] Women were also discouraged from talking about their experiences of rape. Many could not even tell their husbands about these experiences.[74]

The fact that relatively few testimonies in such archives as the Fortunoff and Shoah Foundation collections mention sexual abuse may not accurately reflect the number of women or children who were sexually abused, but only the ones who were willing to talk about such experiences in a record that would be visible for their families to view. Some of this reluctance to mention sexual abuse may also be due to our own – as interviewers – hesitancy to ask about sexual abuse. As Deborah Dwork reports, when she asked the child survivors that she interviewed why they had agreed to speak with her, "In every European language, the same answer was given: 'Because you asked'."[75] It is not the fault of women and child survivors that testimonies about child sexual abuse in the Holocaust were not revealed: it is likely our own. We did not ask – or believe.

THE SCOPE OF THIS BOOK

This book is a partial record of child sexual abuse during the Nazi era. It adopts an "issue-based" focus that centres on the types of sexual abuse experienced by children – predominantly Jewish children but also, to a limited extent, German children – and the types of perpetrators of this abuse, including Nazis, their collaborators, and rescuers of Jewish children both within Nazi occupied Europe and far beyond its borders. It is not a history of the Holocaust, or of World War II. Nor is it a comprehensive history of children's experiences in the Holocaust although some historical context is provided to contextualize sexually abusive events. Nor is this book an analysis of child sex abuse as a psychological and social phenomenon, although the reasons behind perpetrators' actions are considered.

Chapter 1 of this book explains the thesis: that the Nazis' antisemitic ideology targeted Jewish children's lives and facilitated sexual abuse of the few who escaped the Nazi net by destroying the fabric of Jewish life and society, thereby endangering the children. Chapter 1 also outlines the methodology of this research and draws attention to the challenges to obtaining information on this subject created by the taboos surrounding the issue of child sex abuse during the Holocaust. Chapter 2 provides an overview of German children's upbringing and particularly issues relating to childhood sexual knowledge and sexual abuse under Nazi rule. This chapter provides a background reflecting the societal attitudes towards children, and to sexuality and sex abuse, into which children were born during the Nazi era, particularly in Germany but likely more extensively across Europe. Chapter 3 provides a brief history of Jewish children's lives during the Nazi era: for those familiar with this focus of the Holocaust, this chapter can be skimmed or skipped. It is provided to establish a context that frames the experiences of children during this time. Chapters 4-6 discuss various forms of child sexual abuse perpetrated by the Nazis or their collaborators, including abuse imposed under the guise of medical experimentation. Chapters 7 and 8 review abuse perpetrated by "rescuers" of Jewish children both in Europe and in other countries to which Jewish youth were sent for safety. Chapter 9 examines the psychological consequences of abuse on the children themselves while Chapter 10 focuses on the current controversial taboo against studying child sexual abuse. The final chapter (11) examines the question of how perpetrators could bring themselves to sexually abuse children. Appendices 1 and 2 provide a tabular record of the 160 children reported in the book who were abused, the types of abuse they experienced, their ages, and their perpetrators.

This book, then, is the story of Jewish children who were sexually abused, in addition to experiencing one of the worst genocidally-based, emotional and physical abuse that this world has ever imposed. Their individual stories are currently only available in scattered reports, and there is, to date, no integrated report or analysis of Jewish children's experiences of sexual abuse during the Nazi era. This book fills this knowledge gap. Worse still, these stories are often ignored, suppressed or hidden, leaving the children's experiences unrecognized and their perpetrators unscathed. This book honours the memory of these children and fulfills the desires of the many who considered it important to record their testimonies so that their experiences can be understood, acknowledged and remembered.

There is, however, no way to tell these stories gently: child sexual abuse is horrific whenever and however it occurs. Moreover, it often occurs within a framework of other forms of abuse: physical, emotional, cognitive and spiritual. The stories recorded by the children themselves through memoirs, diaries and testimonies provide a vivid account of their experiences and illustrate these life-changing and sometimes life-threatening events. Where possible, I have preserved the children's own accounts of their experiences. The resulting narrative cannot be softened, much as readers might wish for this. Academic analyses that summarize accounts of abuse into statistical reports of incidence – as is provided in the Appendices to this book – tell only a small portion of the story.

CHAPTER 2: GERMAN SOCIETY

Child sexual abuse in Europe in the 20th century emerged against a backdrop of harsh and conservative childrearing principles. Child rearing practices during the early and mid 20th century in particular, reflected rigidity, conservatism and – as judged in today's world – cruelty towards children. Before the advent of either contraception or abortion, women faced harsh choices when becoming pregnant unwillingly: infanticide, unmarried motherhood and, often, poverty resulting from social condemnation and exclusion from their family and friends. Alternatively, women could abandon their babies on a doorstep, send them to an orphanage or similar institution or be forced into a marriage of convenience.[76]

"Baby farming" became one further option: Women could conceal their pregnancies, go to the countryside for birth and hand their baby over to a "baby farmer" who would ostensibly care for the child. Many of these baby farmers were conscientious, but some simply starved the babies to death or gave them laudanum to end their lives. Their bodies were then dumped on the street, buried privately or thrown into a river.[77] Criminal cases against baby farmers were reported in the UK, Australia, New Zealand, Germany and Denmark. In Germany such caregivers were called *Engelmacherin* or angel makers, acknowledging the likely death of their charges. Criminal baby farming was eliminated in the UK by 1920 and by the 1940's adoption became an option for unwanted babies.

Child care practices were equally harsh. Breastfeeding by birth mothers was not common with wet nurses being employed when possible. Girl children were neglected leading to a male-female imbalance[78] with differing expectations being placed on girls compared to boys, reminiscent of Dickens' *Dombey and Son.*[79] Children's crying was regarded as screaming and was not to be responded to, day or night. From six months, babies were subjected to regular enemas; many cities had enema stores where children were taken to be fitted with the proper size enema.[80] Children were beaten with straps and punished with cold water baths to harden them. Other punishments included being placed on red hot stoves, tied to bed posts all night long, forced to kneel for hours a day, and having feces forced into their mouths after "accidents."[81] Frau Karma Raubat in Germany recalled that:

> In the German ideal of upbringing, whatever was creative was killed. If it danced out of line and did something that did not reflect the authoritarian father or mother, it got thrashed [...] In Germany when a child of nine months still wets his pants, it is a catastrophe. And mothers among themselves were proud [if they could say] "Ja, my child is already clean." That was such a tradition.[82]

Children were told horror stories of being taken away by ghosts or other monsters – as often occurs in fairy-tales – if they were not obedient.[83] Variations on such threats made to "disobedient children" are found across Europe. In Poland a child would be told: "A Jew's going to come and get you"[84] or "The Jews will turn you into matzo."[85] In Kazakhstan, a child would be told, "A Russian's coming to get you."[86] In many eastern European countries, children were threatened with a fictional witch-like character: "If you do not listen, Baba Yaga[87] will come and get you."[88] And Jews during the Holocaust might threaten, like Rebecca to her four year-old daughter, Miriam, "The Germans will come."[89]

As Hans-Georg Behr, a German child growing up in the Nazi era recalls:

> The child had been cured of any notion that he was the centre of the world, and had learned that it was less painful to be inconspicuous [...] Spanking hurt the bottom, slapping hurt the face, and the two together were known as a good hiding.[90]

And:

But the child himself must use only the right kinds of words, [such as breaking wind and not farting] and if he didn't he often got a smack on the head to teach him not to use the wrong ones [...].

If you came in from out of doors you had to wash your hands. If you had touched something you had to wash your hands. If you had been playing you were washed, and there wasn't any hot water until midday. And when you had your "best clothes" on, you had to keep perfectly still, because the tiniest little dirty mark on them meant trouble.[91]

Given this authoritarian and restrictive approach to child development it is not surprising that Hitler's approach to child rearing reflected similar harshness:

My pedagogy is harsh. Weakness must be chipped away. The youth that will grow up in my fortresses will frighten the world. I want a brutal, authoritarian, fearless, cruel youth. Youth must be all of this. It must be able to bear pain. It must not have anything weak and gentle. The light of the free, marvelous beast of prey must once again shine from their eyes. I want my youth to be strong and beautiful [...] Then I will be able to create the New Order.[92]

Hitler's followers endorsed this. Goebbels, for example, reports spanking his daughter Helga when she required disciplining. He regarded this as "the best possible corrective"[93] and "from time to time he found himself obliged to give them a "thrashing" to beat the "stubbornness" out of them – as Goebbels saw it, a tried and tested educational method."[94] We now know, however, that corporal punishment and abuse lead to considerably maladaptive consequences for children.[95]

Sibylle, the daughter of an ardent SS officer, also reports that she and her three brothers were subjected to a fascist regime at home:

Hidings were routine. If I tore my dress – a beating: if I got poor marks – a beating: if I talked back to my parents – a beating. And if, as sometimes happened, minor transgression picked up, then there too was a beating. The ritual never varied: we had to fetch the tool ourselves, lie down across a chair, and then it began. There was no point in trying to resist. And no talking back either [...] Mother was in charge of my punishment, and Father took care of my brothers'.[96]

As Sibylle said, "I believed that parents had the right to kill their children."[97] Uwe Timm similarly, reported that "Violence was *normal*. Children were beaten everywhere. Out of aggression, out of conviction, for educational purposes, at school, at home, in the street."[98] He recounts a story of a boy who took his scooter on a cycle path: "A cyclist came past and hit him in the face, just like that. The boy fell off his scooter. 'Quite right too', said a passerby."[99]

As they grew older, children could be sent to other homes to work as servants or apprentices where they were often beaten and sexually abused. At schools, teachers and older students were also sexual abusers. For example, Hans-Georg Behr was sent to a boarding school run by Catholic Priests. He was enticed into masturbating another boy while there, and boys went to each other's beds at night in the dormitories.[100] Masturbation was forbidden although the boys indulged in it more and more as they got older: "you would be expelled from school if the Fathers caught you."[101] He, however, was forced to give oral sex to Father Anselm and was slapped about the face when his actions were not satisfying enough. It was well known in the school that Father Anselm was forcing boys into sexual activities with him.[102]

Many civilizations regard masturbation as a normal and healthy aspect of sexual pleasures, but, over time, these relaxed views were replaced by more conservative approaches that viewed masturbation as a sin that carried serious medical consequences. In the 17th century in Puritanical communities such as in New Haven Connecticut, masturbation was even regarded as a crime punishable by death.[103] Some doctors investigated cures for chronic masturbation including the American doctor John Harvey Kellogg (1852-1943) who went so far as to recommend burning off the clitoris of girls and sewing shut the foreskin of boys in attempts to prevent masturbation. Less severe recommendations included eating a bland diet, to which end Kellogg invented the breakfast cereal Corn Flakes in 1894. Kellogg was not alone in his views; Sylvester Graham (1774-1851), an American minister, had previously invented "Graham Crackers" for the same purpose.[104]

ABSENCE OF PARENTALLY LED SEX EDUCATION

Parents generally did not give information about sex to their children. Instead children frequently learned about sex by personal exposure to others or information/misinformation gleaned from strangers. Behr's experience was possibly not uncommon. He describes his first encounters with sexuality:

> The child [...] peered through the blinds [...] one of the kitchen maids had hitched her skirt up [...] there was another figure there too, [...] then the whole thing reminded the child of what the bull had being doing to the cow on the farm the other day, which he hadn't really been allowed to watch. But what was going on down there lasted much longer and was much more exciting, so exciting that the child had to put his hand on what he called his little bunny and play with it until it felt itchy. The child couldn't remember when he had discovered this game, [...]The child remembered [...] Mother making something which looked like a sack out of stout white cotton, and then she had said, "You're not to play with your little willy or it will turn black one day, and then it will fall off." [...] the child had to go to bed with the [...] sack which buttoned up at the back, with only his head and arms sticking out of it.[105]

After soiling the sheet by accident at home one day his mother placed an open book in his room. The passage it exposed reveals the puritanical attitudes that pervaded thought about sexuality at the time:

Soiling oneself [...] is in the realm of carnal sin [...]
leading to intellectual and physical weakness,
degeneration and complete breakdown [...]
Associated diseases such as hysteria, hypochondria,
profound mental disturbance, etc., as well as male
impotence [...] are caused more particularly by too
lavish a diet given to children. [...] The book also
identified a sufferer; "Pale grey sallow complexion,
pale lips, bluish eyelids, rings around the eyes,
unsteady gaze, soiled linen. Then fatigue and
general wasting despite a good appetite, withered
skin, sweats, trembling, backache, dull pain in the
thighs and calves. Gradually the speech becomes a
stammer, the voice is weak, the hair has no lustre,
splits at the ends and easily falls out."[106]

One day while playing in the garden Behr looked up to see a
Russian workman, the gardener – standing in front of him:

[...] his smile made the child suspicious because he
had a hand inside his trousers, and they were swelling
as if he had a stick hidden in there. [...] then his
trousers flapped open, and out jumped a bunny such
as the child had never seen before, enormous, with a
big purple knob on top, dark-skinned with a lot of
black hair at its root [...] the bunny came further and
further out of his trousers, with the child gaping at it
in wonderment. "You like that eh? Want to see it?"
whispered Ivan [...]. "Yes," breathed the child. [...]
he took the child's hand and led him into the tool
shed. [...] the bunny was even bigger than beside the
sandbox, and when the child felt it, it was all hard
[...] Ivan showed the child what to do [...] Then Ivan
played with the bunny himself. The child helped as
best he could [...] suddenly the bunny spat straight in
the child's face.[107]

In the days that followed, Ivan encouraged the child into oral sex
with him[108] and later returned the action.[109] Behr also observed two of
his neighbour's youngest children (Hans was aged 12) indulging in
sex.[110] He watched as his older brother Stefan masturbated as well[111]

and later joined with him in his game.[112] Like Behr, Stefan was introduced to sex at an early age. Stefan was the child of committed Nazis. Like many children, Behr was introduced to sexual activities by his friends rather than being guided by his parents:

> One time, I must have been about eleven or twelve, some of the boys went into the bushes with a girl. They pulled down her panties, lifted her skirt, and they all looked. I stood near them and wanted to run away when Gerhard, he was the leader, called me and said I should stick my finger in. I tried to run away, but the others held me and dragged me over to where the girl was. She wasn't scared at all and only laughed. Come on, do it, they all yelled at me and pushed me towards her. I threw myself on the ground and cried and begged them to let me go. They did, but for a long time afterward the boys kept kidding me about it. And what's even worse was that the girls did too.[113]

ATTITUDES TOWARDS VICTIMS OF CHILD SEXUAL ABUSE

Attitudes towards child sexual abuse in the Nazi era reflect a mixture of fear, cruelty and distortion, not unlike widespread cultural attitudes towards child sexuality at that time. For example, in 1932, Anni Nagel was accused of sexual activity before her eighth birthday. The older boys involved accused Anni of starting it herself. Anni also named her aunt's husband, a thirty-two year-old man, as having abused her. He admitted having sex with her but also accused her of initiating it. Anni was incarcerated in a reformatory for her incitement of her uncle: she had to be taken off the streets. Officials assumed that girls were more likely to have instigated sex than been the victim of abuse. Society was to be protected from such children. After spending time in a reformatory, Anni was allowed home. In October 1939 she was again abused, this time by her stepfather. Her testimony was discounted and she was accused of lying. She was fifteen and pregnant. Her illegitimate son was placed in a children's home and she was sent to a reformatory, Breitenau. She died on 1 June 1942 of tuberculosis having spent ten of her seventeen years in "care."[114]

In August 1940, Sauerbier, soon after taking over management of Breitenau, appealed to the Professor of Psychiatry and Director of the Marburg Psychiatric Asylum to suggest a medical preparation that could be added to the reformatory girls' food to curb their "sexual drive." The head of the Marburg asylum replied:

> One only gets through to these girls by disciplining them: if those sorts of things happen here, then we lay them in bed and put them on water soup and the most restricted diet until they are small and ugly. Then things tend to go alright for a longish period till [sic] the next outburst of this type occurs. In my experience, you get nowhere by dosing them. I would also recommend that in such cases you proceed against these girls with all severity and set about them without any consideration. That still has the quickest success.
>
> With best wishes and Heil Hitler![115]

Reformatory pupils were obliged to work hard without complaining, despite hunger, taunts and beatings. They had to show the "right attitude" not only to their custodians but in their letters home as well. Ironically, these letters revealed that the parents agreed with the authorities: children truly feared, with good reason, that their parents had condemned them too.[116]

THE HITLER YOUTH AND SEXUAL EDUCATION OF BOYS

Herzog suggests that it is difficult to juxtapose the Nazi's "upbeat defense of heterosexual enjoyment"[117] with the terror and mass murder that characterized Nazism. It is also difficult to conceive of the Nazi's cruel sexual abuse of many victims, including child victims. Given, however, the Nazi distinctions between the so-called, desirable Aryan population and the demeaning depictions of non-Aryans and especially Jews, it is quite possible that such sexual cruelty was simply incorporated into the Nazi's derogatory conception of "the other," thereby justifying their victims' torture and demise through any means, including through violent sexual acts.[118]

The Hitler Youth provided a means for indoctrinating most of the youth of Germany into Nazi ideology, including influencing their attitudes towards sex and child sexuality. Formed in 1926, regular attendance was as low as 25% until membership became compulsory in December 1936 when it grew to incorporate in the region of four to six million – about 90% of Germany's youth.[119] Joyful exploration of sexuality was part of Hitler's ideology. But among the Hitler Youth, sexuality was, for the most part, willing sex among young people, not sexual abuse.[120] Sex with children was defined as criminal sexuality in Nazi Germany.[121] The Hitler Youth followed many of the rules of the *Jugendbewegung* (German Youth Movement): young German men and women spent time together in the nude in camps, hostels or just in the local woods. Surén gymnastics, created by Hans Surén, a military man and a fascist, favoured strengthening the male body with medicine ball exercises, preferably in the nude. His books reached a circulation of one million. Much of what was sold as healthy family living in the nude would otherwise have been banned as pornography involving children and minors.[122]

Nevertheless, the Hitler youth also incorporated sexual exploitation and cruelty at times although this was quickly hushed up:

> In one particularly serious case in 1935, just as Goebbels was beginning his exposure of sex scandals in the Church [as part of the Nazi attempts to discredit the Church and Church institutions], a boy was sexually assaulted by several others at a Hitler Youth camp then knifed to death to stop him talking. When his mother found out what had happened and reported it to the Reich Commissioner Mutschmann, he immediately had her arrested and imprisoned to prevent the scandal coming out into the open.[123]

During World War II, many German children were evacuated from Berlin for their safety just as children in the UK were sent to rural districts to avoid the feared invasion of the UK by Hitler's air force and armies. Between 1940 and 1945, about 2.8 million German children were sent to these camps: about 5,000 were established.[124] Jost Hermand was among the first cohort of children to leave in the autumn of 1940. At ten he was also one of the youngest boys in the school to be sent to a *Kinderlandverschickung* (KLV) camp, (a short form of *Verschickung der Kinder auf das Land* (relocation of children to the countryside) run by the Hitler Youth. He was one of the smallest and most vulnerable boys in the camp and with a slight stutter and puny build, he was always the last to be picked for team sports. There was an established pecking order in the dormitories with the sport kings occupying the top bunks, the weaklings – like Jost – the bottom ones. The youngest and most vulnerable boys were bullied, humiliated and sexually abused.[125] Jost remembered bitterly that he "knew exactly whose shoes he had to shine and who in turn would shine his, even which of the boys he had to satisfy manually at night and who had to satisfy him."[126]

Children's experiences of school life – and sexual harassment or abuse – appeared to be common in many countries during the 20th century. Physical, emotional and sexual abuse were common experiences of children in Germany, the UK, Ireland, Australia and Canada during this century, often facilitated by religiously run institutions such as schools, welfare home, homes for unmarried mothers, and orphanages.[127] A pervasive authoritarian, disrespectful and harsh approach to children's needs characterized the emotional climate of these institutions that, in turn, created opportunities for sexual and other forms of abuse across Europe, the UK, and North America. Today's world is still struggling to come to terms with this.

Sex Education of Girls in the Hitler Youth

Despite this emphasis on sexual enjoyment and its abuse at times, little education about reproductive bodily functions, sex or sexuality was given to girls in the Hitler Youth as was common practice in the western world at the time. Ursula Mahlendorf – an ardent Nazi supporter and member of the Hitler Youth – recalls her first experience of menstruation and her ignorance about such maturation.

> When I went inside, I noticed that my panties were wet and I was bleeding [...] That evening, when the bleeding still had not stopped, I told Mother. She looked at me in consternation and horror, and I had the feeling that I had done something terribly wrong.

> [...] "you will need to wear napkins once a month; you must not bathe or swim during this period; it will probably be painful; you must not be alone with men." My belly started hurting the moment she mentioned pain. [...] judging from her look, I did not dare ask any questions and felt guilty. She gave me some folded rags and several safety pins and told me to fasten them to my panties. I had no one to ask what was wrong with me. [...] The closest I could figure out was that this condition was something that she was ashamed of, something despicable, sexual, and therefore lower class [...]

> After two months of agonizing, I decided to ask Frau Gurn's kitchen help, a farm girl named Martha, if she knew what was the matter with me [...] She seemed less intimidating to me [...] She laughed at my naivete. "Didn't anyone tell you that you are a woman now? Women have their period. When your boyfriend fucks you, you might get pregnant. So you'll have to be careful."[128]

Two years later, she did receive a lecture on intercourse and impregnation from her Hitler Youth leader, Lotte. All fourteen-year-old girls, about forty of them, met with her:

> "[...] rather than your hearing about sex in the gutter talk of the street, as you no doubt will in future years," Lotte continued, "I will provide you with factual information." [...]

"You will enjoy having many children for the Führer, and that is why you must keep yourself pure." Of course, I knew what that meant. Don't talk or think about sex and keep clean.

"When your future husband makes you a mother, he will put his member into you like a sword thrusts itself into its sheath, and his seed will impregnate the seed in your belly."

Silence – that was it!

I still have difficulty understanding how a young teacher could be as alienated from her own body as to use such a violent obscene metaphor.[129]

Ursula's assessment regarding the Nazi imagery – of violence, strength, cruelty, aggression and obscenity – in the analogy used to describe intercourse is telling. It is also reminiscent of views on rape during the 19th and 20th century. Some of the most important medical textbooks informed doctors that female victims who became pregnant must have consented. These texts also insisted that it was not possible to rape a resisting woman. As the physician Horatio Storer wrote:

In his article published in *The Quarterly Journal of Psychological Medicine and Medical Jurisprudence* in 1868, it is "impossible to sheath a sword into a vibrating scabbard." Metaphorically, the penis was coded as a weapon, the vagina, its passive receptacle. Merely by "vibrating," this receptacle could ward off the attack. Despite being refuted by a growing number of physicians, such views were widely held into the mid 20th century. From the 1970s this issue came to public attention and was scrutinized and criticized in the UK.[130]

THE EFFECTIVENESS OF NAZI SEX EDUCATION FOR CHILDREN

Hitler Youth education about sexuality did not prevent sexual contact between children but at times promoted it. A school medical inspection in an east Prussian district reported that many of the girls had recently had intercourse. Examination of girls under fourteen years old in Marburg, revealed much the same figures. In Frankfurt, five Hitler Youth boys aged between fourteen and sixteen lured some fourteen-year-old girls into an attic. Three of them held the girls down while the remaining two raped them. In two other cases, schoolgirls of thirteen and fourteen visited soldiers' billets several times looking for sexual experiences, not just with one man but with several.[131]

The law courts were increasingly flooded with child sexual cases such as those reported in 1942:

- Three boys and three girls, all thirteen, met to engage in group sex.

- Two other boys aged thirteen and sixteen procured three nine-year-old girls for the same purpose.

- A sixteen-year-old boy hired himself out as a male prostitute.

- A girl at primary school lectured her classmates on sexual technique and the use of contraceptives.

- Some fifteen- and sixteen-year-old girls mutually agreed that French prisoners of war could "do it far better than Germans."

- Two fifteen-year-old girls moved in with some antiaircraft gunners and spent several nights practising positions.

- Other girls made a business out of sex but were ignorant enough to accept payment out of small change.

- One fifteen-year-old was reproached by her mother for persistently associating with SS and soldiers. The girl was unmoved and retorted: If she got herself pregnant, she'd be just what the Führer was always asking for – a German mother.[132]

German laws regarding sexual crimes against children were flawed, and considerably influenced by current social norms regarding sexuality among girls and boys. Sexual contact with those younger than fourteen was forbidden in Germany according to clause 176 section 3, from the 1871 *Reichsstrafgesetzbuch*, a statute unchanged by the Nazi regime.[133] This law states that "A punishment consisting of confinement in a penitentiary for a term not to exceed ten years shall be imposed upon any person who: (3) commits lewd acts with persons under fourteen years of age, or induces them to commit or to submit to lewd acts."[134] There is also a caveat about mitigating conditions: "If extenuating circumstances are present, the punishment shall be imprisonment for a term of not less than six months."[135] While sexual abuse crimes perpetrated against German and other "foreign" youth below fourteen were prosecuted and are reported and analysed in detail by Flaschka,[136] no mention is made of any sexual abuse of Jewish children in these multiple criminal trials of Wehrmacht soldiers. German "morality" regarding crimes against German and other "racially inferior" children were also illustrative of the differing values placed on male and female children. No matter what the crime, abused boys were never regarded as complicit or responsible in any way for their abuse in the way that girls were: they were never seen as soliciting or collaborating in their abuse as such acts would threaten their potential heterosexuality and such homosexuality was strongly disapproved of by the Nazi regime. Boys were never "raped" according to this understanding. Perpetrators who raped boys were regarded as having committed "sexual contact with a child" or a violation of the laws against homosexuality. Young girls, on the other hand, were judged to be sexual beings and their crime was influenced by the judges' views regarding their physical development, their perceived compliance with their rapist, unwillingness to protest or fight against their abuser, or their racial background, with girls from socially deprived families being regarded as complicit in their abuse more often, and therefore partially or totally to blame for their own sexual abuse.[137]

Hitler understood the importance of indoctrinating youth from an early age and the Hitler Youth provided a vehicle for this. As Mann writes:

> In *Mein Kampf*: All education must have the sole object of stamping the conviction into the child that

his own people and his own race are superior to all the others. [...]

The Führer's best bet lay, from the very beginning, in the inexperience and easy credulity of youth. [...] because whoever has them has the adults of tomorrow, and can flatter himself he is the lord of the future.[138]

How successful was Hitler in indoctrinating youth? Clearly the Nazi era that followed Hitler's rise to power is evidence of his accomplishments. The effectiveness of his brainwashing indoctrination is also evident from the deeply unconscious voice of a child of the time:

Just after Hitler came in they had an emergency operation, a little Aryan boy with appendicitis. Peritonitis had begun; it was a matter of life and death [...] in the silence of the operating room, deep under anaesthetic, the child began to scream, suddenly, shouting phrases cut so deep into his soul that they remained even during the death under ether, "Down with the Jews! He cried out, "Kill the Jews, we have to get rid of them!"[139]

Clearly, harsh childrearing practices, coupled with inadequate and inappropriate attitudes towards child sexuality did not prevent child sexuality or child sexual abuse either of boys or girls, or German or non-German children. Some adherents of Nazism never relinquished their views. Some perpetrators, in fact, continued to indulge their predilections for child sex victims long after the end of the Nazi era. For example, Paul Schaefer, a former doctor and corporal in Hitler's army fled to Chile in 1961 to avoid charges of sexual abuse. He established a secret sect called Colonia Dignidad near Buenos Aires. This centre apparently served as a torture centre for the Chilean Secret Service under Pinochet where former Gestapo and Nazi officers gave lessons. He was arrested in August 1996 along with twenty-two other sect members and sentenced in 2006 to thirty-three years in jail for twenty-five counts of child sexual abuse committed between 1993 and 1997. A number of former residents of his colony testified that he systematically abused the colony's young children, many of whom were taken from their parents at birth.[140]

Long lasting Nazi attitudes did not only survive among those with distorted bents such as Paul Schaefer. In 1996 and 2006, surveys of children born in Germany asked about their opinions of Jews. The German General Social Survey reflected the views of 5,300 people from 264 towns and cities across Germany. Those born in the 1930's held the most negative and the most extreme antisemitic opinions – even fifty years after the end of Nazi rule. These views were stronger if they came from an area where antisemitism had been prevalent even before the Nazis.[141] The rising rates of right wing, nationalist, populist, and often antisemitic, anti-Jewish or anti-Israeli prejudices that have emerged across Europe and countries beyond Europe's borders in recent years are worrying aftermaths of Nazi thinking and reinvented influence.

Jewish families living in Germany or neighbouring countries, at the time of Hitler, were exposed to similar societal values as those experienced by German children. With fewer than 1% of Germany's population being Jewish, and with considerable assimilation into German society at the start of the Nazi era, and with many Jewish children attending German (as opposed to parochial Jewish) schools, all members of society would have been exposed to similar childrearing practices in existence at the start of the Nazi era. Jewish child sex abuse during Hitler's reign needs to be viewed against this background.

CHAPTER 3: JEWISH CHILDREN

Children were caught up in the increasing antisemitic persecution imposed by Nazi policy from the start of the Nazi era. Such antisemitism served to create legitimate targets for abuse of all kinds, including economic, social, physical, emotional, and sexual. Antisemitism also provided the groundwork for implementing the genocide of all those regarded as non-Aryan, and primarily Jews, and Jewish children. In Germany, *Ostara*, a low end publication, edited by Lanz von Liebenfels, an eccentric former religious cleric, imagined "blue-eyed, blond Aryans waging a monumental struggle against the 'race defilement' danger posed by what he termed 'monkey people.'"[142] Alfred Rosenberg, a Nazi party member from 1919 and editor of the Nazi Party newspaper the *Völkischer Beobachter* from 1923 endorsed these views. His book, *The Myth of the Twentieth Century* was widely disseminated with over a million copies printed by 1942. Permeated with antisemitism, it promoted German "purity of blood." He characterized all of history as "a conflict between the forces of light (the Nordic or Aryan peoples) and the powers of darkness (the Jews)." According to Rosenberg, the Jews had to be eradicated.[143]

Nazi era racial policy did not emerge in a vacuum however: it was created on a soil fertile with anti-Jewish ideology fostered for over two thousand centuries by Christian churches.[144] As early as the fourth century, Catholic teaching invoked antisemitic accusation, based on both theology and economics. These views were strengthened in the thirteenth century and thereafter with blame being placed on Jews for the death of Christ. The age-old accusation of ritual murder of non-Jewish children as an essential ingredient for making unleavened bread for the Passover celebration – the blood-libel – continued throughout Europe and survives today in the Arab world.[145] Added to these beliefs was the enormously popular forgery of *The Protocols of the Elders of Zion* depicting a Jewish plan for world domination.[146] First published in Russia in 1897, as a Russian fabrication, it was rapidly translated and widely circulated throughout Europe, England and North America in the 1920s, and nowhere more so than in Germany in the 1930s. Hitler charged his propaganda department, through Goebbels, to disseminate the *Protocols* worldwide in several languages and to defend its authenticity.[147] Such anti-Jewish sentiments provided clear precursors to Nazi era racial policy and practice.[148]

Antisemitism was further flamed by Germany's frustration and economic burden following World War I, rapid inflation, the global economic crisis of 1929 and its resulting unemployment, and the readily available and traditional scapegoat of the Jews. This despite the fact that in 1933 so few of Germany's population (less than 1%) was Jewish and by late 1939, Jews made up no more than 0.28% of the estimated 68 million residents of the Reich.[149] The Nazis reinforced these antisemitic ideas even in reading materials designed for children's consumption such as Elvira Bauer's book *Trau keinem Fuchs auf grüner Heid und keinem Jud bei seinem Eid* (*Don't Trust A Fox in A Green Meadow Or the Word of A Jew*) published in 1936 by *Der Stürmer*.[150] A hundred thousand copies in seven editions were circulated. The book links the Jew with a malicious and deceptive fox – a traditional image of the Devil – and writes warnings against Jews such as: "Like a fox, he slips about / So you must look out!" Bauer likened the Jewish presence in Germany to a plague that must be exterminated, thus justifying the destruction of the Jews even for very young children. In contrast, in her book, Bauer portrays Germans as hard-working, honest, handsome and courageous. Not surprisingly, such sentiments probably contributed to the willingness of many to comply with Hitler's ideology regarding Jews, and even to commit crimes against children.

Hitler and the Nazis operationalized these anti-Jewish principles both in Germany in the 1930s and then later, as the Nazi party gained power, throughout much of Europe. The antisemitic virulence of Martin Luther's later years was also used to further Nazi ideology. His scathing tract *On the Jews and their Lies*, depicting Jews as Christ killers and criminals bent on ruling the world was prominently displayed at party rallies. In this, he advocated burning synagogues, schools, and homes, and driving Jews "like mad dogs out of the land."[151]

Between 1933 and 1939, 1,400 anti-Jewish laws were passed in keeping with this antisemitic philosophy.[152] Anti-Jewish laws were imposed from the earliest months of Hitler's regime restricting Jewish religious, educational, professional, economic and cultural life. Some affected children directly. On April 25, 1933, the *Law Against Overcrowding of German Schools* introduced a restricted quota for non-Aryan students in German schools and universities.[153] Jewish children were expelled from schools after being segregated and identified as Jews leading to antisemitic reactions from their former friends and classmates as well as their teachers. Only two days later, on April 27 1933, the practice of Jewish ritual slaughter of animals for meat was prohibited. Simultaneously, the antisemitic children's book *Der Giftpilz* (*The Poisonous Mushroom*) depicted Jews in the process of slaughtering an animal with the accompanying text: "Again the animal falls to the ground. It is slowly dying. The Jews, however, are standing around and laughing about it."[154] Young German children were actively recruited to join Nazi youth groups and were indoctrinated on such antisemitic images and concepts.

By the end of 1934 about 50,000 Jews had left Germany to seek safer havens.[155] Additional laws against Jews were passed in late 1935. On November 1, the *Reich Citizenship Law* disqualified Jews from German citizenship.[156] Jewish children became social outcasts, lacking recourse when Aryan children brutalized them. The sentiment extended to even veterinarians refusing to treat the pets of their Jewish owners.[157] By 1937, more than 60% of Jewish children had been forced out of German schools.[158] Such ideas spread: Between 1935 and 1938, Poland eagerly modeled its policy regarding Jews on Germany's. Jews were attacked throughout Poland and tens of thousands of Jews emigrated to Holland – like Anne Frank's family – and to France, Belgium, and Palestine. In 1938, the Romanian government stripped Romanian Jews of their citizenship.[159] Interestingly, University quotas for Jews also existed at this time in American Universities while American discrimination restricted Jewish presence in education, jobs, and housing as well as from immigration. Far from a German creation, antisemitism had become in vogue globally.

In March 1938, Germany annexed Austria adding considerably to the Jewish population of the Reich. A targeted program of persecution, expropriation and forced emigration followed as the accumulated Nazi promulgations against Jews in Germany – the Nuremberg Laws – were immediately applied to Austria. In less than a year, more than half of Austria's Jewish population of 190,000 had fled, escalating into a major international refugee problem.[160] Further, Polish Jews living in Germany were denied their Polish citizenship while Germans tried to expel them back to their homeland. The family of Herschel Grynszpan, who was seventeen years old, was among those who were forced to leave their home in Hannover, but not allowed entry back into Poland. In retaliation, Herschel, living in Paris at the time, went to the German Embassy in Paris on November 7 and shot a diplomat, Ernst vom Rath, who died two days later. To avenge vom Rath's death, Propaganda Minister Joseph Goebbels gave the signal, approved by Hitler, for a nationwide pogrom against Germany's Jews. The actions that followed, known as *Kristallnacht,* resulted in 267 Jewish synagogues – almost all the synagogues of Germany and Austria – being burned, with Jewish cemeteries, hospitals, schools, and about 7,500 businesses and homes looted and often burned. Ninety-one Jews were killed, others were beaten, and around 30,000 male Jews were sent to the newly enlarged concentration camps of Dachau, Buchenwald and Sachsenhausen. Fire brigades allowed synagogues to burn down while protecting nearby Aryan property.[161] Police arrested many of the Jewish victims. Jews were blamed for the pogrom and fined one billion Reichsmarks – or 400 million US dollars at 1938 rates. Children were directly affected by these events. In addition to the fear and terror provoked by the wild actions of rampaging neighbours, many of their parents, and particularly their fathers, were attacked, humiliated and brutalized in front of them, and then arrested and deported to camps.

SOLVING THE "JEWISH PROBLEM"

With the influx of Austrian Jews, other solutions to Germany's self-created "Jewish problem" had to be found.[162] The Final Solution was not long in emerging. In January 1939, Hitler's address to the Reichstag included his standard antisemitic tirade but also a threat to "annihilate the Jewish race in Europe."[163] Eight months later, on September 21, 1939, just a few weeks after Germany invaded Poland on September 1, Richard Heydrich, head of Nazi Germany's secret police, initiated the actions that were intended to exterminate the Jews of Europe.[164] Jews were moved from the countryside to the cities and confined in specified city areas – ghettos – which were readily served by transportation networks so that they could, ultimately, be sent to "the east" to labour and concentration camps – and more often than not, to their deaths. Whether these actions were planned from the start – an intentionalist theory – or emerged "on the fly" as situations changed and differing solutions were adopted as reality changed – a functionalist explanation – is still debated with the latter being more readily accepted today.

German forces crushed Polish resistance within one month of invading the country. Poland's Jewish population, 3.3 million out of 33 million Poles (10%), came under German control, giving even greater impetus to the need to solve the "Jewish Problem." In addition to Heydrich's moves to ghettoize Jews in preparation for their deportation to camps, Hitler authorized the euthanasia program to replace the eugenic sterilization program that had been in place since 1933.[165] Signed in October 1939 and backdated to the start of the war on September 1, 1939, the euthanasia program targeted Germans and Austrians (both Jewish and non-Jewish) who were physically or mentally disabled. It authorized killing them using multiple techniques including gassing.[166] Estimates vary, but between 70,000 to 200,000 people[167] including at least 5,000 German children, were murdered.[168] The euthanasia program's ideal of racial purity, its methods of murder, and its administrative personnel played key roles in the ensuing Final Solution.[169] The restriction of Jews to Nazi enforced ghettos began in Poland on October 8, 1939, followed shortly after, on October 12, with the start of deportations of Jews from Austria and Moravia to Poland. It also marked the beginning of Jews over the age of ten being forced to wear publicly identifying emblems such as a yellow Star of David on their clothing, although the timing of this injunction, and the placement, design and colours of badges varied from place to place. This six-pointed star, a symbol of Judaism, was turned into an insignia of deep humiliation and a form of torture. Now immediately recognizable, Jews were easily monitored. Gentiles could instantly shun them. Fortunate were those who were merely snubbed in the streets, for the yellow (or white in some places) hexagram identified its bearers as targets for state-sanctioned exploitation, abuse and even death. Jewish children quickly became targets of such physical and verbal abuse.[170]

MOVING TO GHETTOS

Many aspects of children's lives in ghettos have been extensively documented.[171] Living conditions in ghettos were horrific: abysmal accommodations, overcrowding that resulted in unhygienic, disease promoting conditions, filth, lack of food, water and toiletry facilities, and restrictions on virtually every aspect of life were the norm.[172] Despite this, people adapted as best they could, and actively made adjustments, where possible, to resist the Nazi-imposed degradation and dehumanization and create a semblance of order, employment, education and entertainment.

Eva Heyman's diary, written in Hungary, at the age of thirteen, comments astutely on the changes that occurred in their lives on moving to ghettos. The Raczes family had been assigned to 20 Szacsvay Street. Eva remarked on the "interesting" use of language regarding the new reality.

> It occurred to me only when we got to Szacsvay Street that we weren't going to have an apartment, because the commission had said: "your place to sleep will be 20 Szacsvay Street." It made a tremendous difference, dear diary, because a normal person has an apartment, while people talk about "a place to sleep" only in connection with animals. I

swear that Agi is right; as far as the Aryans are concerned, we've become like animals.[173]

Children's lives were equally devastated, if not even more so, than those of adults. Many lost parents, siblings and other family members. Some parents were killed before their eyes or were snatched away from them. Many children were left without support and alone. In his diary of the Warsaw Ghetto Emmanuel Ringelblum wrote, "Death lies in every street. The children are no longer afraid of death. In one courtyard, the children played a game tickling a corpse."[174]

Many young people undertook tasks far more demanding than should ever be imposed on a child. For example, because they were less conspicuous, smaller and less likely to be perceived as criminals, many took to providing for their families as best they could. They became smugglers, crossing the boundaries of the ghettos to trade or steal whatever they could in the way of food to contribute to their families' survival.[175] Punishment for being caught by the Nazis or by local militiamen was vicious, with beatings being the order of the day. On Friday 1st January 1943, Yitshkok Rudashevski, a fifteen-year-old boy in the Vilna ghetto writes of such abuse in his diary:

> Elke, the son of Khone Rone, lives on Shavler 4 (they lived with us). He slips out every day and brings potatoes, flour, through a hideout. The family is a large one and so the little boy looks for a way to survive. On one of these days the Jewish police seized him, and the small, frail Elke was given twenty-five lashes. Four policemen held him and [Meir] Levas himself the commander of the gatekeeper [commander of the Jewish police who guarded the ghetto gate] beat him so mercilessly, so murderously. The little breadwinner was brought home badly flogged.[176]

PHYSICAL AND EMOTIONAL ABUSE

Such public displays of horrific physical abuse were common events in ghettos and could not be avoided by children or young people,

Marcel Tuchman, in the Przemyśl ghetto in Poland, tells of three men, one of whom was his uncle Wilhelm, who tried to cross the ghetto border, but were caught:

> It was a Sunday, a lovely sunny day, and Schwamberger [Josef Schwamberger, S-Oberscharführer, Ghetto A] brought his wife and five-year-old son to witness the diabolical scene. It was reminiscent of the films depicting how the Romans tortured the early Christians. The punishment ordered by Schwamberger was to strip the men naked in a public place and deliver twenty-five lashes each on their naked bodies. Schwamberger's Ukrainian flunkies delivered the punishment with hateful, merciless passion. The physical pain and humiliation suffered by the victims seemed to satisfy and entertain the voyeurs.[177]

Not everyone was willing to endure such degrading humiliation and torture. People feared not only death, but the degrading events that might lead to it. Survival was sometimes not viewed as more important than the awful experiences that might accompany it. Many doctors collected medications that were ultimately used in mercy killings or suicides to avoid indignity and suffering.[178]

Ghetto life was intolerable, and all those living in them were expendable, according to the Nazis. Chaim Rumkowski, the head of the Lodz ghetto Judenrat, acceded to Nazi demands to send the ghetto's children to the camps. His infamous appeal to the Jewish community of the ghetto to give up their children for deportation remains etched forever in the history of this period. But children were not valued as workers; Rumkowski believed that only Jews who were "useful" might be saved in the ghetto. In addition, if the children were not sent, then adults would have to be chosen to fill the deportation quotas demanded by the Nazi's.

> I have to cut off the limbs in order to save the body! I have to take children because otherwise – God forbid – others will be taken. I have come like a thief to take your dearest possession from your hearts […] I did succeed in one thing – saving all

children past the age of ten. You see before you a
broken man. Don't envy me. This is the most
difficult order that I have ever had to carry out. Give
into my hands the victims, thereby to ensure against
further victims, thereby to protect a community of a
hundred thousand Jews.[179]

Parents' hysterical and understandable reactions to these demands
and their inevitable implementation were devastating. But so too were
the reactions of older children who escaped this particular *aktion*.
Faigie Libman (nee Schmidt), now in her eighties, but ten years old at
the time, still recalls her memories of this event with horror.[180] She
had been allowed to take only one toy into the ghetto with her when
her family was forced to relocate. She chose her very special Shirley
Temple doll, which was her pride and joy and the envy of all her
friends. Her mother had dressed Faigie as a far older child and had, by
saying she was twelve, managed to get her a workplace in a factory in
the ghetto. When Faigie returned from work on the day of the children's
aktion, she found every one of her friends and playmates had been
taken. She was so devastated that she believed "the end of the world
had come." She "smashed her doll to smithereens."[181] In contrast Adam
Czerniakov, the head of the Warsaw ghetto *Judenrat*, chose to commit
suicide rather than comply with this Nazi demand. This response to the
Nazis' demand did not, however, result in saving the children.
Ultimately almost all perished.

Parents went to unheard of lengths to protect their children to the
extent of formalizing marital relationships in an attempt to prevent
separation. Aliza Barouch, in the Greek ghetto of Baron Hirsh in
Saloniki, reported that boys and girls were married fictitiously in order
not to be separated. She married a young boy in a *marriage blanc* (a
marriage without consummation) ceremony; she was fifteen at the
time.[182] Such "marriages" were a manipulation of the marriage laws –
and the requirement to at least pretend to marital behaviours – in order
to survive. In most cases these probably provided only a short reprieve
from deportation from ghettos.

To escape these horrors, and when ghettos were positioned close to
forests, some – and particularly those who no longer had ties to the

ghettos such as family members whom they cared for – fled to the forests to join partisan groups. While few such groups were virtually exclusively Jewish – such as the Bielski group – others were comprised primarily of Russians who sometimes displayed little affection for their Jewish neighbours. Women joining Russian partisan groups, although not reputedly in Jewish groups, were often expected to pay for their protection with sexual favours. Children in partisan groups assumed adult awareness and, sometimes, involvement in sexual activities at a younger age than would have been the case in most family settings. As Tec writes regarding the Jewish Bielski partisan group:

> The Bielski children, wearing cut-down, cast off adult clothing, mimicked adult behaviour, going off on their own to play at Germans and Partisans, but also spending much time spying on the adults and watching the ebb and flow of sex under the trees. Among the Bielski, one small boy called Garfunk charmed everybody by springing to attention before Tuvia [one of the Bielski group leaders] in the morning and announcing "Commander, allow me to report that in our *ziemlanka* [bunker] whoring has been taking place."[183]

Few families survived their ghettoization intact. The survival of Dr. Zalman Grinberg's family is exceptional and reveals the lengths to which some were forced to go in their attempts to stay alive. Faced with a Nazi roundup of children in the Kovno ghetto in Lithuania, he injected his five-month-old son with a sleeping drug and buried him in a barrel in a remote part of the ghetto. He inserted two breathing tubes – cut from his stethoscope – through the lid of the barrel. Two days later, following the *aktion,* he rescued his son, still alive, took him to his wife who fed him, and injected him again, before smuggling him out of the ghetto to a non-Jewish friend who agreed to care for him. Shortly afterwards, both he and his wife were transported from the ghetto, she to various camps and he to work as a physician in a German hospital in Danzig. Amazingly, they all survived and were reunited after the war.[184]

THE EINSATZGRUPPEN

By the end of 1940 the number of Jews killed by Nazi Germany had reached around 100,000, but in 1941 1.3 million Jews were murdered by four *Einsatzgruppen* killing units, one by one, supported by local police, collaborators, and the *Wehrmacht*. The *Einsatzgruppen*, the infamous SS death-squads, accompanied the *Wehrmacht* as they invaded Soviet territories on June 22 in Operation Barbarossa, committing mass murders, as they progressed deeper into Soviet territory. Such massacres as that at Babi Yar, where 33,771 Jews were individually murdered in two days contributed to such alarming numbers. These atrocities were common.[185]

The actions of the *Einsatzgruppen* that accompanied the *Wehrmacht* during Operation Barbarossa have been well documented.[186] These German troops were, usually, assisted by locals. Aron* (aged less than ten years) in Ukraine, reported that Romanian collaborators went house to house with lists of people who had helped the partisans.[187] They took them all to jail. Some days later the *Einsatzgruppen* marched all the Jews into a field, made them dig one big grave, stood them in line, shot them, and then covered them with lime. Aron* saw about 300 people treated this way. Such atrocities occurred in village after village as the troops advanced further into Russian territory. In many, if not most places, Jews were already confined to village ghettos which were then, immediately before the arrival of the *Einsatzgruppen* and on their advance orders, surrounded by police guards or barbed wire by locals a night or two before being taken to mass graves and massacred.[188]

There are numerous records of the *Einsatzgruppen's* specific cruelty towards children such as the report by Rene Chevalier who had witnessed the requisition of Jewish women to do the harvesting as there were no more animals to pull the carts filled with hay:

> They came in the morning with their children. The German who was guarding them couldn't stand their crying and whenever it irritated him too much, he would get hold of a little child and bludgeon it to death against a cart. In the evening, all that remained were the women, carts and hay.[189]

The *Einsatzgruppen* in the Ukraine killed parents on the edges of a ditches: babies were torn from their mother's arms, toddlers fell into the ditches alive, or both mother and baby were shot with one bullet before falling into the burial ground.[190] Ohlendorf, the head of *Einsatzgruppen* D, testified at the *Einsatzgruppen* trial after the war that he thought he was acting humanely in circumscribing the manner in which his victims were killed. He claimed that he would not allow his men to bash infants' heads against hard surfaces, but instructed them to have the mothers hold their children close to their chests so that one bullet through the head of the child would kill both the child and the mother. Heinz Schubert, a subordinate of Ohlendorf, and tried at the same time, however, noted "it was of the greatest importance to Ohlendorf to have the persons who were to be shot killed in the most humane and military manner possible, because otherwise [...] the moral strain would have been too great for the execution squad."[191] It was not, apparently any attempt to be humane towards the victims that led to Ohlendorf's instructions, but concern for the perpetrators. Such concern for their sensitivities did not seem to be needed by many of the killers, whose were ready to kill children without compunction. As Desbois reports: "An old lady told me that she had seen a young, Jewish woman place her baby on the sidewalk. She said the German soldiers had made an old Jewish lady pick up the baby but because she had been too weak to carry him, they had killed them both."[192] Anna Dychkant, seventy-seven, of the Busk, region of Lviv, remembered a young Jew who was holding twins in his arms. A German went up to him, shot at one child, then the other and then shot the father with a third bullet.[193] In La Risiera prison, in Italy, under *Einsatzgruppen* command, one survivor recalls, "An SS man passed his cell, leading a curly-haired toddler by the hand. The child, Jewish, tripped and fell. The man kicked him in the head with the full force of his heavy boot. The child's head literally exploded."[194] Clearly, cruelty to children and their parents was an accepted part of the *Einsatzgruppen's* mandate to exterminate Jews.

The Nazi policy to eliminate Europe's Jews – the Final Solution – probably went into effect during the summer of 1941, after the *Einsatzgruppen* killings had begun in June.[195] The German army had been thwarted in their attempt to occupy the USSR rapidly, before the winter, erroneously expecting little resistance. Faced with a large Jewish population, the killing process – one Jew at a time – proved too slow. In September, experiments at Auschwitz indicated that Zyklon B could be used to kill Jews in gas chambers. By late autumn, stationary gas chambers were being constructed at the Belzec and Auschwitz camps in Poland. On December 8, the day after the bombing of Pearl Harbour and the entry of the United States into the war, the first large-scale gassing of Jews took place: 700 Jews from villages near Chelmno, Poland, were executed in trucks filled with carbon monoxide gas. By this time too, mass murder of Jews by individual killing as was the practice of the *Einsatzgruppen*, was perceived as being too stressful for the killers and too inefficient. Instead, the death camps would be further refined.[196]

FROM GHETTOS TO CAMPS

The movement of Jews into ghettos across Europe served only as a staging point before transporting those who survived the intolerable living conditions, the *aktions*, and the rampant disease in the ghettos, to concentration camps.[197] During 1942 and 1943, the Nazis liquidated the ghettos by deporting and murdering their remaining inhabitants.[198] The *aktions* stimulated the movement of Jews to hiding places, to concealment on the Aryan side of the ghettos and to placing their children with Christian families or institutions in the hope of saving their lives.[199] Children were often among the first to be taken through these mass *aktions* as was the case in the Lodz ghetto.[200]

Children were usually forcibly deported to concentration camps together with their families but were sometimes sent alone. For example, children of parents who were in the Dutch underground were taken to Westerbork (a transit camp in the north of Holland) prior to being sent on to Auschwitz. Dozens of the children were sick when they arrived in Westerbork, including babies under a year old and children as old as fourteen years. The younger ones did not even know their own names. All were exhausted and hungry. Those in Westerbork managed to care for most, but all who survived were sent on further transports.[201]

In France, during the second half of 1942, 4,000 children who had been separated from their parents were brought to Drancy in sealed cattle cars before being sent further to Auschwitz. The children ranged from fifteen months to thirteen years, smelled bad and were dirty. Showers were arranged for about a 1,000 but only four towels were available. Almost all had dysentery. Many had contagious diseases including diphtheria and scarlet fever. As in Westerbork, the little ones did not know their names. All were transported to Auschwitz and were gassed immediately on arrival.[202]

Cruelty met children on arrival in extermination camps such as Auschwitz or Treblinka. Gisella Perl, who served as a prisoner doctor in Auschwitz reported that:

> The children, little blond or dark-haired children coming from every part of Europe, did not go with their mothers into the gas-chambers. They were taken away, crying and screaming, with wild terror in their eyes, to be undressed, thrown into the waiting graves, drenched with some inflammable material and burned alive.[203]

Perl's reports are echoed by Lucie Adelsberger, who also served as a doctor in Auschwitz:

> I saw the flames of the open fire next to it and watched as they tossed the dead (and sometimes not quite so dead) bodies of the children onto it. I heard their screams, saw how the fire lapped at their tender bodies. No metamorphosis of my being, regardless of whether in this life or the next, will ever expunge this horror from my soul.[204]

During the summer of 1944, large numbers of children were thrown alive onto fires in the death camps. Sometimes a more merciful SS man would shoot the child dead to save it from the gas chamber or the fire.[205] Additional instances of extreme cruelty to children exist: Dr. Jacob Wollman of Lodz reported that the SS clubbed about five hundred children to death with their rifle buts.[206]

At other times, on arrival in camps like Auschwitz, mothers were sent to their deaths together with their children. Some chose to stay with their children; some gave them to an older woman or a relative. The women, like Sophie (in *Sophie's Choice*[207]) who was forced to chose one of her two children for survival, had to live with their heartbreaking, choiceless, decisions.[208] Parents sometimes tried to hide their children on arrival at the camps, to avoid being separated from them but such decisions were terrifying and with unknown consequences for the children:

> When it came [their] turn [...] to march past the SS officer, [...] Samek and his wife [...] had given their two-year-old Miriam a sedative and put her in a knapsack slung over Samek's shoulder. The column advanced slowly [...] In the tense silence the wails of a baby suddenly rose. [...] A Ukrainian guard ran out, plunged his bayonet several times into the knapsack from which the criminal sounds had come. In seconds the knapsack was a blood-soaked rag. *"Du Drekiger Schweinehunde!"* [filthy dogs] the SS officer shouted indignantly, bringing his riding crop down on the ashen face of the father who had dared to try smuggling his child past. Mercifully, the Ukrainian guard's bullet put an end to the father's ordeal then and there. Thereafter it became routine for guards to probe every bundle and knapsack with their bayonets. [...]
>
> "Take off the knapsack!" she [Adek's wife] hissed. As if in a trance, he did so [...] he edged over to the end of the row of marchers and carefully deposited the knapsack on the curb. It took no more than just a fraction of a minute."[209]

Those who were "lucky" enough to be chosen for life on arrival in camps were subjected to multiple bodily and emotional assaults including nudity, shaving of all bodily hair, sometimes tattooing as in Auschwitz, removal of their clothing to be replaced by degrading prison-wear or randomly allocated used clothing, as well as other more intimate and sexually humiliating experiences. Resistance to these abusive impositions was futile and often fatal. For example, Ursula* testified that a woman refused to remove her clothes when sent to the crematorium in Majdanek. When a member of the *Sonderkommando* tried to undress her, she hit him. They tied her up but she still objected to undressing. A German put her straight into the fire alive.[210]

Nudity and voyeurism were widespread in camps. The Holocaust created multiple opportunities for the SS and their accomplices to expose women and to humiliate them. Hana Muller Bruml in Kodowa-Sackisch, a subcamp of Gross-Rosen, from October 1944 to liberation in May 1945, tells that she was forced to attend classes on how to use a micrometer. The German *Meister* (foreman) who taught these classes offered, one day, to take her and her four friends to have a shower. They had no towel or soap and had to put on their old dirty clothes again, but it was a wonderful relief just to be under water again. "It took years before I finally allowed myself to remember why he did it. He stood in the corner and watched five naked young women taking a shower. He got his jollies!"[211]

In addition, at Stutthof, Gabis reports that:

> Afterward there was another room with a cement table. Everyone had to lie down and have a gynaecological check to see they're not hiding anything. It was done by men; they were 'doctors'. I was young, I was a virgin, but there were older women who had had children. The men dug into them, really dug. They were aggressive. I remember very well there was a young woman with us who had hidden things. She had hidden a watch and some jewellery and in the gynaecological check they found them and took them out. She was crying afterward. "Not only did I lose my jewellery, but I'm not a virgin anymore."[212]

There were few children in camps. At some point, however, there were as many as 500 children in Ravensbrück which was designed to hold 6,000 women but held 50,000 in January 1945.[213] Most of them were sent on to other camps and did not survive.[214] In 1942, a separate camp for women and children was established within Majdanek's men's camp. Most of these children were murdered within a year.[215] Bergen-Belsen had a small children's section.[216] Auschwitz also created a children's barrack. It was the brainchild of a German political prisoner who convinced the Germans that children could be put to work and should not, therefore, be killed. The SS agreed to let him prove it and put him in charge of a barrack that housed only children. Ten-year-old Thomas Buergenthal was sent here, and most of his fellow inmates were older than he.[217] Ruth Elias reports that the Family Camp BIIb in Auschwitz also had children. This camp was headed by Freddy Hirsch, a German Jew who worked tirelessly to assist them.[218]

In 1943, in Buchenwald, communist elder Ericj Reschke also persuaded the SS to set up a children's barrack – Block 8 – to "teach them a sense of German order and discipline." Block 8 shielded the children from sight and afforded them some protection. The number of children in this Block rose from 150 in 1943 to 400 in 1944. Most were Jewish. The group set up a further barracks – Block 66 – in which Elie Wiesel was housed. Block 23 was yet another block established for children.[219] The expansion of these youth barracks suggests they were seemingly effective, from the Nazis' perspective.

Despite the multiple award-winning film *Life is Beautiful*[220] that depicts a father successfully hiding a young boy in a camp, children were scarcely ever able to be hidden in camps. On occasion, babies were smuggled into the camps in luggage, and were discovered in the clothes sorting sections such as the Kanada barracks in Auschwitz. They were killed upon discovery.

Glass reports that children's life experiences in camps manifested in horrific nightmarish dreams of tortured and mutilated parents, imprisonment and death by horrific means such as drowning, burning and gassing. Children entertained themselves with macabre games that reflected the abuse, annihilation and death that surrounded them: they simulated beatings, imitated doctors selecting inmates for death, acted like guards punishing prisoners, or played the roles of parents collapsing in snow.[221] A further game was called *Appell* [roll call]: those playing it acted out the roles of perpetrators and victims.[222] Hanna Hofmann-Fischel reported to Yad Vashem later that children:

> played *"Lagerältester"* and *"Blockältester"*, "Roll Call" shouting "Caps Off!" They took on the roles of the sick who fainted during roll call and were beaten for it; or they played "Doctor" – a doctor who would take away food rations from the sick and refuse him all help if they had nothing to bribe him with. Once they even played "Gas Chamber". They made a hole in the ground and threw in stones one after the other. These were supposed to be people put in the crematoria, and they imitated their screams. They wanted me to show them how to set up the chimney.[223]

Few families survived the camps intact such as those of Walter, Ruth, Albert and Marion Blumenthal, having not suffered physical or sexual abuse other than the general and horrific starvation and disruption in camps and the death march.[224] In Poland, where nearly one million Jewish children had lived in 1939, fewer than 100 intact Jewish families remained at the end of the war.[225] More realistic and typical narratives are those penned by Hanna Lévy-Haas, a prisoner in Bergen-Belsen who describes conditions of total family collapse,[226] and Rena in Auschwitz, who watched as hundreds of tiny children were marched to the gas chambers clutching their stuffed toys for comfort.[227] Barefoot children froze to death in Treblinka while they awaited their turn in overloaded gas chambers,[228] and Bullenhuser Damm is infamous for the hanging of twenty Jewish children aged between five and twelve.[229] In reality, most families sent to the camps were destroyed.

CHILD MASCOTS

Some children in camps were subjected to uniquely distressing psychological manipulation. The use of Jewish children as "child mascots" provided a form of cruelty, manifesting as apparent kindness that was exploited on occasion. These were children abducted and indoctrinated into an SS way of life: turned against their own people and exploited to murder Jews themselves. Christian Wirth, the commander of the "Clothing Works" in Lublin, treated a ten-year-old Jewish boy kindly, giving him sweets and a pony. One survivor remembers:

> I have personally seen that this SS commander led a Jewish boy, who was about ten years old, whom he kept and whom he fed chocolate and other goodies, to kill with a machine gun here and there 2 or 3 Jews at a time. I myself stood about 10 metres away when this boy carried out such shootings. The SS commander, who rode a white horse and who had given a horse to the boy, joined in the shooting. These two human beings together killed – in my presence – among the several occasions - some 50 to 60 Jews. Among the victims were also women.[230]

Similarly, Mark Kurzem reports on the story of his father, Alex, who was adopted into a Latvian *Einsatzgruppen* squad as a five-year-old Jewish child. SS officer Colonel Karlis Lube, who served with the group, protected him during the war: he was dressed in *Wehrmacht* uniforms.[231]

The methods of initiating these boys were often emotionally manipulative:

> The commandant of area three had a *piepel* who was about twelve years old [...] He came to the camp with his parents [...] One of the SS officers motioned to the boy to come over. The officer patted his head and said; "Do you want to become a *kapo?*" You'll be dressed nicely, you will be treated to chocolate bars, and you will go around giving orders like one of us."

> At first the boy was confused. But his parents who thought that he had found favor in the eyes of the officer, motioned to him that he should agree to the invitation. [...] The boy [...] was appointed an official *kapo*. [...] On the third day [...] the camp

inmates were ordered to gather around the gallows
[...]

An eyewitness reported:

> "We all stood breathless. No one of us in our wildest
> imagination could believe the scene that unfolded
> before our eyes. We thought this was a macabre joke.
> The parents stood on the scaffold, their backs to the
> gallows, an indescribable look on their faces. It
> seemed as if they too, imagined that the commandant
> was playing a hoax. The boy stood frightened, his
> head bowed. The commandant then said to him,
> "You are still young, we want you to have a good
> time here. Your end will be similar to those of all the
> others – death. But I want you to live. Therefore,
> from now on you will be my son, a German like all
> Germans. All those who are gathered around you will
> have nothing in common with you. Because from
> now on you are one of us – they are Jews. You are
> now a *kapo*, and like all *kapos* you will not think
> twice about hanging two filthy Jews. Is it not so?
> Now show us all that you are not a Jew."
>
> The boy's hands trembled as he tied the noose
> around his parents' necks. The father stood rigid
> and pale, the mother sobbed quietly. As she exhaled
> her last breath, she motioned as if she were thrusting
> away someone, something, with her dying hands.
> To me it appeared as if she was trying to blot out the
> memory of the horror.
>
> At Maidanek [sic] this boy was the chief degenerate.
> He would walk about with his wooden club in his
> hand and break heads capriciously[232]

The diabolical irony of a Jewish child being coerced into being
implicit in the murder of his fellow Jews, and in some cases, even the
murder of his own parents,[233] is almost incomprehensible. Against this
backdrop of cruelty to children, the addition of sexually related cruelty
is not surprising.

AVOIDING THE CAMPS

Some managed to avoid the hardship of the camps, but encountered sexual abuse in other settings. For example, one Polish father "sold" his daughter to a man in Argentina in the 1930's– probably for economic gain or necessity. She was placed in bordellos to serve a life of sexual slavery. Her older sister, Cila, lived with a German camp commander in Bergen-Belsen and did not suffer the same fate as prisoners during the war.[234] Jewish women who lived with Germans during the war might have escaped death, but frequently lived thereafter with highly conflicted feelings about their memories of the period, while also being subject to extreme social condemnation. Maja was one of these.[235] She was a particularly brutal Jewish *kapo* in Auschwitz who shared her privileged bunk in the barrack with a German SS officer whom she later married. She later reported:

> Now I'm considered an outcast, a criminal by those who knew me then. There were others who were far worse than I during those years! [...]

> A nameless, faceless SS man came every night. I feared for my life and thought it would ensure my survival in Auschwitz. I loathed him then: I knew that he was a criminal and a killer. But as the months went by I got used to him. He kept me out of the gas chamber. He gave me food. I did not think of the future then. I lived one day at a time. Whatever I did was my way of surviving [....]

> After the war I spent two years in Germany in a displaced persons camp. He found me there but I refused to see him or talk to him Then I came to New York. He followed me again. He kept coming back into my life. I knew his past and he knew mine. I was tired of running and hiding. We decided to start a new life together. Can you understand? I didn't do anything wrong![236]

Sexual abuse did save some young women. Shoshanna often wondered why her father's two aunts – now hapless women – had been chosen for survival when they were young girls in Auschwitz:

> Basza [sic] had the sheer luck of being in the right place at the right time. But the unfortunate Boba, with her delicate air and sickly ways, had been among the first to be designated for annihilation. Seven times, she claimed, she had come before Mengele for selection at Auschwitz, and each time she had had her patrons. Her very frailness and rarified, subtle beauty had, it appeared, been a magnet for lesbian guards in the SS who persisted in smuggling her back to the right-hand side from the left. No-one [sic] ever asked about the services she had had to render in return for her life.[237]

Sexual violence is a complex issue. It is dehumanizing, degrading, humiliating and terrifying in addition to being sexually abusive. Sexual abuse and violence has often been conceived of as a common spoil of war (despite the gross moral violation it represents) and in many current conflicts worldwide, such as in the Rwandan genocide,[238] it was, but in the Holocaust, sexual abuse of Jewish women and girls was not a formal component of Nazi ideology. Theoretically at least, the *Rassenschande* laws forbade this, and certainly child sex abuse was illegal in Germany even before and during the Nazi era,[239] although this did not stop such abuse from happening. The ensuing chapters deal with the sexual abuse of children, and primarily Jewish children, during the Nazi era.

CHAPTER 4: ABUSE

Sexual harassment and abuse of children occurred throughout the Nazi era. It took many forms ranging from witnessing sexual acts, through voyeurism, fondling, rape, and even more perverse sexual activities. While all sexual abuse is abhorrent, and the extent of trauma experienced by any victim is not dependent on the externally perceived severity of the sexual abuse (for example fondling as possibly less traumatic than rape), for pragmatic reasons, the various types of abuse experienced have determined their inclusion in the chapters that follow. In this chapter, the sexual "climate" of the Nazi era is examined as are various forms of sex abuse that are generally classified as of "lesser" intrusiveness than rape. It is fully acknowledged that the actual experience of any one of these types of abuse is likely to be dependent on a myriad of factors such as the age of the child, his or her family situation, the perpetrator's identity, the feeling of betrayal that might accompany the event, the resources available to the child for help, the extent of physical and emotional harm that is done, and others. Discussion of rape itself is delayed to a later chapter.

Just as existed among German children, Jewish children across Europe were raised within a culture that decried openness about sexuality, particularly with regard to children. Magda Herzberger from Rumania (Cluj, Transylvania) comments on the lack of sexual education and awareness among children.[240] So too does Pnina Granirer, writing of her life as a Jewish child in Romania in the Nazi era:

> In today's [early 21st century] open and permissive
> culture, with young children receiving sex education
> in public schools and seeing sexual imagery all
> around them, it is difficult to imagine that seventy
> years ago, sex was a mysterious and forbidden

territory. Of course, we thought about it and imagined all sorts of answers to our questions, but there were no manuals to read and no one to ask. For younger children, the answer to, "Where do babies come from?" was still the stork story.[241]

Sexual education of children was a taboo subject. Anna tells that when she was a small child in Budapest, Hungary, and Attila was a boy a few years older, he asked her if she knew how babies come. He tells her:

> "The father takes his thing and puts it in the mother's thing and they rub themselves together up and down, up and down, up and down, that's how."
>
> [...] It couldn't be true. Not my parents [...]
>
> "Anyu" I said to Shoshana [her mother] upstairs, "how does a baby get inside its mother's tummy?"
>
> "Don't ask me about this." Shoshanna says, her hands coming to rest on the mound of her belly. "When you are old enough, I will tell you all you need to know."[242]

Despite her mother's reticence to share this knowledge, she recalls her grandmother enforcing that she was changed into pajamas instead of nighties as soon as she could toddle, and that her mother checked that her hands were always above the covers when she went to sleep,[243] just as Hans-Georg Behr's mother had done to him in Germany.[244]

WITNESSES TO SEXUALITY

Even if children were not informed about sex and sexuality, they were often exposed to sexual behaviour throughout the Nazi era, and often cruel, sadistic or misogynistic actions. Pnina Granirer tells of an incident that frightened her and her cousin Gabi when they were about ten or eleven years old, in Romania:

> We had just been to the movies at the Trianon Theatre
> and were heading back to Gabi's home. Just as we
> were about to cross one of the ubiquitous dark filthy
> alleys serving as unofficial public urinals, a man
> suddenly appeared from the shadows, flashing his
> huge penis and making obscene gestures. Terrified,
> we ran as far as we could away from this menacing
> figure. We had never seen a penis before and after
> this experience we did not want to see one again.[245]

While Pnina's story might reflect life at any time, anywhere, for children growing up in cities, exposure to sexually related actions in the Nazi era were often more sinister events for children. Erika*, who was around ten years old at the time, and living in Poland, testified that an SS officer came up to her mother, who was very beautiful, started playing with her hair, and undid the braid. He took her mother, ostensibly to find her sister. At that moment Erika's* father came home and said "Where are you taking my wife?"[246] The SS told her father that he had nothing to say in the matter. The SS man then took her mother towards the bedroom. Her father angrily lifted the SS man and threw him down the stairs. Her mother was shaking – saying "you could get hurt." Her father said he didn't care – the SS had no right to take his wife. The SS man stood up, took his gun and walked away. The next day, however, the SS came and took all their furniture and her mother and father away. Erika* was told that her father had been taken to work. She never heard from them again. She said, when giving testimony decades later, "You cry, you wipe your eyes, and you accept."[247] There was nothing that she, as a child, could do.

Sexual humiliation, amongst other atrocities, became a part of the Nazi terror perpetrated against Jews. For example, *Kristallnacht* - a precursor to the ghettoization of Jews - provided an opportunity to rampage and terrorize young girls as experienced by Susan and her younger sister:[248]

> Susan remembered being woken that night
> [Kristallnacht] by shouting and screaming as eight
> young storm troopers burst into the family home and

began to vandalize everything in sight. They locked her parents in a bathroom, then attacked Susan and her younger sister. The girls were dragged out of bed and Susan's nightgown was ripped to shreds. Her parents could be heard shouting and crying but were unable to intervene. Then the SS thugs ordered Susan to get dressed, but as she opened the wardrobe they pulled it down on top of her and left, assuming they had killed her. Fortunately, it had fallen onto an overturned table.[249]

GROWING UP: EXPERIMENTING WITH SEXUALITY

Life in the ghettos rapidly eroded childhood sexual innocence. Children were educated in ghettos even though this was prohibited by the Nazis. As Maria Ember says boys and girls were, unusually for that time, schooled together: "And in the air there was a little sexual contact and awakening too. In the schools in Hungary before the Second World War, we were not coeducated. It was a new thing, boys and girls together."[250]

While sexual abuse is customarily thought of as rape, forms of sexual interactions that took place during the Nazi era, and that were precipitated by the exceptionally stressful conditions of ghetto life with its ever-impending threat of deportations at any moment, led to sexual activities among young people that – from within a perspective of "normal" society – might never have occurred. As Nate Leipciger recounts in 1939, in Sosnowiec "It was if they knew they were on borrowed time and might as well enjoy whatever they could before it was too late. [...] I heard rumours that young people were partying all night and having sex parties."[251]

The experiences of fifteen-year-old Janina Bauman in the Warsaw ghetto on May 30, 1942, reveal a similar example of situations that were precipitated by the Nazi era. Her friend Zula went to a party and stayed overnight, in itself an unusual activity in this era of sexual naiveté:

They were playing games […] sitting on each other's knees and kissing. From time to time they would drink vodka straight from the bottle. Somebody passed Zula the bottle and she drank too. [They] switched the light off and lay down on the floor, all next to each other. She fell asleep straight away, but woke up after a time and heard a couple making love next to her. She thought the other couples were doing the same in the dark […] she began to sob. A boy came over to comfort her and wanted to make love to her. She was very frightened and refused […] The boy […] told Zula that with life as it is we shouldn't wait for our one true love before making love, because we might never live that long.

We've been thinking about and talking about what he said all day. Perhaps he was right, perhaps we've been wasting the last nights of our lives not even trying to find out what love is? Yet the very idea of doing it drunk and in the presence of other people makes me sick. I would rather die not knowing.[252]

Zula's tearful reaction to hearing others having sex nearby reflects the minimal exposure or understanding that she might have had about such parties or such sexual activities. Two months later, on 21 July 1942, Janina described her budding relationship with Roman, aged sixteen, a little older than herself. Their opportunities to be alone together were limited in the overcrowded ghetto conditions, and family members continually walked into and out of the room they were in, winking at them in their attempts to give them some privacy. She was uncomfortable and asked Roman to go.

As we were saying goodbye Roman whispered something strange in my ear. He said the only way we could be left alone is to go to an hotel. There is a secret hotel in the ghetto, he said, and he's got enough money to book a room for a single night. We could go there tomorrow if I wanted to.

She puzzled over this option and decided to go with him, but the mass deportations from the ghetto began the next day.[253]

Janina Bauman's decision, although unfulfilled, was not unique in the unnatural ghetto environment, but was unlikely to have been considered (or even been possible to contemplate) in a "normal" family setting. Vladka Meed revealed at a 1983 Conference on Women's Experiences in the Holocaust that men and women needed to be loved at this time. As she said, "A 17-year-old girl told me, 'I would like to live with a boy because I don't know what is going to be tomorrow and I have never experienced to be with a boy.'"[254] While such sentiments may not be all that different from those of teenagers today, they were exacerbated by the events of the Holocaust including the breakdown of normal family life, the separation from fathers (and their parental control or guidance) who might have been arrested, killed or fled to find safer living places for their families elsewhere, the close quarters in which people lived, sharing a single room with all members of their family or indeed with other whole families, and the resulting lack of privacy for all. As Freda,* who was sent from Prague to Thereisenstadt, testified, she witnessed sexual activity, in consequence, at a young age.[255]

Normative behaviour was destroyed by such ghetto conditions. In addition, Nazi perpetrated sexual abuse compounded the children's naturally increasing sexual awareness with forced sexual events. Mary Berg's (Miriam Wattenberg's) Warsaw diary entry of December 1939 (she was fifteen at the time) reports on bizarre sexual voyeurism by the Germans at the expense of the ghetto inhabitants:

> The cruelty of the Germans is increasing from day to day, and they are beginning to kidnap young boys and girls to use in their nightmarish "entertainments." They gather five to ten couples together in a room, order them to strip, and make them dance to the accompaniment of a phonograph record. Two of my schoolmates experienced this in their own home.[256]

Children in ghettos also witnessed sexuality. For example, in the Lodz ghetto, children worked as "coal miners:" they were dump pickers looking for anything that could be burned to create heat. The children dug in muddy ground to find pieces of "coal" that could be sold to better-off homes. These "coals" were dug out in places where once there had been a house, a fence, or any kind of structure. They could be pieces of wood, stones or rags. They did not burn, but if placed in a burning fireplace, might turn into coals and cause the fire to smoulder for a little longer.

> In the coal mines girls take off their one dress before stepping into the pit. Boys of 10 or 11 and girls of 13 and 14 get to know the secrets of their mothers and fathers right there in the coal pit. They take care of their physical needs right there and then in full view. No time for amenities.[257]

Children also reported sexual violence in their testimonies of their experiences in ghettos. For example, in the Lask ghetto in Poland, Sala Pawlowicz was stripped naked as a young teenager and beaten by a Polish-German policeman.

> "But I can't have you, scum, because you're Jewish and filthy. What a shame!" He swung the whip across my breasts, "Here's what you can have for being a dirty Jew – instead of me – this!" He lashed the whip again and again and I fainted.

> I found myself lying naked in the street.[258]

> While in Sala's case the laws of *Rassenschande* deterred this policeman from raping her, they were not always an inhibiting force and multiple women and girls were raped.[259] As Sala describes, Germans made selections of Jewish girls they wanted in the streets, dragged them off and raped, assaulted or tortured them before either shooting them or throwing them aside.[260]

An additional component of sexual violence and abuse in the Holocaust was, however, the fact that this usually private behaviour frequently, but not only, occurred in public. In Sala's case, for example, she reports that the beating she received from the policeman occurred in a room with several other Germans who "laughed and pointed obscenely at her."[261] The use of dogs to attack and abuse women is also frequently reported as a public event. [262] Such public displays of atrocities – designed to deter unwanted behaviours or to humiliate and terrorize Jews, or simply to boast and aggrandize their perpetrator – is termed "paratheater" and is well documented as a means of implementing Nazi ideology.[263]

FONDLING

Inappropriate touching of children occurred in multiple settings including in ghettos. While fondling itself was an egregious assault, and might have been the ultimate intention of some perpetrators, it is also possible that these sexual advances might have been interrupted before reaching full sexual intercourse. For example, Dana S. from Lvov tells:

> I was playing with friends [...] A German soldier came over, tall, with a part in his hair [...] He took me by the hand. I was scared. He squatted down and started to grope me under my dress. He took out a tomato and said, bite it. I knew that no possible good could come of this because I knew about "Snow White" and the apple. And he was just as wicked. He showed me his gun. I remembered, would I be shot if I ran to [my] apartment which I could see. I ran, but he didn't shoot [...] my mother made a bath and hugged me and put me to bed. She didn't ask any questions. I felt really grateful and it was OK.[264]

Agi Stein-Carlton (thirteen years old) and her eight-year-old brother Andre Stein lived in a ghetto cellar in Budapest, Hungary. She remembered that the superintendent of the cellar, a devout Catholic, would come around and, taking advantage of the darkness, would feel up the women including her: "No one said a word [...] I would feel his hand creep up my body. I was mortified. First I though it was a rat and I screamed."[265]

USING SEXUALITY TO SURVIVE

The testimonies of two sisters, in Skarzysko Kamienne, Plaszow, provide credence for the lengths that some girls went to in order to survive. They report that young girls entered into relationships with a policeman for protection.[266] These two sisters are not the only ones to report sleeping with a policeman to save their lives. Rita* lived in a Lithuanian ghetto and, as a fourteen-year-old, worked for the underground. When the ghetto was liquidated, she was hiding with twelve other family members and friends in an attic – they lived there for about a month – but they were all exposed by a Lithuanian and were herded off to the police. Rita* had sex with a policeman and was thus the only one to be let go. She was rescued by the underground and survived.[267]

Sex was sometimes offered in exchange for survival, or at least, in an attempt to survive, although it is not always possible to identify these types of activities in reports. Some testimonies reflect instances which may or may not indicate that sex was used for survival by using euphemisms for sexual exchange. An example of this is a story told about two gendarmes who held up a woman and a young boy, Noam,* in the Warsaw ghetto. Noam* later testified that the gendarmes held them against a wall ready to shoot them. The woman, who was exceptionally beautiful (a crowned beauty queen) begged the officers not to shoot them. Instead she offered to go with one of the gendarmes apparently to collect a fur coat from her apartment for him while the child stayed with the other gendarme. She went to the apartment and gave him the fur. While this story may well be a true one, it is possible that sexual exchange, rather than only the exchange of a fur coat, might have also been involved to save their lives.[268] Such phrases make identification of sexual abuse from testimonies difficult. This story is related not to claim that sex was exchanged for freedom in this case, but to illustrate the difficulties involved in identifying all cases of sexual abuse from reports.

Sometimes girls used sexual activity after being raped to secure their survival. For example, as Tova (aged thirteen) says: "The men who raped me were also the ones who kept me alive"[269] When Tova's family in the

Lodz ghetto in Poland got sick, they were transported to the camps but she was left behind with a family that shared their room. While the wife was out of the house, the husband raped Tova. He was a handsome man and he and his wife were very cultured and intelligent people. Tova worked in a clothes factory, mostly with other children. The Jewish foreman came up to her and her older friend and told her friend that she looked like his wife. He offered to give them both better jobs. Tova did not want this but her friend readily agreed. "The man came around, told me and my friend to wash ourselves, and then he used us for his sexual needs. I didn't want to have sex, but it seemed we had no choice."[270]

When they first arrived at the factory they were shaved. Two or three German men watched and loudly and lustfully judged her older friend's body. Some of them raped girls, in front of everyone. One day a German combat engineer ordered them to move to another factory, a long way away. The soldiers who herded them openly killed some of the girls along the way. The combat engineer raped her without looking into her eyes. She imagined that she could keep this man's viciousness at bay by being a good worker and doing everything he asked her to do sexually. On the day of the death marches this man kept her and her friend back, so saving their lives until the Americans came. As Tova reported:

> There were others who had used us for sex, including the Jewish foreman, who had not provided for us. It doesn't matter if men are Germans or Jews, all men are rapists [...]

> The rapes took place in the face of the loss of my family, our abiding hunger, and the wide-ranging tortures we and others endured. I was in such a shock that I didn't care much where I was, what people said to me, and whether I was raped or not. I was finished.[271]

After the war, Tova was alone. She never spoke about being raped during the Holocaust. Years after coming to Israel she married but she never wanted to get pregnant. She tried to abort her first pregnancy but did ultimately have children. Tova's thoughts about these rapes swirled within her: "Were they rapists or saviors?"[272]

WITNESSING SEXUAL ABUSE

Even on transport trains from ghettos to the camps, children were exposed to sadistic sexual activities that they would never have encountered in normal life. Liza Silbert reported that Ukrainian guards raped young girls every night while on the train from Vilna ghetto to Kaiserwald concentration camp near Riga, Latvia.[273] Marion Loew testified that on a train transporting her from Sarajevo, Croatian Ustashi guards stopped the train in the middle of nowhere and forced the prisoners to watch as a Serbian woman was gang-raped while her husband was also made to watch: the remaining guards stood around laughing. Both the husband and wife were then killed. Marion was ten years old at the time and had nightmares about this scene for years.[274]

Children's barracks in camps provided no security against the sexual manipulation of others. In Birkenau, some learned that they could trade sex for food:

> Jehuda Bacon remembered how a friend of his with a pretty sister became her pimp, charging a packet of cigarettes a time. Bacon believed that the boy did not understand what he was doing, beyond the pleasure of acquiring cigarettes and demonstrating his power. The practice spread even to the younger children. As one boy aged eight progressed from trading goods with a Kapo in another part of the camp to arranging for his mother to become the Kapo's girl friend [sic], so his food and dress attracted universal envy.[275]

In 1959, Jehuda Bacon told his story to an Israeli interviewer. Bacon related that the *Sonderkommando* men frequently "dealt with the most beautiful woman separately, namely they kept her back till [sic] last. Then they threw her last, and with a certain piety, into the oven on her own too, not with the others."[276]

Whether this story is true or not, young teenage boys listened to these stories of sexual pimping, or sexualized treatment of even those who were gassed to death, in their shared barracks at night. They also learned "to sell bras and make-up to the women in the camps, crucial items that helped distinguish the healthy-looking 'prominents' from the rest during selections."[277]

VOYEURISM IN CAMPS

Voyeurism was not only indulged in by the SS, the Nazis, and the *Wehrmacht*, but by their collaborators. Such voyeurism was not just sexual harassment but was intended to dehumanize the targets of the Nazi genocide. Nudity, public exposure, shaving of all bodily hair usually by men, inadequate and dirty clothing, a lack of undergarments, no means to manage menstruation for those who continued to have their periods, were all intended to deprive women of their modesty and to humiliate them as women and girls, and not just as Jews. Such dehumanization through sexually linked activities were uniquely created by the conditions imposed on Jews in the Holocaust. In March 1944, in the Ukraine, Sylvia Aron, who had lost both her parents, recalls one humiliating incident above all others:

> Before we returned to Romania, we appeared before a committee consisting solely of men. They sat behind a table. [...] We came in naked, one by one, and stood before them as they asked us questions and personal details and wrote them down. My sister was older than I, about thirteen, and as she left the committee she burst into tears, her whole body trembling from that humiliating encounter.[278]

Selections for transports from ghettos and labour camps were based on multiple criteria, including age, usefulness, employment status, and no doubt such factors as financial ability to bribe authorities, knowing influential people, or simply luck. In some cases, sexually abusive and humiliating methods were used to select those who could stay or those who must go. For example, at Neusalz – a women's sub-camp of Gross Rosen labour camp – a selection was arranged where women had to appear individually before a panel of SS officers. A large circle had been drawn in chalk on the floor of the room, with an X in the middle. Each girl was forced to walk around the complete circle naked, and then to do so on her knees. One of the officers measured each women's chest and thighs, examined her muscles, and checked her teeth and inside her mouth, assisted by the female SS guards. Each woman's back was then marked "A" for the strongest, "B" for average, or "C" which meant transport to Auschwitz.[279] Such abusive examination methods were probably both sexually evocative for onlookers, as well as intimately dehumanizing for the girls. Humiliation of girls through nudity, invasive examinations of their mouths, forced embarrassing positions requiring them to crawl on their knees, having male SS officers measure their chests and thighs, all observed by a panel of men, were all deliberately degrading and diminishing, sexually repulsive actions, but perhaps titillating for the men.

Sexual humiliation and voyeurism went hand in hand in other situations as well. As Rena says, on arrival and in camps.[280]

> Our own boys, our own men are forced to see our nakedness, forced to shave our heads, our arms, our legs, our pubis. Sometimes they are friends, sometimes they are relatives; mothers get shaved by their own sons, sisters and brothers suffer this embarrassment.[281]

She writes further that:

> The German officers parade back and forth looking at us as if we were interesting specimens in their insect collection. There is one beautiful girl whom they stare at unrelentingly. She keeps her chin up, her eyes down. She is gorgeous despite her baldness. How anger-defying it is to stand and be visually defiled by these murderers. What I wouldn't do for a tap with hot water and a scrub brush to wash the Nazis eyes from my flesh.[282]

Rena's own words powerfully express the girls' humiliation and shame as well as their anger and revulsion at the Nazis manipulation of their sexuality and their dehumanization.

INAPPROPRIATE TOUCHING

Sexual predators did not stop at just looking: there are many reports of inappropriate touching. Eva Grinston reported that a man on the train transporting her from Czechoslovakia to Auschwitz "became very tactile" doing something she did not understand: she was able to break free. She was about thirteen years old.[283] It is not known whether the man was Jewish or not. Maria Scheffer, at around eleven years old, reports having to strip naked in front of many men in Auschwitz prior to being manually assaulted by a German soldier.[284] Shari Braun in Augsberg concentration camp reported that an older man of about thirty-two grabbed her breasts when she was fourteen.[285] Marina was transported to a small camp near Auschwitz; a Ukrainian guard often stared at her. She was eleven, with long blond hair, and green eyes and had not yet reached puberty. One day he called her over, took her to his cabin, closed the door and talked nicely to her. He stroked her hair and said he would look after her. The first time he let her go but she was too afraid to say anything to anybody. The guard kept making advances, took her to his cabin, touched different parts of her body, moving his fingers under her shirt. She was too frightened to move. Soon after, she and her family were sent to Auschwitz. The guard was there too. She was undressed, shaved, and tattooed. The guard who had abused her saved her even though her sister, who was seven years older, was not saved. All the rest of her family except her brother were gassed.[286]

Others tell similar stories. Lily Wolf, aged sixteen, in an internment camp near Budapest, agreed to have sex with a man of about thirty for about three weeks, in exchange for his willingness to rescue her family. He did so.[287] Erica Gold (aged approximately fifteen) in Riversaldt internment camp, reports allowing a guard at the solitary confinement block where her mother was imprisoned to "touch her breasts" each day for ten days in exchange for allowing her to take bread to her mother.[288]

Many of these instances of rape, and sexual violence, happened in public and involved other members of the community or family being forced to watch or even participate. In this context, sexual violence is as much a psychological weapon as a physical one and targets not only the individual being violated, but all those around her/him as well. It is a weapon of dehumanization, terrorism, humiliation, and a physical weapon as well ... it could even be considered a biological weapon in that it can spread disease or cause pregnancy. Sexual abuse under the Nazi regime, with its multiple consequences for both victims and perpetrators, became a far more common event than would likely ever have occurred had the Holocaust not happened.

BESTIALITY

While all sexually directed violence requires human agency, some conducted it through animals. George Reinitz, a young boy in Auschwitz, tells of a particularly cruel Ukrainian guard in the camp who had a dog called "Man" who was trained to attack Jews in the camp. "He would tell his dog 'Man' to attack the 'Dogs' – that was his name for Jews –'Dogs.' And the dog would attack us by going for our private parts."[289] Similarly dogs were used to abuse girls in Majdanek and extensively across the camp system.[290] Several survivors recall how Hildegard Lachert used to command her dog to attack female inmates, although the age of these girls is not known.

> I heard a women [sic] start to scream. It was Wladka, a polish woman [...] 'Brigida' [Hildegard Lachert] had set her large German shepherd on the girl. The dog bit her hands, which the girl was holding in front of her face to protect herself. Then the dog began tearing her clothes [...] 'Brigida' kept spurring him on. Then 'Brigida' assembled us for a kind of roll call: we were forced to stand in a kind of triangle formation, with the girl in the middle, and watch her punishment. I found out later that the girl had become pregnant by an SS soldier, a man 'Brigida' also liked. That was the first time in my life I saw what an umbilical cord looked like, and a fetus. Two girls had to carry Wladka away on a stretcher. [...] After the dog had torn her clothing

from her body, she was covered in blood. You could see shredded bits of flesh hanging down, and the long umbilical cord."[291]

HUMOUR

Even amidst the despair of the camps, sexual humour managed to emerge and served as a coping mechanism that helped people tolerate an intolerable situation.

"Look at your Kapo," Tadziu says to us as we all put down our baskets. We look down the road and see her coming towards us on extremely bowed legs. Her red hair gleams in the sun above her curving limbs as if she had a huge ball between her knees. She waddles towards us.

Tadziu teases, "here comes innocence between parentheses!"

Like a bubbling gurgle of water, a sound wells up from inside of us, erupting quietly from our chests. We are completely surprised. I barely recognize what is happening or what we are hearing and doing [...] we laugh."[292]

Humour, and particularly smutty, sexual humour, served to save the life of one Jewish adolescent, eighteen-year-old Abraham Cykiert. He was a poet in Auschwitz – not generally thought of as a skill helpful for survival. He obtained paper from a clerk in the *Schreibstube* [records office] on which he wrote his poetry. "Can you also write left-handed poetry?"[293] asked the Schreiber, which question Abraham did not understand.

The Schreiber then pulled out a sheet of paper filled with jottings and scribbling. He handed it to Cykiert. The young poet from Lodz blushed as he read gutter rhymes, obscenities, abominations. "Try it." said the Schreiber.

The next day Cykiert showed his latest creations to the Schreiber who was so pleased he paid the teenager with a hot bowl of soup. "Can you recite as well as you write?" he asked. Cykiert nodded. "The following night he took me to the weekly binge of all the inmate VIP's in the camp: veteran prisoners who assisted the SS in running the place. They were sitting around a table laden with delicacies: cheese, sardines, sausage, fruit. The alcohol flowed freely. There were other inmate-performers with me: singers, actors, musicians. We performed from the back of the room while they devoured the food. We were not allowed to touch anything, but when the party was over, we could share the leftovers. I read my pornographic lines and they rolled with laughter. I was consequently accepted as the group's permanent jester. Every week, each of us had to come with new material – to this day I am ashamed of the poems I was forced into writing. Decades passed before I could start writing again.[294]

It is not known whether any of Cykiert's bawdy writing survived the war, although he did live to write and contribute to Jewish life until his death in 2009.[295] His titillating writings for the *kapos* and camp guards, however, remained a source of shame for him throughout his life.

Voyeurism, fondling, and unwanted witnessing of sexual acts or even sex offered in exchange for survival, were humiliating and degrading experiences. While living conditions in the ghettos were impoverished, over-crowded and abusive; they did, however, reflect a level of normality of life in comparison to later situations encountered in extermination and labour camps. Sexual abuse of men, women and children in camps reflected one more abysmal level of horror against a background of life at a minimal level of existence. Ghettos, at least, still retained a semblance of humanity. While labour camps were horrendous places, extermination camps, with their secret locations, prohibitions on revealing what happened within them, and their unbridled cruelty and murderous intent, granted even greater freedom for physical, emotional and sexual abuses.

CHAPTER 5: RAPE

Rape occurred during the Holocaust despite rules against sexual contact with Jews.[296] Rape of boys involved contravening laws prohibiting homosexuality as well. Men, women and children were all raped. Perpetrators of rape often murdered their victims in order to silence them, but some victims survived to tell their stories.

The rape of children affected by the Holocaust was frequently instigated because opportunities to rape, and to rape with few or any repercussions, were facilitated by Nazi policies or the situations created as a result of the war. Rape occurred in homes when Jews were evicted; in ghettos, where children were targeted on the streets; when children were cared for in orphanages; on transport trains to camps; in camps; in hiding, apart from family members or caregivers to whom they could turn to for help; and when sent far from Europe into the hands of strangers. Rape was not uncommon among the *Einsatzgruppen* and *Wehrmacht* as well as among partisans. Most of these situations were the direct result of the enormous disruption in their lives that ensued from the Nazi determination to murder all Jews and particularly all Jewish children. The opportunities this created, combined with a highly autocratic society, in Germany in particular, that endorsed male dominance and both female (and child) submission to male authority, made rape more likely. The lack of accountability for rape of Jews and Jewish children by Nazis and their collaborators facilitated, at least, if not encouraged, these perpetrators' actions. Rescuers of children who hid them and then raped them were also less likely to be held accountable to anyone: fear of betrayal by the children and not having anyone to turn to for help would have limited children's recourse to assistance, giving their rapists freedom to do what they wished with the children. While the Nazis did not endorse child rape legally, or overtly include this in their ideology, their genocidal actions certainly facilitated the sexual abuse of Jewish children and did nothing, that we know of, to prevent or punish it. This chapter focuses firstly on the rape of girls followed by that of boys. As in society today, there are far more reports of female rape than male rape.

RAPE IN EVERYDAY LIFE

Anna*, not yet nine years old, stayed alone in her home in Romania during the day while her mother worked, sewing for the German army.[297] She recounts the terrifying experience of a German breaking down the door to her house. He threw her on the floor, swore at her, and assaulted her. She lost consciousness. Later, a Jewish man, Morris, came to check on her and found her unconscious on the floor. Morris called Anna's* grandmother who took her to the doctor. Anna* was in pain and "bleeding everywhere." [298] The doctor gave her sedatives for a few days. Anna's* grandmother told her mother that Anna* had a cold and that she would keep Anna* for a few days. Anna* did not understand what had happened to her although she guessed she had been raped. As she testified, little girls did not know or understand these things. A few weeks later, Anna's* mother managed to put her in an orphanage where she would be safer. It took many years for Anna* to talk about her rape. When recording her testimony, she said, "It is very important for generations to come to know what I went through."[299]

While there are many who consider that reporting instances of child sexual abuse or rape during the Holocaust is unnecessary, Anna's* words contradict this sentiment. Even though it took her many years to disclose her experiences, when she did, she overtly expressed how important it was for generations to come to know what had happened to her. It was so important that she recorded her testimony for the Shoah Foundation archives decades later, although it might have been far easier to stay silent. Her words speak for the many who were unable to come forward to give testimony.

Sex is usually a private affair, but sexual violence may not be. Rape was not only a one-on-one, private occurrence but often occurred in public or involved multiple perpetrators. For example, in France, the Germans went through a village looking for resistance. They heard rumours that there were Jewish children in the school. The headmaster denied it, but the Germans did not accept the lie, and upon finding the children:

> They tie the smallest children, boys and girls, to the chairs. And tell them to suck the soldiers' organs like their mothers' breasts. Then when the soldiers have had their way, the children are told to imagine it as milk and swallow happily, and their teachers are to make sure they do not cry as they swallow.[300]

This group sex abuse is not only indicative of the perpetrators willingness to abuse children but also their pleasure in doing so as a group, in public – in front of other soldiers and the teachers.

In Poland, society disintegrated after the German occupation. Bands of marauders roamed the countryside robbing and terrorizing, as well as raping women and girls. In 1941, Chaya Finkelstein lived with her husband and four children in Radzilow. The youngest child, Chana, was four at the time. Germans and Poles burst into their home. Chaya fought the intruders to help her husband get away:

> They beat the children, and Chaya defended them like a lioness, kicking and biting the attackers, taking most of the blows herself. She broke through to the cellar where one of the intruders was trying to rape her daughter Szejna, [about eleven or twelve years old] and tore her from his grasp. By the time midnight struck, the house had emptied out, but Chaya, the most heavily wounded of the family, was covered in blood.[301]

Many others also report being raped in Poland. Nina Rusman testified at a trial against the German officer who had raped her. She was thirteen or fourteen, became pregnant, had an abortion which was botched, leaving her bleeding and needing medical care. She was left infertile.[302] A Jewish doctor testified: "One continually hears of the raping of Jewish girls in Warsaw. The Germans suddenly enter a house and rape fifteen- or sixteen-year-old girls in the presence of their parents and relatives."[303] Rape also occurred in other countries occupied by Germany. Jezcchiel F [sic] testified to a representative of the World Jewish Congress in Vilna that the Germans would rape women and girls in their homes after locking up others in the household. The more educated girls were taken to military barracks to be raped and killed.[304] The selection of more educated girls in this instance is in keeping with the Nazis' deliberate actions to first remove the intelligentsia among the Jewish people for either punishment or extermination – in accordance with the Nuremberg laws that removed academics from official positions.[305] Alternatively it could have been a more vindictive motive to target the "best" Jews for humiliation and abuse, as evidence of the Nazis' power over Jews and a clear message of the Jews' inferiority.

RAPE IN GHETTOS

Rape of youth, mostly girls but including at least one boy, is reported in ghettos including Warsaw, Lodz, and Lvov in Poland, in Theresienstadt, and Tacovo in Czechoslovakia, in Budapest and Satoraljaujhely in Hungary, and in Riga in Latvia.

In the Warsaw ghetto, Vivi* reports the rape and murder of a thirteen-year-old girl by a member of the SS.[306] In the same ghetto, Izolda escaped death although she could not escape being raped. She was sexually abused by a policeman in the ghetto in 1942. One day she was stopped by the policeman who eyed her closely, hailed a rickshaw and drove her to the Hotel Terminus where he ordered her inside and into a room where he identified her as Jewish and ordered her to take off her clothes.

> The policeman unbuckles his belt with the holster, takes off his uniform and shoves her to the bed. His breathing is hoarse, loud, long, he smells of cigarettes and sweat. She thinks: Will he demand money? Take me to the station? Ask for my address? The policeman stops moving. She thinks: Will he follow me to Wesola? Will he find my mother? The

> policeman gets up and dresses. He stands in front of
> the mirror and combs his moustache and hair. Put
> your clothes on, he says. Now go outside and get
> back in your rickshaw. You see how lucky you are,
> running into a decent person…He salutes and heads
> back to Nowy Swiat.[307]

At first, she was happy that he didn't demand any money, or take her to the police station, but then she started to regret that she didn't ask him for anything – seeing that he was "a decent person" – a place to stay, a safe address for herself and even for others. She regretted letting such a great opportunity slip by: she ran into a decent person and didn't ask for a thing. While shock and horror might be the reactions we would expect from a child following rape, Izolda's response reflects the streetwise response of children in the ghettos. Survival of the child or her family members was more important than any other personal loss or trauma that she might have experienced. Her reaction also indicates the depths to which life in the ghettos had deteriorated, that simply not demanding money from her or reporting her to the police allowed her to think of her rapist as being a "decent person." Her reaction is indicative of the extent to which the Nazi policy of Jewish denigration had been successful, leading to Izolda's gratitude towards her abuser for letting her go without further victimization.

Further incidents of rape occurred in the Warsaw ghetto. G was about fifteen: She remembered seeing a young SS officer seek beautiful Jewish women, go to their houses, and rape them. Afterwards he would shoot them. He always came prepared with a horse-drawn hearse. Since G was quite pretty, her mother and cousin made paste from flour and water and put it on her face with the hope that she would be less vulnerable if she appeared less attractive.[308] Disguising pretty girls by disfiguring their faces and clothes with dirt or some kind of paste was a common defence used by many mothers to protect themselves or their daughters. Such actions confirm the attitude that the girl is responsible for attracting her rapist. This attitude was, and to an extent, still is, prevalent in many societies. Among the Nazis and their collaborators, there was little responsibility imposed on men to avoid raping women and particularly Jewish women. While it was not overtly encouraged as a spoil of war for example, as far as we know, it was not punished either, leaving men free to seek and abuse their victims.

There are numerous reports of rape of young girls in ghettos, although it is not always possible to identify their ages. Bernard Z in the Tacovo Ghetto in Czechoslovakia reports that Hungarian guards would take young girls and do what they wanted with them.[309] In Riga ghetto, Sia Hertsberg (nee Izrailewitsch) recalled that, as a child, she had gone to bed with a safety pin securing her pajama pants as the elastic had given way just before bedtime. During the night the Latvian police raided their apartment collecting Jews for deportation. One of them pulled her aside after her mother and family had been thrown out, and with his gun in one hand had forced her down on the bed and tried to pull her pajamas off with the other. The safety pin would not allow them to be removed. While he was struggling with this, a member of his troop – who had seen what was happening and who knew Sia – called his officer aside requesting that he assist him, saving Sia from further physical harm although leaving her emotionally distraught.[310]

Dalia* was about eight years old and living in Budapest, Hungary. She went to visit friends of her parents, a married couple, one of whom was a paediatrician and the other a general practitioner. When Dalia* arrived, they were being assaulted outside a Wallenberg safe house by the Hungarian Nazis' Arrow Cross. She and the couple and others were taken to the Danube. They had to undress to their underwear, were shot and pushed into the river. She does not know how it happened but she went into the water alive but with a bloodied hand. She floated down the river until she came to a flight of stairs leading up the river bank. She climbed up and came upon a man with a Nazi armband and a gun. He held her up against a wall and put a gun to her head. He took out his penis and, grinning, said to her "which one should I shoot you with?" He looked tormented. She said "Uncle, please don't." He laughed and let her run away.[311]

Poznanski, in the *Diary from the Lodz Ghetto* (entry dated September 2, 1944), wrote of the rape of a Jewish girl by Hans Biebow, the German head of the ghetto.[312] Biebow grabbed the sixteen-year-old daughter of Dr. Sima Mandels and her engineer husband in the hallway, dragged her into his office, and tried to rape her. She started screaming. Biebow shot her in the eye. Biebow ordered her entire family to be shipped out immediately. Two other testimonies also report rape by Biebow: Esther H reports that Biebow and another German kept Rita, a beautiful Czech girl, and both raped her.[313] Later, she was murdered. Bina W also reports being raped by Biebow.[314]

After the liquidation of the Vilna ghetto, a group of 112 people, including 30 children were hidden by a Polish woman in exchange for furs, silks, and tens of thousands of German marks. When the group could no longer meet her increasing demands (for five kilograms of gold) she denounced them to the Germans, just two weeks before Vilna's liberation. A letter survives, written by two women in the group who threw it out of a vehicle that took them to Ponar, and to their deaths. It describes how eight-year-old girls were raped in the presence of their mothers and how adult men were sexually mutilated with pins and needles by German and Lithuanian police for five days before the group's murder.[315]

RAPE IN PRISON

There are very few accounts of girls who were raped in prisons, possibly because few of them survived to tell their stories. Opportunities to escape from prison were even more rare than from many other situations. Nor was there any chance of avoiding sexual assault if the jailor wished it. Aliza Barak-Ressler and her family, in Slovakia, were betrayed while in hiding and were imprisoned. She was ordered to clean the offices of the guards. One day a guard that she had not seen before, a "broad shouldered, balding, elderly looking man" came to watch over her.

> I was totally absorbed in what I was doing, when suddenly I felt the man breathing on my neck, giving off a stink of alcohol. He pressed against me from behind, put his arms around me in a tight grip and hissed, "Leave the chair and come with me. I won't hurt you. You are a beautiful girl, it's such a

pity" – and then he suddenly burst out laughing. He bent his head and was about to kiss me. I pushed him away forcefully and slipped out of his clutches. Terribly upset and frightened, I still managed to say, "Excuse me, Sir, leave me alone. I am a little girl of fourteen. You must have a wife at home, so why do you need me?" The guard, stunned at my brazenness, backed off and looked at me, and then as though pushed by some hidden hand, left the room."[316]

Fifteen-year-old Irene Binzer was held in solitary confinement for a year in a Serbian prison in Yugoslavia. The head of the Cetnici (the Serbian nationalist group working in collaboration with the Germans) held the key to her prison cell and sexually abused her, virtually daily. As she testified "He raped me over and over and over and over and over." She still recalls him vividly as "tall and thin with a red beard and red hair, and ugly."[317]

RAPE IN LABOUR CAMPS

Dozens of labour camps were set up in a part of Ukraine called Transnistria. Tens of thousands of Jews from Bucovina, Bessarabia, Moldova and the Ukraine were destroyed there by typhus, dysentery, starvation, cold and by bullets. Sonia Palty was fourteen when she was deported with her family to Transnistria.[318] They were moved to a state farm run by a man named Mr. Gogleata. He welcomed them as follows:

"You stinking kikes" [...] Marshall Antonescu sent you here to work and die [...] Ha! Ha! Ha! I would rather you die first and then work. Ha! Ha! Ha! Last year in January, when I participated in the Legionary Rebellion, I sent lots of you to Heaven [...] pardon me [...] to Hell. You rotten kikes, you have no God. You have the Devil in you. If you won't break your back working, this farm will be soaked in your blood. Roll-Call! I want to hear all of your names, and to see each of your faces. I want to see who I am dealing with. As far as your girls are concerned, I have always had an eye for Jewish girls. They smell nice. It's been a long time since I had a Jewish girl in my bed.[319]

He was true to his word, made no effort to conceal his lust for Jewish women and particularly the younger ones. One night, young Mioara did not return from working in the fields. Sonia Palty recalls:

> After a frantic search, we found her badly beaten, swollen, covered with blood, with both her legs broken. I gently touched her hand. She slowly opened her eyes, and stared at me for a few seconds with a blank expression. She looked like she had just been awakened from a deep sleep. Her lips were swollen, cracked and bleeding. Her beautiful long golden hair, which she always kept nicely groomed, was matted with sweat, some strands sticking to her bleeding face. She could hardly speak. I had to lean over and put my ear close to her mouth to be able to hear her whisper, "They bit me, the beasts. They gang-raped me. They burned my skin with cigarettes, they beat me. At first, I screamed, I struggled, I bit, and I swung my arms and kicked my feet. Then four of them held me down, and the first one to have his fling with me was Gogleata. I could no longer struggle or scream. Then he invited the entire army squad to have their fun, the beasts. I will feel them on me for the rest of my life. Then, they just threw me away."

> We took care of Mioara as best we could. After a few days, when she felt slightly better, she asked me to always remember what had happened to her. How could I forget? How could anyone forget?[320]

Palty saw Mr. Gogleata again after the war at the Ministry of Agriculture conference in Budapest (1947), by then incorporated into the Soviet Union. She told her manager about him and was asked to write a report on her experiences. She did so. Two years later she was summoned to the Security Centre of Investigation – a locally dreaded, fear-provoking summons. There, she was reminded about her memo with the officer saying "We have examined the facts [...] There was a war, as you know, and he did his duty. How shall I put it?! At the moment engineer Gogleata is an indispensable staff member. An important employee of the state."[321] Palty reports that she looked him in the eye and said "I understand! An indispensable staff member!"[322] Smiling, the officer let her go free. Clearly the fear and terror instilled by the postwar Soviet regime was not to be countered by survivors, Jewish or otherwise, in post-war Soviet society. Nor was rape considered a significantly serious abuse to warrant any repercussions for the perpetrator – and especially a senior "respected" official. Dismissing reports of rape as unimportant, or too embarrassing to pursue an influential perpetrator, is not unique to the Holocaust but is a practice that pervades global society even today.

RAPE IN CONCENTRATION CAMPS

There are some reports of child rape in concentration camps.[323] The abuse of Jewish female inmates in Ravensbrück applied to women and girls of all ages. Sara B was transferred to Ravensbrück when she was only five years old. She was brutally abused by two SS officers in a special room reserved from that purpose:

> It is very difficult for me to even talk about this because it was one of the most horrible of my experiences [...] Someone came to get me. And I was given some candy [...] And I was taken into a building into a small room [...] There were two men there. And there were some other people in the room [...] I was put on a table [...] or a tall bed [...] I was very violently sexually abused. And I remember being hit. I remember crying, and I wanted to get out of there. And I was calling people. And screaming. And I remember [...] One of them told me that they would stand me up on my head and cut me right in half. They wanted me to stop screaming. And [...] it was [...] I've had nightmares about that for most of my life. And then I was taken

back to where my aunt was. It was something we didn't talk about." [324]

Eliahu Rosenberg, who escaped from Treblinka, reported in 1947 that John Demjanjuk who was convicted in 2011 in Germany as an accessory to the murder of over 28,000 Jews while acting as a guard at the Sobibór extermination camp in occupied Poland, raped women and young girls.[325] Others have reported that prisoners were forced by the Germans to perform a play about rape.[326]

Many camps created brothels to service the SS and their accomplices in the camps, as well as privileged prisoners.[327] It was typically women, or perhaps young girls, rather than children, who were forced to serve as these sex slaves. Nevertheless, children in the camps knew about the brothels and did, in an odd way, benefit from their activities. George Reinitz, in Auschwitz at about the age of eleven or twelve, recorded his exposure to the women forced into sexual slavery:

> I saw that there was a ditch running alongside the road. I looked down. To my horror I saw babies crawling in the ditch. [...] I learned where the babies in the ditch had come from. Women carrying young children who arrived in Auschwitz were divided into two groups. Some [...] were sent to their death upon arrival and the other group were used as slave labour [...] the Nazis selected women they considered to be the prettiest to serve as prostitutes [...] their [...] babies were tossed in the ditch to die.

> The sex slaves were kept on the top floor [...] the youth of the camp would gather outside this building and the women imprisoned in it would throw candies to us. The Nazis gave these poor women some extra sweets after abusing them and the women shared them with us.[328]

Although women were raped in concentration camps, there are few surviving reports provided by those who were children at the time, largely because few female children were ever admitted to such camps.

RAPE BY THE EINSATZGRUPPEN OR WEHRMACHT

The *Einsatzgruppen*, the infamous SS death-squads, accompanied the *Wehrmacht* as they invaded Soviet territories on June 22 in Operation Barbarossa, committing mass murders, such as that at Babi Yar, as they progressed deeper into Soviet territory.

Cruelty accompanied these troop movements including multiple accounts of rape of young girls. For example, Leonid testified that in Minsk a young girl of fifteen or sixteen was raped by a German: when her mother came to help her screaming daughter, the mother was shot.[329] Similarly, Violida Starokostiantyniv from Ukraine, who was ten at the time of the mass shootings of Jews, reported that her sixteen-year-old Jewish neighbour was gang-raped by German soldiers: "All night long we heard her screams, but we could do nothing."[330] The guards standing outside the ghettos of Brest, in Belarus, recalled that the Germans went in every night to rape young girls, in full view and in full knowledge of all.[331] Villagers in Brousk recalled that sexual slaves were imprisoned by the Gestapo and by the end of the year most of them were pregnant: they were then shot by a neighbouring unit from Sokol.[332] Nachum Apelfeld of Berdychev, Ukraine, testified: "that two German soldiers took a woman and a girl to an empty office and raped them. The girl's name was Gusta: she was our neighbour's daughter. Gusta Glozman was fourteen or fifteen-years-old."[333] Carla* was about ten years old at the time and was dressed as a boy in *lederhosen* with her hair cut short to avoid being raped.[334] Her sixteen-year-old cousin was raped by over forty soldiers in Ukraine. Her mother was also raped while they made her father and her brother watch. As her uncle was screaming, the rapists killed him. Forcing husbands or other family members to watch rapes and other atrocities was a means of emasculating men who were helpless to save their loved ones.

As the German-Romanian army descended on the Khotin district in Bessarabia (Western Ukraine), many of those who were raped committed suicide. In Skoriany, eighty Jews were killed within a few hours after the city was occupied. Romanian soldiers ran from house to house, gathering together victims to rape.[335] Similarly, once the district of Soroki was occupied, the soldiers of the 11th German army murdered its Jews. Later, the army decided to open a brothel for soldiers and officers, and it forcibly assembled a group of Jewish girls from nearby for this purpose. Some girls attempted to run away to the forests, but many were tracked by bloodhounds and recaptured. The brothel was opened. The girls served in groups, each group for twenty days, after which they were all shot.[336]

Some reports of physical abuse include suggestions of sexual abuse as well. Many of these emerge from testimonies emerging from Ukraine although they occurred throughout occupied lands. For example, Petrivna in Ukraine, testified that she had seen everything: She saw her Jewish classmate who sat next to her at school arrive at the killing site and then be shot. She saw her friend in the pit, naked, and then was forced to trample on her friend's corpse. Petrivna also remembered that

> Hummel [head of the local Gestapo] took two Jewish girls out of the line, a seamstress and a very pretty young girl, who were to his liking. They were taken to Hummel's house and were not killed that day [...] our eyes were full of the image of these three village girls running down into the pit, trampling on the bodies, throwing sand, and coming out again on the orders of Hummel, trying to catch their breath before the next shooting.[337]

SEXUALIZED BRUTALITY

Horrific sexualized brutality appears repeatedly in reports. Avigdor Shachan writes:

> Jews of the village of Seumpea [...] had fled to the neighbouring town of Falesti [...] later a German unit entered the village. [...] One of the Germans present "excelled" in his utter bestiality. He forcibly grabbed infants from their mothers' arms, and then "played" with them, stabbing them with his knife, cutting off their heads and breaking them over his

knees as if they were but pieces of wood, and all this in the presence of their mothers. At the same time, his comrades were involved in raping young girls and in cutting off women's breasts, while throwing some of the men into the pit while they were still alive to "save ammunition." When they had completed this slaughter, they returned to the village and went on a hunt for any remaining Jews. Those who were caught were gathered together and skinned alive, after which they were strung up in the local poultry slaughterhouse. The bodies remained there until they rotted, and then they were buried.[338]

Similarly, one of Aron's* aunts was raped with a bayonet and had her breasts cut off before being shot. Such actions reflect a level of sexual sadism that is hard to comprehend but was likely intended to dehumanize, destroy, and emasculate the Jews, and provide a perverted sense of power, authority, and dominance to the perpetrators. It is also significant that sexually associated body parts were targeted as opposed to less intimate parts of the anatomy. Such actions might have been perceived as a means of preventing reproduction among the "enemy" in congruence with the Nazis' prevention of Jewish reproduction to implement the genocide of the Jews.[339] Alternatively, such abuse might have simply been vicious, sadistic cruelty. Sadly, such sexually related brutality is not unique to the Holocaust, but pervades literature on modern genocides as well.

Multiple accounts reinforce the occurrence of such sexualized brutality in the Holocaust. For instance, on 7 January 1942 the people's Commissioner of Foreign Affairs of the Soviet Union, Vyacheslav M Molotov published an account of eyewitness testimonies which, during the Nuremberg trials, became known as the Molotov Note. The document testifies to the rape and brutalization of L. I. Melchukova, a sixteen-year-old girl, in a forest in Ukraine. She was later seen nailed to some boards with her breasts cut off. [340] Also, in Belorussia, Lilya S Gleizer was an eyewitness to the Minsk pogrom in July 1942.

> Before the eyes of mothers [...] the drunken
> Germans and policemen raped young girls without
> a trace of shame either in front of each other or in
> front of onlookers. They took their knives and cut
> out sex organs, forced bodies, both dead and alive,
> into the most disgusting poses, and cut off noses,
> breasts and ears.[341]

The bravado of such public rape, cruelty, and sexualized brutality without any apparent censure by onlookers, and in fact, apparent 'enjoyment' of their shared crimes, arouses a spectre of brutality, horror and disgust that is not readily countenanced even in the worst of genocides or war. Yet it is not an isolated incident. For example, in Greece, on June 11 1944 a Waffen SS battalion commanded by Fritz Lautenbach, passed through the town of Distomo. Just outside the village the SS troops were attacked by partisans. The SS troops returned to Distomo and took vengeance by killing the population with unparalleled viciousness. Pregnant women were eviscerated and their intestines wrapped around their necks. Women and little girls were raped, some decapitated, others had their heads crushed or were otherwise executed. Houses were burned and all the animals killed. Between fifty and sixty percent of the dead were children.[342]

There seems to have been no limit to the sexual aberrations that were perpetrated by the Nazis or their collaborators: rape, gang rape and sexual torture accompanied the German war in eastern Europe. Rape of a woman often ended with her murder, though for some, even death did not mean the end of debasement: some corpses continued to suffer the indignities of sexual abuse.[343] Kulski reports, for example, that during the Warsaw uprising by Poles, on September 16, 1944

> I noticed a couple of soldiers dragging a body to the
> shade of an apple tree, not 100 metres distant. I
> focussed my field glasses upon them. They were a
> couple of Ukrainian SS men, and the body – dead or
> nearly dead – was that of a young girl. They placed
> her on the soft grass, spreading her legs wide. One
> of them waved his hand and four other soldiers
> emerged from behind the trees.

> They encircled her and the first two at once started to take off their trousers. One of the Ukrainians mounted the body of the girl; the others crouched around watching. The girl did not struggle. While the first one finished, and before the second mounted the body, the girl's legs flopped limply. She was dead.

> Our standing orders are not to fire until the enemy enters the side gate into the compound. But now a shot suddenly rang out and the Ukrainian collapsed on the body of the girl. The others started running back toward their lines.[344]

RAPE OF BOYS

While some accounts report abuse of boys in ghettos, most boys appear to have been assaulted in camps, where a number were used as sexual slaves of *kapos*. For example, Agi Stein-Carlton (thirteen) and her eight-year-old brother Andre Stein lived in a ghetto cellar in Budapest, Hungary. Andre was raped. He had to collect bread in the morning. One day he was late coming back and everyone began to worry.

> Then Andre turned up. I could tell that he must have seen the face of the devil. He looked like a sleep walker. His face was covered in what looked like dirt. His clothes were tattered and soiled. My first thought was that he had been in a fight. I rushed to hold him in my arms. His body was trembling like a leaf in the wind [...] He ran into the darkest corner of the shelter and disappeared before our eyes. When I put my arms around him, his body felt dead like a slab of ice. His face felt crusty. From the smell on my fingers I realized with horror that his face was covered with coagulated blood. I wanted to feel his body with my hand and search for an open wound, but he abruptly pushed me away.

"What happened to you?" I asked, whispering right into his ear. I swear on Mother's head that I won't tell anyone. Just tell me."

"I don't know" he whispered back "I think I had been killed."

Little by little I got it out of him. When I did I wished I hadn't. [...] Without either of us fully realizing what it meant, it became obvious that he had been raped.[345]

Adolescents were raped as well. One Jewish survivor reported that at age sixteen he had been raped by two SS men when he and his family had been deported to the Riga ghetto.[346] However, perhaps some of the worst sexual exploitation of children was that imposed on young boys in the camps.[347] When transports arrived in Birkenau and Auschwitz, approximately 3-15% of able-bodied men and women were selected to work in the affiliated labour camps. Up until 1944, no children were retained for work in the camps, but from then onwards many were, as labour became more scarce with the continuing war and deployment of men to the army.[348] A small percentage of male children above the age of eleven escaped the gas chambers, largely to serve as sexual slaves of *kapos*.[349] Leon* was one of these.[350] So too was Julian Reuter who, at the age of fourteen, was assigned to work in the *Sonderkommando* at Birkenau dragging corpses from the gas chambers to the crematoria. He recorded that the *kapos* sought out young boys to work for them as sexual slaves. One of them in particular, a Jewish homosexual *kapo*, would provide food for the boys if they "played around with him."[351]

In many camps, some prisoners turned first to homosexuality, and then, when young boys arrived in the camp, to pederasty, to satisfy their sexual needs.[352] Although there was, as of 1943, a brothel in Buchenwald, it did not put a stop to the abuse of young boys. Youngsters were tempted into providing sexual services by the offer of food, or were simply coerced into doing so. Such youngsters, known as "doll-boys" or "dolly-boys"- *Puppenjungen* or *Piepels/Pipels* - sometimes became morally corrupt by emulating the cruelty or viciousness of "their" *kapos* believing they would be protected by their masters.[353] In Majdanek too,

Eisenberg[354]confirms that a number of boys aged twelve to fifteen, mostly Jewish, were selected as runners or messengers/errand boys of the SS. They were privileged and treated with luxuries while they served as the sexual slaves of their masters. These boys exercised great power in the camps for as long as they were protected by their masters and some would beat prisoners without pity as did their *kapo,* thus blurring the line between victim and persecutor. *Piepels* were abused in labour camps as well as in concentration camps as experienced by Nate Leitciger in Fünfteichen, a subcamp of Gross Rosen that supplied workers for one of the Krupp industrial plants. At the age of fifteen Nate was abused by his *Stubenälteste* (room senior) Janek[355] only to be replaced some months later by a newcomer to the camp, a young boy about two years older than Nate.[356]   Stazek, another *kapo* then took an interest in Nate, abusing him, and making Nate masturbate him.[357]

Leon Greenman, a British Jewish inmate, in Buna-Monowitz and Auschwitz-Birkenau remembered that there was a *kapo* named Schiller, who was a notorious bully. He recalled that one young boy of about sixteen used to work with them but then stopped doing so while he became better dressed and seemed happier. He was being used by Schiller. Greenman never noticed it until one night, after lights out, he heard Schiller say in German, "Not so, but so, yes, so is good."[358]

These *piepels* served the *Blockältesters* and the *kapos* who gave the best favours: they were extremely skilled at manipulating their lovers.[359] As Haas notes, "whatever capacity for human tenderness the supervisors possessed was glimpsed only in these distorted relationships."[360]

Heger,[361] writing about homosexuality in camps, notes the contradiction in this aspect of camp life.

> The men with the pink triangles were always 'filthy queers' while the very fellows who insulted and condemned them in this way had no qualms about the relationships of the block seniors and capos [sic] with the young dolly-boys. This was also the attitude of many SS officers. Homosexual behaviour between two 'normal' men is regarded as an

emergency outlet while the same thing between two gay men, who both feel deeply for one another, is something 'filthy and repulsive.'[362]

Heger was himself offered lighter work by a *kapo* if he would become his "lover" and have sex with him. He agreed.[363]

A number of testimonies bear witness to sexual abuse of boys in the camps. For example, Frans* was abused by a German in Mauthausen who told him that if he would give him oral sex, he would look after Frans* and get better food for him. Frans* told that there were many *piepels* in camps working for a high *kapo*.[364] Gunter* was in a subcamp of Auschwitz, Altenhammer, and worked for an SS officer, preparing his baths, who abused him sexually.[365] Harry* tells of Hendrik, a homosexual who would choose the most beautiful boys between ten and fourteen for his own purposes.[366] Branko Lustig,[367] Kenneth Rowan,[368] and Sam Steinberg[369] also served as *piepels* for *kapos* or political prisoners in the camps. The majority of the boys were between fourteen and seventeen years old[370] including fifteen-year-olds Paul Molnar and Rudolf Satovitz. Gilbert, also aged fifteen to sixteen years, when approached to provide sex to a *kapo,* refused and was sent to work in a *Sonderkommando.* Before being sent to his death he was forced to become the *kapo's piepel*: a steep price to pay for his life. He reported later "He raped me again and again, and I swore I was going to kill him, and later on I did. I never told that to anyone."[371]

There are rare reports of young children being abused including that of Peter, Anka Nathanová's eight-year old nephew, who was sexually abused by guards in the Czech Family Camp in Birkenau before being gassed.[372] Even more rare are reports of female *kapos* abusing young boys as happened to Abraham Malach at the age of nine years. The *kapo* ordered a young attractive woman to wash him and fondle him and then took him to her bunk. He reports "and as a nine-year-old boy lying beside her, on top of her, and in any kind of position, whatever she tried must have been futile."[373]

Elie Wiesel reports a scene in the life – actually death – of a *piepel* in *Night,*[374] but the most prolific, and controversial, writer regarding *piepels* was Ka-Tzetnik, the pseudonym of Yeheil Dinur. In *Shivitti De*

Nur he writes "Flames come out of the nether regions of Auschwitz. In the fire's entrails is Cain's burnt offering – pieces of boymeat, pieces of an eleven-year-old nicknamed *Piepel*, the sexual plaything of a block chief in Auschwitz."[375] Yeheil Dinur writes in *House of Dolls*[376] and *Piepel*[377] (his second and third novels) about the fates of his younger sister and brother who were children in the camps, and sexual slaves. Dinur has been scorned, criticized, and condemned for addressing such taboo subjects about the Holocaust. "The fear of dealing with such material is so great that Dinur has even been cast in the role of rapist."[378]

> Dinur's inclusion of sexual slavery in the narratives he composed is seen by turns as obscene, pornographic, melodramatic, voyeuristic, vulgar, even as kitsch. [...] he is personally attacked for his supposed lack of good style and his lack of literary constraint. He is [...] demonized for fantasizing and insidiously passing off as real the horror of institutionalized rape and sexual slavery. The pervasive animosity towards Ka-Tzetnik in critical writing is a contemporary example of an ancient ritual of repression: when you do not like what you are hearing, stone the messenger.

> Innumerable horrors are told over and over in fiction and nonfictional accounts of the Holocaust, but when it comes to sexual slavery, suddenly, according to Porat, the readers' sensibilities, the public's psychological interests, a moral imperative even, eclipse the survivor's rights to speak and be heard.[379]

Why have Dinur's description of *piepel* life in concentration camps been so condemned? Is it simply because they are fictional? Or is it because they are so realistic that they evoke challenging, even frightening, experiences that we cannot face with equanimity? Or that we are unable to accept this as part of the Holocaust experience? Or, even more atrociously, because they refer to the experiences of children? Perhaps they embarrass our sensitivities and fear of confronting sexuality? And especially sexual abuse of children? Possibly, all of the above? Ka-Tzetnik's writings are evocative, insightful, and a remarkable exposure of the probable life of a *piepel*. An extract that illustrate this life most powerfully is provided here, taken, not from *Piepel*, which is more widely known, but from a later book – *Atrocity*[380] (also called *Moni* in some editions):

> He so wants to serve Franzl with all his heart. He wants to be devoted to him, shine his boots, serve his meals, see to it that there was always fresh underwear, clean socks in his locker, the bed neatly made. He so wants Franzl to like him in bed. He is ready to let Franzl try anything he wants on him. At first it had hurt terribly. […] But after a while he got used to it. […] Oh, how he wishes he could give Franzl what he wants in bed. He doesn't let out the slightest groan any more during the lovemaking. Why won't Franzl understand? Why does he kick him out of bed?[381]

> In the Block Chief's bed I had no choice. In fact, there I went all out so the Block Chief could be satisfied with me. And you know that often this lovemaking went on all through the night. All night death was staring at me right in the eyes and still I dozed off in the middle of lovemaking. The Block Chief would grab me by the throat, and only when my eyes tore open I realized that I had dozed off. A moment ago, I knew that if it weren't for the fact that the Block Chief was all worked up just then, my eyes would never have opened again. He kept me alive just so he could shoot his load. And then, with the last ounce of strength in you, you try to keep the lovemaking going and to keep the Block Chief's mind off your life with all the lovemaking tricks you learned in your year in Auschwitz. […] Oh those nights in the beds of the Auschwitz Block Chiefs! Nobody, nobody knows about them. And nobody ever will.[382]

While this is a fictional account, it is possibly a very realistic depiction. Written by a Holocaust survivor, shortly after the war and supposedly reflecting his siblings' experiences, it is likely to reveal images that are reality-based. Such writings are little different from the testimonies provided by boys who served as *piepels* in the camps[383] and as emotionally evocative as Wiesel's description of a hanged *piepel*.[384] Denouncing Dinur's writings will not eradicate the reality that young boys were sexually used and abused as *piepels* in the camps. Clearly sexual abuse of young boys occurred in camps and was, as Heger notes, regarded as standard and "acceptable" fare.[385]

Sexual abuse of boys is reported less frequently than that of girls, most likely because it occurred less often, as in everyday life today, but also probably because most boys abused in camps were unlikely to survive when discarded by their *kapo*. If the *piepel* was unable to find another *kapo* to take them on as a sex slave, they were not likely to survive. Those *piepels* who adopted arrogant or superior behaviours – as the "favoured ones" – as some, but not all, did, were probably less likely to receive support or help from other prisoners. While the "law of the jungle" certainly existed in the camps, with every person for him/herself, the help of others could be lifesaving as well.[386] Children in camps – including *piepels* who had outlived their *kapo's* attentions – were particularly vulnerable and least likely to survive the camps without help.

RAPE OF JEWS BY JEWS

There are some rare reports of Jews, particularly people in authority, abusing Jewish children. Rita H from Pabianice in Poland reported that "*Judenrat* leader Rubinstein [...] started molesting me when I came for milk for my mother. My friends [would say] that this is the only way to get favours from him."[387] Chaya also reported that one of the ghetto officers in the Jewish police force in Poligon was caught raping children.[388] Perhaps the most egregious account of Jewish rape of Jewish victims emerges from the reports of Chaim Rumkowski, the head of the *Judenrat* in the Lodz ghetto. Lucille Eichengreen reports Rumkowski's sexual assaults against herself, aged seventeen at the time, as well as three other children in the Helenowek orphanage in the ghetto.[389] While he ostensibly did much to support the work of the orphanage he also took the opportunities offered to him by his visits there to abuse young children, including Luba who was sixteen,[390] Bronia aged eleven,[391] Mania aged eight,[392] and Yulek who was thirteen years old.[393] Although reputedly impotent, he isolated the children in his office with him, undressed them, touched them intimately, kissed them, and forced them to masturbate him. Bronia, a growth restricted child, recalled

> Once the doors are shut, he victimizes me. I try to get away but his iron grip on my arm fastens me to him. My tears and pleas do not move him; he remains indifferent, even hostile. I am revolted when his groping hands touch me in places I cannot mention, and I cannot tolerate his smelly breath or the slobbering lips he presses to my face. I feel sullied, disgusted, and ashamed, because I am often reduced to the level of praying for his death.[394]

Rumkowski took care to groom one of the children, Mania Zylbersztajn, who was

> 'exceptionally beautiful' She smiled frequently, and was a well behaved, extremely bright girl. Rumkowski took a liking to her and treated her to rides in his carriage. As winter came rides were no longer possible [...]

> During his visit in December, he made himself comfortable in the director's office [...] After an hour he asked for Mania. She greeted him and smiled happily when she entered. Rumkowski took her by the hand and locked the door behind her. But soon we heard the child's shrill cries and agonized shrieks. We did not know what to do! Like fools and cowards we dared not knock on the door – and so we waited. When Rumkowski finally opened the door, he pushed the sobbing Mania out of the room in a distinctly rough manner.

> Mania's face was ashen, and streamed in tears. The right sleeve of her dress was torn at the seam, and in her bulging skirt pocket were her crumpled panties [...]. She changed markedly. She was withdrawn and had stopped playing the violin.[395]

Six weeks later Rumkowski planned to come to the orphanage again. Mania ran away in the middle of the night before his visit, and was found shot dead at the border fence of the ghetto.

Lucille herself was forced to manually stimulate Rumkowski.

> Rumkowski entered, slammed the door shut and swept a chair across the floor. He sat close to me as I tried to inch away, but he clamped onto my shoulder like a vise from which there was no escape. With his free hand he grabbed hold of my hand and before I knew it placed it on his penis. He forced me to rub it back and forth and I tried to pull away – but his fingers gripped my hand tightly and his nails dug deeply into my flesh. I was filled with horror, fear, and loathing, and I did not know what to do as he continued to coerce me. Back and forth went my hand, with Rumkowski hoarsely commanding *"Make it work!'* […] For twenty minutes or so, I lived a nightmare; they were long, slow minutes, and they seemed like an eternity […]
>
> From then on the same ordeal was repeated over and over again.[396]

Rumkowski's legacy is severely tarnished by his infamous call for the children of the Lodz ghetto to be relinquished by their parents for transport "east" rather than adult deportees. Accounts of his child sexual abuse, despite his – or perhaps because of his – reported impotence detract further from his image. His grooming of eleven-year-old Mania prior to his assault of her is typical of pedophiles,[397] although his use and abuse of his position of authority and the opportunity offered by the ghetto and its children's orphanage,[398] indicate that his predilection for children benefitted from Nazi policies and practices that created these circumstances.

A few additional reports of rape by Jewish men, exist. Regina and her family were sent to Auschwitz, where she was separated from her brother. Later, when she was thirteen, she was injured and was admitted to Mengele's hospital where she found her brother. He had lost all his hair and nails and was just skin and bone. His arms were covered in bruises from the injections he had received. He knew he was dying but still recognized her. They embraced thinking he only had hours to live.[399] She begged for a job in the hospital. She was told to carry buckets of soup from the kitchen to the patients. There was always a lot left over because so many died each day. She took the extra soup to her brother. They both got stronger and her brother started to walk again. The doctors continued to experiment on her brother by giving him injections and by cutting him. They wanted to see how long he could survive and withstand the pain.

> Then they told us they needed blood for the soldiers. And it was to come from the children in this camp. Everyday a bus came to take the children; every evening it would bring them back on cots, sucking oranges. The next day the same children would be taken. Within 48 or 62 hours these children died […] I did not have any hope for us anymore. Finally, they came to get all of the children left […] We [Regina and her brother] hid in a ditch while the trucks took all the others away […] We discovered some men who were also Polish Jews who had hidden and stayed behind. We went into the basement with these men where they had a hiding place behind cement blocks. They said it wouldn't be long before the Russians would be coming.
>
> But […] before we [both Regina and her brother] were liberated one of them […] tried to rape me. I couldn't scream because I didn't know if the Germans were all gone, and I was afraid they would hear me and come and kill us all. But I bit that man so hard he was bleeding, and he couldn't go on with it. I was only thirteen years old. […] After this we continued to live in hiding, all of us together. I saw him day in and day out. He did not apologise to me; he thought he had the right to do what he wanted. He's dead now, but I have never forgiven him for what he has done. The thought of being raped, of having my body invaded, is worse to me than death.[400]

Hannah* tells a similar story of sexual assault by a man who may have been Jewish.[401] She was sent to Theresienstadt. One day she went to the toilet but was followed there by a man who sexually assaulted her. She was only nine-years-old, but managed to fight him off. She thinks it was another prisoner although whether he was Jewish or not, is not known. She was terrified but never told her mother. Men used to visit their families in the barracks which is where it happened. She said "I gave it to him!"[402]

These few cases, together with that of Tova[403] who was raped by a Jewish foreman in the Lodz ghetto, and Noel[404] who was raped by his mother while in hiding, comprise the few cases of rape of children by Jews that have materialized from an extensive review of the available evidence.

In most cases, rape of young girls was a deliberate choice made by individual perpetrators – Nazi, German, *Wehrmacht,* or Allies. These rapes were not forced by the Nazis, were not clearly a part of their overt ideological framework, and were, likely, mostly ignored when known about. Perpetrators clearly took advantage of the power discrepancy created by war and the opportunity this presented for abuse.

CHAPTER 6: MEDICAL EXPERIMENTS

For some, the Nazi medical experiments have come to epitomize the ultimate Nazi horrors and a significant feature of the Holocaust. Nazi medical science played a central role in achieving Nazi ambitions to create a Master Race and to eliminate those not deemed worthy enough to live. The period between the arrival of prisoners in the camps and their murders provided the Nazis with a window of opportunity to conduct medical experiments on prisoners, mostly hidden from public view. These experiments were designed to enhance the survival of Germans, the refinement of hereditarily desirable characteristics or to facilitate the prevention of reproduction of "undesirable" people.[405] Brigadier General Telford Taylor, prosecutor at the doctors' trial, described this Nazi science as Thanatology: the science of producing death.[406]

The numbers of victims involved in medical experimentation in the concentration camps has evaded certainty for decades. The numbers involved were certainly substantial: for example, there were over 1,000 in the malaria and typhus experiments and several hundred women operated on in Block 10 at Auschwitz for experiments on their reproductive systems alone.[407] At the Nuremberg doctors' trial, it was decided that 2,000, overall, died in experiments involving about 350 perpetrators.[408] At that time, no consideration was given to survivors of these experiments, only to victims who died. Survivors were considered to be only a few or perhaps only hundreds. There were actually tens of thousands.[409]

Weindling and his colleagues have accurately confirmed 15,744 victims of experiments. A further 12,002 people have claimed to be research experimental subjects and in many cases their descriptions can be matched to known details. This gives a total of 27,748 persons. Of these, 3,878 are probably Jewish victims.[410] A further 50,150 people are known to have been included in large scale research such as infection of 2,500 prisoners of war with hepatitis on Crete; Ritter's research on 21,498 Roma and Sinti; Kraut's studies on 6,802 forced labourers; feeding 10,000 concentration camp inmates and hundreds of Greek civilians with "Mycel" sausage made from cellulose. The total of coerced research is therefore 77,898 victims.[411] In addition, approximately 20,000 civilian and military personnel became unwilling test subjects, bringing the total to around 98,000. Most of these experiments occurred between 1942 and 1945, with 1944 as the high point in research activity.[412]

Interestingly, the laws against experimentation without consent, on children, or dying people, and where animal subjects could replace humans, were in place in Germany in 1931, and were not repealed by the Nazi regime.[413] The decree had neither legislative status, nor the force of criminal or civil law. Its clauses on consent and responsible experimentation stood as guidelines for best practices. Despite these guidelines, these laws were extensively contravened during the Holocaust. The Nazi view of Jews, and those they considered subhumans or of lesser value than so-called Aryans offered justification for these contraventions in Nazi eyes. As subjects destined for extermination anyway, their prior usefulness as research guinea pigs was deemed optimal.

MEDICAL EXPERIMENTS INVOLVING CHILDREN

In addition to multiple experiments on adults, numerous experiments in various camps were carried out involving child subjects. These are summarized here while those experiments involving sexually related activities are reported more fully thereafter.

The Rhineland Bastards: The Germans sterilized 145 mixed-race children whom they diagnosed with "idiocy" or congenital syphilis out of approximately 600-800 so called 'bastard' children emerging from mixed-race relationships.[414] Hans Hauck, born in 1920, said that when Gestapo officers collected him and the other children. "We were all too scared to object. I suspected something would happen, but did not know about sterilization and castration."[415] He had to agree not to marry or have sexual relations. He was held for fourteen days with other scared, mixed-race adolescents while research was conducted on the group. Later, he joined the German army as part of his patriotic duty.

Euthanasia Program Psychiatric Research: The Nazi eugenics and euthanasia programs are well documented. Approximately 350,000 to 400,000 were sterilized under the eugenics program,[416] while the euthanasia program killed over 200,000.[417] In all, fourteen research centres were associated with eleven killing centres/hospitals.[418] These research centres provided morphological analyses and anatomical dissections of the bodies killed. Several thousand children were selected for so-called "special treatment" as part of the euthanasia program: they were experimented on, starved to death or injected with fatal substances.[419]

A number of centres are known to have conducted research on children prior to their murders. From August 1943 until the end of December 1944, fifty-two children and youths aged two to twenty-two were examined in the Heidelberg Hospital. Of these, twenty-one were killed by the drugs Luminal and Morphium-Scopalamin in the Eichberg asylum in late 1944. In addition, at the Wiesengrund special unit at the Wittenou Psychiatric hospital in Berlin, the psychiatrists Ernst Hefter, Gerhard Kajuth and Gertrud Reuter diagnosed, conducted morphological research on, and killed eighty-one children. The children were subjected to comprehensive physical and psychological examinations and photographed totally naked.[420]

Harvesting Brains: Between August and October 1940 about 100 children from Brandenburg Gorden psychiatric hospital were killed in a gas chamber at the Brandenburg prison. Forty brains of a group of fifty-six children and adolescents were sent to Drs. Hallevorden and Heinze.[421] Child brains were also sent to Willibald Scholz at the pathological histological research department of the Kaiser Wilhelm Institute for Psychiatry in Munich. These pathologists were indifferent to whether these were natural deaths or murder victims.[422] Some children were deliberately killed in order to determine which structural brain features corresponded with observed behaviour, such as Valentina Zachini:

> Valentina was born in June 1932 in Nottingham, Britain, to parents who were circus performers, and American citizens. The child psychiatrist Gerhard Kujath at the Berlin Charite diagnosed the child as microcephalic in January 1937. Kajuth filmed Valentina's movements and reflexes, causing her distress and pain. By October 1941 she was on the dissection slab, dissected by Ostertag and Klein. It was Klein who later worked with Hans Nachtsheim at the Kaiser Wilhelm Institute for Anthropology, and in 1945, dissected the lymph glands of twenty Jewish children killed at Bullenhuser Damm School.[423]

Experimental Procedures on Children: Karl Gebhardt conducted experimental operations on children with disabilities. In 1938 he reported a series of operations on thirty-five children to the German Society for Surgery.[424] From 1939 children underwent harsh experimental treatments for tuberculosis. One case was of eight-year-old Manfred Bartke, who was held immobilized in plaster for four years, from 1939 to 1943.[425] George Bessau at the Charite hospital in Berlin subjected nineteen children to a "Bessau inoculation" for tuberculosis using a specially formulated so-called vaccine produced by I.G. Farben's Behringwerk. The children were mainly orphans or illegitimate. There were two experimental series. From July to September 1942, nine children aged from ten to fourteen years old were experimented on. From November 1942 until March 1943, ten infants between two and six, including three-year-old Guenther E. were studied. The abscesses on the children's legs were researched by Salzman. In all, eight of the infants and one fourteen-year-old died.[426] Hensel conducted a series of tuberculosis experiments at the psychiatric hospital of Kaufbeuren in Bavaria from December 1942 to May 1944. Of thirteen children involved, nine were mentally disabled, and one was both deaf and mute. The children were inoculated in May 1943 and all died over the following year.[427]

Fever Therapy Research: Hefter tested "fever therapy" – the idea that sickness can cure. A child whose therapy began in August 1942 died on 27 August 1942. One child died from a fever cure on 20 October 1942, and another infant died after three weeks on 24 October 1942 aged one year. A five-year-old boy with Down's syndrome died from the therapy on 22 December 1942. Hans Klein (the pathologist who later dissected glands from the Bullenhuser School children) working under Ostertag, conducted the dissection finding the cause of death to be an overdose of Pyrifer.[428]

Pressure Chamber Experiments: The geneticist Hans Nachtsheim, at the Kaiser Wilhelm Institute for Anthropology, obtained children for a pressure chamber experiment with oxygen reduced gas on 17 Sept 1943. Six children, aged eleven to thirteen, were obtained from the Gördon psychiatric hospital for what was called "research for the benefit of others." One child lived on after 1945 but the fate of the others is unknown.[429]

Typhus Experiments: A prisoner doctor, Jan Cespiva, testified that eighty-six mothers were infected with typhus and their progeny then tested to see if the placenta acted as a barrier against infection. These were mothers in the "gypsy camp" – Roma and Sinti women. None of the mothers or newborns survived.[430]

Twin Studies: Mengele's twin studies involved the largest group of children studied in any one Nazi research program. Estimates of the number of twins studied range from 900 to 1,500 pairs (i.e. 3,000 children) with less than 200 survivors. The majority of twins were between eighteen months and thirteen years old. All infant twins (under a year) died within six to ten weeks.[431]

His experiments caused illness, deafness, blindness or death. If diagnoses were disputed he would kill either or both twins and conduct autopsies. For example, disagreement arose regarding whether twin gypsy boys aged seven had tuberculosis or not. Mengele killed them both, autopsied them and found no evidence of illness.[432] On the whole, however, he kept the twins alive.[433]

Mengele was intrigued by eye colour. Vexler Jancu, a Jewish inmate doctor, saw eyes laid out on a table in the "gypsy" camp. They ranged from very pale yellow to bright blue, green and violet. Another witness, Vera Kriegal saw a wall covered with eyes in one of Mengele's laboratories "pinned up like butterflies."[434] Mengele collected eyes of those with heterochromia (different eye colours in the same person). On one occasion he had eight gypsies from one family with this characteristic killed and their eyes collected. His assistant noticed that only seven pairs of eyes were retrieved, so cut one blue eye and one brown eye from two corpses and added them to the collection.[435] Mengele tried to change the pigmentation of eyes, to artificially create the desired Aryan appearance of blue eyes and blond hair, by injecting different coloured dyes such as methylene blue. Thirty-six children in Birkenau were used for these tests which resulted in painful infections or blindness and in one recorded case, death. After the tests, the children were gassed.

Mengele's research on twins imposed considerable pain and anguish on many of the twins that could have lasting, lifetime, effects.[436] For example, the Reichenberg brothers, Laszlo and Efraim, (one was sixteen the other was eighteen) arrived in Auschwitz in July 1944 and passed as twins in Mengele's research unit. Laszlo was a singer while Efraim "could not carry a tune."[437] Mengele injected substances into their necks that caused pain, swelling and vomiting in both boys as well as an inability to speak. The procedure was repeatedly administered over the next four months. Crude surgery removed both brothers' vocal cords. Laszlo also had his right lung removed. He died one year after the war having been hospitalized from the time of liberation. Efraim moved to Israel after his brother's death in 1948. From 1965 onwards, he could no longer speak at all. In 1967 he underwent a twelve-hour operation to recreate vocal cords so that with the aid of, ironically, a German made instrument, he can now talk.[438]

Mengele also conducted research on people with physical anomalies such as hunchbacks, some of whom he had shot so that he could dissect their bodies. For example, twin bothers Guido and Nino were given chocolates and extra clothes: a few days later Mengele sewed them together at the wrist and back, with veins interconnected, and their wounds festering, to resemble conjoined twins. The boys screamed all night until their mother managed to give them a fatal shot of morphine.[439] One anonymous survivor confirmed the story of the twins Guido and Nino in testimony given before a six-person tribunal/ mock trial of Mengele held in Jerusalem, in February 1985.

> Scores of Mengele's twins died, many of them from a particularly bizarre experiment in which the blood supplies of different pairs of twins were inter-changed. Vera Alexander, a witness, described how two children, one a hunchback, were sewn together back to back, their wrists back to back as well. There was a terrible smell of gangrene and the cuts were dirty. The children cried every night.[440]

MEDICAL EXPERIMENTS INVOLVING SEXUAL BEHAVIOUR

Mengele's research on twins is also reputed to have focused on sexual activities. Although twins were always examined nude, he was apparently proper and "never rude" in his examinations.[441] There are reports, however, that Mengele tried to change the sex of some twins: female twins were sterilized and males castrated.[442] Eva Mozes Kor, a noted twin survivor, reported that blood from boys was transfused into the bodies of older girls while their blood was transfused into the young boys. The doctors told the young girls that they were going to make them into young men. She also reports that "One twin had his sex organs removed in an attempt to turn him into a girl. Some girls had their uteruses burned."[443] Similarly, another survivor reported. "We two each received 350cc of blood from a pair of male twins which brought on a severe headache and high fever."[444]

Some of Mengele's research was directed towards understanding some hereditary principles including the cause of multiple births in order to promote reproduction of the Aryan race. Rumours suggest that Mengele used the sperm of twins to impregnate German women to see if they would bear twins and to see if male twins who had intercourse with female twins would again bear twins.[445] In like vein, Lagnado and

Dekel report that several twins believe that Mengele had pairs of twins mate.

> There are hushed testimonies to that effect. Although all the twins deny first-hand knowledge, and many insist it never happened, there were rumours around the barracks that such perverse experiments were indeed taking place. No twin will elaborate on what he or she knew: even in the nightmare world of Auschwitz there were taboos, and this was the ultimate one. We will probably never know for sure.[446]

There are, however, some reports that confirm this belief. Survivor Moti Alon who arrived in Auschwitz at the age of nine in 1944 confirms that some aberration of sexual behaviour among the twins did occur. He remembers being forced to watch a quadriplegic dwarf and a Roma woman being made to have sex and that the children were forced to watch without turning their eyes away. This is confirmed by the testimony of other twin survivors, such as Efraim Reichenberg[447] and Moshe Offer.[448] As Ephraim writes: [449]

> "Among us in the experimental barrack for male twins and dwarfs was a misshapen, hunchbacked gnome, a little less than four feet tall," recalls Efraim Reichenberg. He was forty years old, had a fissure in his skull, and could only walk with the aid of two crutches. He had been a watchmaker in Budapest, and we came together on the same transport [...] Nearly every day he was put in a room and stripped naked. The SS brought him gypsy women infected with syphilis, and forced him to have sexual intercourse with them. The SS doctors stood watching. Every morning when he arrived, and at the end of the day before he left, they checked him thoroughly to see if he had already caught the disease. When he first told me, I didn't want to believe him but one day I saw him through a crack in the door. A male nurse was holding him, forcing him down on a woman, because he was no longer able to. The unfortunate man didn't last long

– he died some time later, not of syphilis, but exhaustion.[450]

That Mengele's research did involve the reproductive organs of twins is also confirmed by Moshe Offer, a twin in Auschwitz, who reports that:

> One day, my twin brother, Tibi, was taken away for some special experiments. [...] Mengele made several operations on Tibi [...] One surgery on his spine left my brother paralyzed. He could not walk anymore.
>
> Then they took out his sexual organs.
>
> After the fourth operation I did not see Tibi anymore.[451]

There was much sexual speculation about Mengele in the camp among inmates. He occasionally manifested a prurient interest in sexual details when questioning pregnant women; according to Dr. Lengyel, he never missed the chance to ask women indiscreet and improper questions. [452] Others report him being much more concerned about lesbianism in the women's camp and about homosexuality in the men's camp than other SS doctors.[453] Some of his research into twins also reflected a similar interest in sexual issues. Two pairs of identical teenage twins testified for the Frankfurt prosecution that he had forced them to have sex with other twins to determine if the women would bear twins in turn.[454]

Many of the more grotesque aspects of Mengele's sexual curiosity and sadistic physical and sexual humiliations are verified by the reports provided by the Jewish Lilliput family of respected entertainers, together with their close family assistant and his family of five, the Slomowitzes. The group included seven dwarfs, and seven children, and as many full-sized spouses.[455] This family became an object of Mengele's special interest and morbid curiosity resulting in them being protected during their years in Auschwitz, and their survival. On one occasion Mengele arranged an exhibition of the dwarf group which they later called, "the performance."[456]

> They mounted the stage [...] to take their places in a line that stretched from one end of the stage to the other. The auditorium was packed [...] The audience stared at the assortment of men, women and children [...] Mengele [...] turned to them and snapped, "Undress!"

> Aghast, their hands trembling, they fumbled with their buttons. The Lilliputs tried to shrink into themselves, and wished they could disappear altogether. They bent their shoulders forward, they attempted to cover their genitals with their hands. "Straighten up!" barked Mengele.[457]

Shimshon Ovitz, only eighteen months old at the time, has no memory of the Lilliputs' humiliation, but notes that

> The SS officers wanted to see us at close range. They marvelled at the doll like figures and peppered us with invasive questions while staring at the Lilliputs' dressing. One of them came close to my mother – she was holding me in her arms – and touched her naked breast. I flung out my hand, so I'm told, and pulled at his swastika with all my might. It fell to the floor, and my mother panicked and started crying, sure he would draw his pistol and shoot us on the spot [...] the officer calmed her down – "never mind, he's just a baby, he doesn't know what he is doing."[458]

As Perla, one of the surviving dwarfs later recounted, Mengele was aiming not only "to discover the biological and pathological causes of the birth of both dwarfs and giants"[459] but also to demonstrate that in the course of its long history, the Jewish people, the Jewish race, had degenerated into a people of dwarfs and cripples."[460]

Mengele showed a salacious interest in the sexual activities of the dwarfs: "Now tell me, how did you live with your midget?" In her memoir of Auschwitz, Sara Nomberg-Przytyk recalls Mengele posing this question to Dora, the tall, full bodied wife of the dwarf Avram Ovitz:[461]

Mengele hinted at the stereotypical notion of the male dwarf as a subhuman characterized by an unusually potent sex drive and wild, unnatural desires. Dora Ovitz blushed, dumbfounded, her blood pounded in her ears. "Speak!" screamed Mengele, and then proceeded to interrogate Dora, vulgarly, in front of her young daughter and the rest of the barrack. Had she conceived her young daughter with her dwarf husband, he demanded, or was the father someone else? Dora tried to respond by praising her husband's intelligence and industry, and meanwhile writes Nomberg-Pryztyk "we all stood there like blocks of stone."

"Don't tell me about that, only about how you slept with him."

Mengele was salivating. The sweat poured down her [Dora's] face in big drops on her clothes. She spoke and he asked questions. I cannot repeat the conversation. It was grotesque, inhuman torture."[462]

While reports about Mengele's research emphasise his cold, calculating manipulation of inmates, it is clear, from multiple testimonies, that he was capricious, mercurial, sadistic, impervious to the concerns of his "subjects" and with a morbidly depraved sexual interest that was frequently acted out even with "his" twin children and prized "specimens" such as the Lilliput dwarfs.

SEXUAL ABUSE BY OTHER EXPERIMENTERS

There are some reports of enforced sexual intercourse involving children other than in Mengele's studies. Some survivors tell stories of having been used for experimental laboratory tests including forced sexual relations with siblings and parents.[463]

Cornelia came from a rich family in Hungary. She was transported to Mauthausen where she was experimented on. She was undressed, her legs were spread and she was given shots into her vagina. When she fainted, she was thrown onto a pile of corpses on a wagon. She awoke in the night with other corpses being thrown onto her. She called "Mommy" and someone lifted her up and put her in the children's barrack.[464] Typhus, fleas and diarrhea spread in this shack, and more experiments followed. This time, they spread her legs apart and put something into her vagina that was painful. She did not have the strength to cry anymore. It burned for hours and she couldn't stand up. She was full of blood and bleeding for most of the time. Her belly hurt. She hardly remembered eating for months. Her legs were thin and her feet were swollen.

> Other experiments involved using children to arouse each other sexually. We were just small kids and had no living signs any more. They forced one 14-year-old (there were others) to penetrate me. I didn't respond but just cried like a kitten mewing. I just wanted to drink. I was so thirsty and hungry all the time. A child younger than me cried too when he was raped by another child who was forced to do so by the guards.[465]

She witnessed terrible things: vaginas taken out of women without anaesthetics, people bleeding to death. She remembered seeing a child injected with air who screamed in agony. The memories plagued her dreams. All this happened in just one year.

After liberation, Cornelia was taken to Israel. She was eight-and-a-half. For the next two years, she was afraid of any noise, startled easily, never spoke and never smiled. She felt ill all the time, had no hair, and stopped developing physically. She eventually married but could never have children because of the sexual and experimental abuse.[466]

Isaac*, born in 1928, was subjected to medical experimentation and sodomy in Buchenwald.[467] He was injected with various substances. His armpits and his groin were shaved and smeared with a paste that caused the skin to burn and sting and that later developed repeated inflammations. Besides this, he was raped for months by a *kapo* in the camp. In 1963, he married a woman, also a survivor, who had been raped by Russian soldiers. This traumatic experience caused her psychological problems and she had several psychiatric hospitalizations until the couple decided to divorce. Isaac* had psychological problems all his life: his sexual functioning was impaired and he was unable to have children.

Block 46 (in Buchenwald) was established on December 29, 1941 to experiment on treatments for typhus.[468] A Dutch prisoner, Peter Shenk was seventeen when he came to Buchenwald and obtained a job as a tailor in this block. He found, however, that in exchange for this job he was sexually assaulted, "chosen a couple of times a month" to be tied up and raped in a room next to the crematorium. In recorded testimony given in 1996, Shenk reported that SS Doctor Ernst Ding was the rapist, but circumstantial evidence suggests that it was more likely Dr. Waldemar Hoven who was the perpetrator as he had also been accused of homosexual rapes by other inmates who worked in the same workshop.[469] Both Nazis had unsavoury sexual reputations.

Ernst Ding at Buchenwald had a reputation as being sexually exploitative of adolescents.[470] Ding was a committed Nazi and SS doctor who is described as "ambitious and deceptive," "nasty and cruel at times," and although posing as a highly trained professional, was an incompetent scientist and a fraud.[471] Telford Taylor, prosecutor at the Nazi Doctor's trial in Nuremberg in 1946, stated that "Nowhere will the evidence in this case reveal a more wicked murderous course of conduct by men who claim to practice the healing arts than in the entries of Ding's diary relating to typhus experiments."[472] From December 1937 in Buchenwald, Ding was involved in castrating prisoners deemed "asocial" or "criminal." Such actions were in accordance with the laws of congenital criminality or voluntary acceptance of castration by homosexuals. Imprisoned after the war for his criminal and cruel acts, he committed suicide in June 1945.

The second in command in Buchenwald was Waldemar Hoven – and most likely Peter Shenk's abuser – who had a dual responsibility of camp doctor responsible for general sanitation as well as being responsible for the health of the SS and camp staff. A prisoner who worked in the home of Camp Commandant Koch, reported that Ilse Koch, his wife (known as the Bitch of Buchenwald) was having affairs with Dr. Waldemar Hoven and Deputy Commandant Hermann

Florstedt. When Colonel Koch was transferred to Majdanek, Ilse Koch stayed behind and was with Dr. Hoven almost all day. Hoven reputedly had a penchant for conspiratorial intrigues, sexual licentiousness and corruption that led to his arrest by the SS in September 1943. He was imprisoned for eighteen months in Buchenwald and then released to assist with the critical shortage of doctors. He was charged at the Nuremberg Doctor's trial and was executed in 1948 for killing prisoners and personally conducting brutal experiments.[473] He murdered between ninety and 100 prisoners per week for almost one and a half years with intracardiac injections of phenol or evipan.[474]

Interestingly, prisoners working in Ding's laboratory were some of the very few who were able to sabotage the plans of the SS.

> Since Ding-Schuler [in 1944, when it appeared that Germany was losing the war, Ding changed his name to Shuler, the name of his birth father, to conceal his activities[475]] demanded large quantities of vaccine, we produced two types: one that had no value and was perfectly harmless, and went to the front; and a second type, in very small quantities, that was very efficacious and was used in special places like for comrades who worked in difficult places in the camp. Ding-Schuler never heard about these arrangements.[476]

EXPERIMENTAL BLOCK 10 AND ARTIFICIAL INSEMINATION

Kai* reports that Jewish men and others used to sneak to Block 10.[477] Sometimes at night, men came to this block, where the young girls and women were held for medical experiments, to have sex with them. Such sex was likely in exchange for food – i.e. exchanged as a means to survive. The men were inmates or those holding higher positions in the camp hierarchy. If caught, the punishment was imprisonment. Kai* was a member of the camp kitchen staff and his report is based on what women told him. It is dated March 1944 and reports that 360 women and young girls were kept as guinea pigs for medical experiments connected with artificial insemination. Kai's* description of the director of these experiments indicates this was Dr. Carl Clauberg. A few of the women were chosen for experimentation among those condemned to death and awaiting extermination. He notes that considering the severity of the experimentation they underwent afterwards and the actions of slaughter they witnessed through chinks in the windows, they were sorry to have been spared.[478]

These is little documentary evidence for experiments on artificial insemination although in addition to Kai*, Olga Llengyl, in Auschwitz, includes definitive mention of this research. It is likely that the sensitivity of the subject has meant that few would report it, as Olga says:

> Twenty miles from our camp was an experimental station which specialized in artificial insemination. To this station were sent the most endowed of the doctor inmates and the most beautiful of the women [...]

> The Germans practiced artificial insemination on a number of women, but the investigations offered no results. I knew women who had been subjected to artificial insemination and had happened to survive, but they were ashamed to admit the experiments.[479]

AFTERWARDS

Some of the estimated 350 doctors involved in experimentation during the Nazi era – like Erwin Ding – committed suicide after the war's end. Some were brought to trial – including Waldemar Hoven who was then executed. Others went on to obtain or preserve their academic status (like Prof Otmar von Verscheur, director of the KWI for Anthropology from 1942, and Mengele's mentor[480]) and to then prosper in Germany or elsewhere. Mengele himself escaped and remained at large, although in hiding and hunted, throughout his remaining life.[481]

Jewish doctors who had been forced to collaborate with Nazi medical services, for example in camps, as prisoner-doctors, were often challenged after the war as "collaborating" with the Nazis and therefore regarded as disreputable. Gisella Perl, a distinguished Jewish doctor was one of these, who did, however, manage to counter these arguments and to expose the ethical dilemmas that she and others facing similar predicaments in the camps, were forced to face.[482] Some Jewish doctors chose not to implement Nazi demands to experiment on Jews and particularly on Jewish children. For example, a female Jewish doctor in Kishinev hospital, Dr. Gefaisman, was ordered by the Gestapo to carry out experiments on Jewish children in the hospital: "She was told that if she did not do so she would be killed. The doctor went home and gave her mother and brother poison capsules, without telling them what these were. Once the two had died, she committed suicide by shooting herself."[483]

Like, Adam Czerniakov, the head of the *Judenrat* in the Warsaw ghetto, Dr. Gefaisman, chose death rather than to abuse children. Doctors under Nazi control faced a difficult ethical dilemma: whether to obey the Nazi's demands to experiment on prisoners, including children, but at the same time, to sabotage those experiments in order to save some lives. Alternatively, they could take their own lives. Dr. Samuels[484] chose the former and managed to save some women's lives and to preserve their fertility before being murdered by the Nazis himself. Dr. Gefaisman chose death.

SEXUAL ABUSE JUSTIFIED BY MEDICAL SCIENCE

Doctors who conducted medical experiments on Jewish and other prisoners regarded their research as scientifically valuable and expressed little or no regret at the Nuremberg doctors' trial regarding the atrocious experiments that they conducted, including a number that involved sexual organs or sexual behaviours, even of children.[485] They took pride in their accomplishments irrespective of the purpose of the experiments and the cruelty they imposed on victims.[486] The continuation of Nazi ideology in Neo-Nazi movements that have sadly gained in momentum in recent years clearly indicates that, like the doctors, not all Nazis were apologetic after the war or repentant of their actions. Antisemitism remains and, in fact, looms larger than in more recent decades on our current horizons. Given this Nazi ideological perspective, murder of those who did not meet desired Nazi attributes was desirable, praiseworthy and acceptable. Adding the dehumanization through sexual abuse of their victims was not necessarily a big step to take.

CHAPTER 7: HIDDEN CHILDREN

As Stein writes: "All children who lived through the Holocaust and survived were hidden children. Those who were visible could not survive."[487] The number of children hidden during the Holocaust is unknown, but estimates range between 10,000 and 500,000.[488] It is also uncertain as to how many were discovered and killed. While concealment in some hiding place is the customary understanding of the "hidden" child, there were alternate forms of hiding that occurred. For example, some Jewish children were too young to know they were Jewish when hidden and, although they survived, they may not have been counted among the survivors. Some who did know of their Jewish heritage chose not to identify as hidden Jews after the war. Almost all these survivors, share one thing – silence.[489] As Lola Kaufman says, "For nearly 50 years I don't and can't speak about what has happened to me – not to Walter [her husband], not to anyone. I was silent when I was hidden and I stay silent even when I am not."[490]

Children were hidden in homes with people who were willing to take them and who were trusted not to betray them; trying to ensure other considerations for the children's hiding places such as a happy family, a stable home, or loving parents were luxuries that could not be indulged in under the circumstances.[491] It was also extremely difficult for the children who had to adopt new names, religions, identities, parents and families, behaviours, living conditions, and often new languages. Flora, for example was hidden in a monastery and cared for by nuns who had taken a vow of silence. Flora, desperate for love and wishing to be held close and hugged, prayed that they would look at her instead of keeping their gaze glued to the sky "Look at me, she wished. Look at me. Look at me."[492]

Desperate parents considered any option they could to save their children, including giving them to Gentile families to care for them, leaving them on the doorstep of non-Jewish institutions with the hope that somebody would be kind enough to look after them, throwing them out of the trains bound for the camps in the desperate hope they might survive, or handing them to resistance workers to be smuggled away to find security with strangers. Parents seldom knew where their children had been hidden, let alone had the ability to keep in touch.[493] Resistance workers who rescued individuals did so under dangerous conditions.

> [...] once she arrived to pick up a twenty-month-old baby. As she stepped out into the street, pushing the infant in a stroller, the Gestapo arrived and closed off all the surrounding streets to prevent escapes. While she walked along people were being rooted out of the houses all around her. She had arrived in the nick of time to save the baby.[494]

Jewish children were hidden in convents, in city apartments and houses, on remote farms, in boarding schools and orphanages. They hid in cellars, sewers, wooden sheds, stables, bombed out and abandoned buildings and any shelter or burrow they could find.[495] They hid behind closets or false walls, in attics, and even in sewers. No locations were totally safe and many were moved multiple times.[496] In Ukraine, some hid in caves.[497] Some were concealed in plain site by passing for Aryan, requiring them to assume totally different persona reflecting Christian rather than Jewish traditions, religious practices and appearances: while living in the open they remained emotionally buried. For many, their home language of Yiddish, or even its telltale intonation when speaking local languages, might reveal their Jewish identity.[498] Hiding was also a terrifying experience for many. Lola, a child hidden by Anna writes:

> If there's an air raid, they [hidden Jewish children] can't leave and get to a bomb shelter. Like me, some of them can't stand up. Like me, they may not know when it is day or night, and never sleep deeply or for long. They sleep a kind of twilight, dreamless sleep.

> Anna's older son is second in command of the Ukrainian police. He comes to the house at least once a week. He does not know his mother is hiding Jews. If he finds out, he will kill us himself.[499]

Estimates indicate that one percent of the non-Jewish population in Europe helped Jews, although exact numbers are not known.[500] Jews were concealed in every country where they lived – France, the Netherlands, Italy, Greece, Yugoslavia, Ukraine, Belgium, Bulgaria, Denmark, Hungary, Germany and Poland. Many rescuers were Christians and a few were Muslims.[501] Many Christian families were brave enough to take Jewish children into their homes, at the risk of their own lives.[502] Hundreds of families also gave shelter to one or two Jewish children, not always knowing their religious identity.[503] In a few rare instances, whole communities hid children, such as in the French village of Le Chambon-sur-Lignon which hid 3,000 to 3,500 Jews – mostly children – between 1940 and 1945.[504]

In Belgium, for example, more than 4,000 young Jews were hidden in institutions and private homes.[505] The sixty-five schools, convents, orphanages, crèches, camps and hospitals that provided this shelter often knew the origin of the children they were taking in and the danger of being discovered by the Gestapo. Some schools did not know their Jewish identity at first, but once discovered were no longer willing to shelter them. As Reinitz, a Hungarian Jewish child in the Holocaust reports:

> Mr Rothschild took his two daughters, aged nine and eleven, to a convent […] without letting it be known that they were Jewish. But […] he gave each of them a siddur, a Jewish prayer book, so that they could pray [and] remember their Jewishness. The girls hid the prayer books under their mattresses. Unfortunately, the nuns discovered the books, and, instead of protecting the girls, they turned them over to the authorities. The girls were taken away to the Jewish ghetto in Budapest. […] The Arrow Cross would round up groups of Jews, take then to the Danube river, force them to remove their shoes and shoot them. This was the tragic fate of Mr Rothschild's daughters.[506]

An international conference of hidden Jewish children was held in New York in May 1991. About 1,600 former children and some rescuers came from all over the world to talk about their experiences, often, for the first time.[507] Some, however, did not tell their full stories, hiding the cruelest parts of their experiences. Only in 2001, some ten years later, at a subsequent conference, did some acknowledge the physical and sexual abuses they endured while in hiding.[508]

The prevalence of sexual abuse among hidden children in the Holocaust is unknown. Some suggest that one in six or 16.7% of hidden children were sexually abused.[509] Others claim that more than 80% of hidden children were treated well, 15% were occasionally mistreated and 5% were treated badly.[510] Rachel Lev-Wiesel and Marianne Amir interviewed twenty-two survivors of child sexual abuse (fourteen men and eight women) who volunteered to tell their stories: they were all born after 1930. Of these, 42% were hidden with Christian families, 33% had hidden together with one parent, 12% had hidden, without their parents, with partisans or in the woods, and 13% were sent to Thereisenstadt. Of the children, 28% were sexually abused by their biological parents (two mothers and one father) or another male Jew, 46% were abused by their Christian foster parents, and 12% by their foster siblings, while 14% were abused by someone else such as the village vicar or a neighbour.[511]

Sexual abuse of hidden children took various forms including voyeurism, fondling and rape, and was perpetrated by boys, fathers, mothers or siblings in homes or shelters where children were hidden, by police officers, friends and farmers. Examples of these experiences follow although it must be remembered that none of these sexual assaults might have happened if these children were not forced into hiding by the antisemitic events occurring in Nazi Germany.

FEAR OF SEXUAL ABUSE

Eva Heyman was hidden in Hungary at the age of 13. She kept a diary that has survived, reporting on the discussions about her potential hiding with a Mrs. Jakobi. The diary entries reflect her naivete about sexuality as well as the concerns of a child who understands little about sexual abuse.[512]

> April 18, 1944: This Mrs Jakobi really isn't an evil woman [...] I don't even understand what Grandma meant when she did say that Mrs Jakobi would sell me to men. Nobody is buying Jewish girls these days, and Agi even said that Grandma only says such things because she is sick [from fear] right now.[513]

> May 18, 1944: Agi told other things, like what the gendarmes do to the women [...] things that it would be better if I didn't write them down in you. Things that I am incapable of putting into words, even though you know, dear diary, that I haven't kept any secrets from you till [sic] now.[514]

> May 30, 1944: I don't want to die! I want to live even if it means that I'll be the only person here allowed to stay. I would wait for the end of the war in some cellar, or on the roof, or in some secret cranny. I would even let the cross-eyed gendarme, the one who took our flour away from us, kiss me, just as long as they didn't kill me, only that they should let me live.[515]

The diary ends three lines later. Eva was murdered at Auschwitz in October 1944.

INAPPROPRIATE CONTACT

Living conditions in the various homes that offered shelter to children were often limited. Personal privacy was curtailed and such events such as bathing became public affairs. For example, eleven-year-old Ruth was in hiding with a childless couple. The couple took a weekly bath in an aluminium tub in the kitchen. In 2007, Ruth testified that

Tante Hanny insisted on washing me. Her presence in the kitchen made me feel uncomfortable, but at the same time I knew that it was my responsibility to be grateful. These people were putting their lives in danger for me. I told Tante Hanny I was too old, that I had been washing myself for a long time. She would not listen. One day the washing turned into a massage. I could not stop her. The expression in her eyes frightened me. In the moment all my fury at her took over, and I splashed her with water. She never touched me again.[516]

ASSAULT BY BOYS/SIBLINGS

More commonly, victims were sexually assaulted and/or raped by siblings in their hidden families. There are many examples of this. Sometimes older boys in the family raped younger girls who had been given shelter and sometimes they raped boys who were hiding with them. Examples of these differing types of rape experienced by both boys and girls follow.

Boris* was moved from the Warsaw ghetto to hide in a secluded forest home in a Polish village where he witnessed his hiding brother rape his hiding sister.[517] He lived with a man and his wife, their son (Leon*) and daughter (Marta*). He was about seven or eight years old. The children in his hiding family were told he was a nephew of an aunt whose house had been bombed in the Warsaw raids. He was able to pass for Aryan as he spoke Polish without an accent, a necessary requirement to avoid suspicion of Jewishness. Leon* and Marta* never saw him undressed and did not know he was Jewish. Boris* did all the dirty jobs: he stole coal from the railways, worked the fields and the garden, drew water from the well. His experience was not unique among many children who were hidden in Aryan homes: they could not refuse to undertake these harsh tasks for fear of consequent betrayal. After the father of the household was killed, Leon* found a yellow star in Boris'* cupboard. Leon* tried to betray Boris* to the Germans to receive the ransom money for betraying Jews. Before going into hiding, Boris* had, however, been given a German hand grenade by a nun who told him to use it if he was ever taken. Boris* threatened to blow up Leon* and Leon* gave up trying to turn him over to the Germans. In 1945, Leon* tried it again and Boris* said "go and ask your mother who you are,"[518] and I will tell everyone that you are also half-Jewish. His mother confirmed this. Leon* then tried to commit suicide, but only broke his leg. After the war Leon* tried to contact Boris* to get help to go to Israel but Boris* told him that if he ever met him, he would cut his throat. Boris'* anger stemmed from other experiences he had had in that house. Boris* reports that Marta* was friendly and the mother "was an angel."[519] He had called her aunty. But Leon* was malicious. He stole and then blamed Boris.* Boris* was beaten with a cat-of-nine-tails for all Leon's* crimes. Boris* ran away but was caught and brought back again. In addition, Leon* raped his sister Marta.* Boris* was there. She screamed, and Boris* tried to pull Leon* off. Leon* was fourteen or fifteen, and Marta* was twelve. Leon* raped Marta* twice and they never told their mother about it. Leon* also tried to rape Boris* but Boris* fought him off. Leon* joined the Hitler Youth. As Boris* testified, "it was his scene."[520]

Difficult situations such as this were experienced by other hidden children as well, although rape was reported more often by girls than by boys. Aniko Berger's story typifies this type of assault. When Aniko was five years old, she was hidden with a family with two sons of fifteen (Pista) and fourteen (Imre). They never seemed to smile and she spent the first two weeks there alone. Every time the boys noticed her it was to make her cry. The boys kept touching her face to check "how soft Jewish skin was" or they reached under her dress to check "how silky Jewish panties were."[521] Shortly after her arrival, she was sent mushroom picking in the forest. The boys followed her, knocked her unconscious, and raped her.

> When Aniko came to her senses again, she opened her eyes and saw that the sky was solid red like blood, without the shred of a cloud. It hurt her to look so she closed her eyes. It was only then that she realised that the pain didn't come from looking

at the sky above: it came from within. Her entire body ached as if it had been ripped into many pieces. She wanted to stand but her legs wouldn't obey. When she rose to her knees an involuntary howl escaped from her lungs. There were blood stains all over her lower body, and she was stark naked. [...]

They made her swear on the head of her "Jewish whore mother'" that she would not say how she got hurt. If she did they would kill her. [...] She teetered on the edge of life for several days."[522]

Older boys in hiding families were often identified as sexual predators. For example, Sabina was concealed by Madame Rothschild in Belgium. Sabina used to wet her pants from fear and developed red rashes in response. An older non-Jewish boy of about eleven or twelve was also living in the house and offered to help her. He would sit himself on the toilet, spread her legs across his hips and tell her to cover her eyes and not to peak. He molested her several times until she peeked and realised something was wrong. She pushed him away and would not allow him to touch her again.[523]

Marion van Binsberger, recalled having to find a different home for her ward, Esther, after learning that Esther was being sexually abused by the older boy in her hiding family. The boy's sister informed Marion of what was happening, although Esther herself had not said a word as she had been threatened with betrayal to the Nazis if she said anything. Many abusers used similar threats.[524]

Condolisa had similar experiences to Esther. Separated from her family at the age of about seven, Condolisa lived in a series of places in France, near Paris. The second family she and her brother lived with was bad in every way. They lived with a mother and her fifteen-year-old son. The teenage boy would come to her bed at night and force her to undress, touch his penis and "do other things" [525] and keep quiet about it. She thinks the boy's mother knew what was happening and permitted it, because she saw how her son looked at Condolisa.[526] Condolisa and her three-year-old brother were moved again, but their situation did not improve. Her brother was beaten, became very fearful, stopped talking and began to wet his pants. She came home from school one day to find open wounds on him. The woman of the house said "Yes, today I taught him. I gave him the pot to pee and shit in, and he did it not in the pot but next to it. I made him eat it."[527] One day she pushed him into the fireplace and he was burned. "Then the woman made him go through the garden to the toilet – a hole in the ground – and he was just a little kid. He could have fallen into it."[528] They remained in that house until the end of the war, about a year or longer.

As an adult, Condolisa had difficulties conceiving and carrying pregnancies to term although she did eventually have two children. She believed that her fear of being pregnant stemmed from the sexual abuse she experienced during the Holocaust.[529]

Assault by Children in the Neighbourhood

A number of other girls report similar types of assault, but by neighbourhood children. For example, Regine was a twelve-year-old in Belgium. One day, on the way back from school with her friend Marie, she was chased by a gang of boys across a field who, when they caught up with her, tried to pull off her clothes. She screamed, kicked and ran free. When she got back to the farm, Marie told the story to her parents, who seemed to think that the episode was all Regine's doing.[530] In another example, Lucy and her family fled Poland in 1938, when she was six and eventually settled in Leninabad in Tajikistan. A few years later, her mother warned her older sister to be careful at all times. "Never enter deserted places,"[531] she said. She was especially afraid of sexual abuse. Local women who wore long dresses believed they were somewhat protected by their clothes but Lucy and her sisters did not wear such clothes. But when they grew taller, her mother managed to find some fabric and to add that to their skirts so that they reached below the knees, with the additional admonishment that "If you see two or more boys or young men, turn around and walk – or better yet, run – the other way. They will not hurt you if they don't see you, so stay out of sight."[532]

One day, Lucy had to fight off a young Tajik man, maybe even a teenager. He grabbed her from behind and managed to hold her with just one hand with a grip of steel around her waist. With his other hand he tried to reach under her dress. She screamed and managed to free herself by kicking and scratching. He didn't like being scratched, so he let go, slapped her face and laughed at her. For him, it was a game.[533]

In each of these cases, the girls were assumed to be responsible for their potential rapes by wearing revealing clothes such as short skirts. The onus was on the girls to avoid the assault rather than on the boys to change their behaviours.

ABUSE BY MALE RESCUERS

Today, child sex abuse commonly occurs in the home, perpetrated by a family member or someone who knows the family well. Such child molesters also found opportunities to abuse children who were hidden in families during the Holocaust. Pauline was one of the children molested by relatives of her hiding family.[534] Lien de Jong was another.[535] While hiding with the van Laar family in the Netherlands, Uncle Evert began to sexually abuse her, first digitally and then with full penetration, from the age of eleven years. Afterwards, he would always tell her "You wanted this yourself."[536] After the war, with both her parents and extended family members killed, she chose to live with one of the other families that had offered her shelter, but where she was again harassed, this time by the father of the family. She reported years later that "This man, whom she thinks of as a father, seems excited by her as a woman."[537]

Abuse by the father of the rescuer's family was common. David's story incorporates many of the most demeaning experiences that children faced: exploitation of his labour, forced conversion to Christianity, humiliation in the home, repeated beatings, voyeurism, inappropriate sexual exposure of others to him, and sexual assault. He was left emotionally scarred for life. He was twelve years old when the abuse started.

125

David's family was sent to Auschwitz from Belgium. He was hidden in a sanitarium for a year on condition that he convert to Catholicism. Soon after his conversion, the director, John, took him to live with his family of seven children. David was required to do all the chores: he chopped wood several times a day for the stove, washed dishes, did laundry, peeled potatoes, polished shoes, scrubbed the floors on all three levels of the house and emptied each child's urine pans. The director was lauded as someone who had saved a Jewish child by conversion, but at home the children heckled David as a dirty Jew. Sometimes he went to John in tears and John would slap David's face. John told him many times that his parents and he were being punished for crucifying Christ. That Jews were doomed for all eternity. If he did anything wrong, John would beat him with anything he could find or David would be sent to bed without supper. John would hit him repeatedly on the right side of his face so that later he lost his hearing on that side and had poor vision in his right eye.

Sexual abuse followed the physical. Eventually John came to David's room and took off David's underwear wanting to see a circumcised boy. After that he came frequently to fondle him. John had a thirteen-year-old daughter, one year younger than David at the time. Every Friday night John would put them both in the tub together and would watch to see if David had an erection. He never did. Nor was John the only perpetrator: whenever David was in the kitchen doing chores, John's wife would come in and sweep the floor with her hands, ensuring the boy could see she was wearing nothing underneath her short skirt.

David's life after the war was difficult and his relationship with his brother equally so. Although David eventually married a good woman and had a large family, he believes his life is not worth living. "Every night before I close my eyes, I pray to God that I won't see the morning. My daily prayer has gone unanswered all these years."[538]

Eight-year-old Anne reveals a horrifying story of sexual abuse by four men in different families in which she was hidden from the age of three-and-a-half until eight years of age, and her (commonly experienced) mixed emotional reactions to this abuse. She revealed to

Paul Valent – the psychiatrist who assisted her after the war – her hiding fathers' regular invitations to join them in their beds. The first man who abused her was always friendly, took notice of her, and played with her: feelings of love that she craved in the absence of her parents.

> At nights he took my singlet off and brushed against me. He took my pants off. […] he […] wanted me to play with him, his penis, and every part of him. […]

> I remember saying something to the lady [of the house] about him squashing me. […] She called me a liar and said she would punish me by putting me in the oven. She took me to the oven, opened it, lifted me, and I thought I was going into the roaring fire.[539]

She was again abused by the man of the house in the second family that hid her.

> He was rough. He picked me up and threw me around. […] Then he pushed me between his legs and he wanted to put his penis in my mouth […] it was too much for my mouth […]. He was moving up and down, and my throat was aching […]. There was this odour, this liquid. I could not stand the smell, the sight, I could not get away […]. Then he began to use me from the other end […]. He hurt me, and he tore me. I was full of blood, and I was very afraid […] it seemed to go on and on […]. This ritual took place many times, perhaps once every two weeks.[540]

> The man kept asking me to hop into his bed. He spoke with a soft lovely voice at first, and each time I thought that he liked me. I liked that even though I knew what I would have to do. But there was no way out, so I did it. Obviously, I did not respond well, because he always became angry, angrier and more violent each time. I had bruises everywhere. I was blue […]

> I could not stand up any more. [...] So he slapped me, threw me to the floor, and yelled at me [...] I became very ill then. I was so sick they had to take me to the hospital.[541]

Anne was hospitalized for about a year and was cared for kindly. She was then taken to a third home but this time – at the age of seven-and-a-half – she learned that her parents had died and would never return, leading her to give up hope. At this home she had to work in the wheat fields. One day she fell asleep in the sun.

> I was woken by this man standing over me wetting my face and mouth with urine. [...] The he put his penis in my mouth [...] I screamed [...] So he hit me about. Lifted up my dress [...] he penetrated me with such strength, such force [...] I thought he was going to go through my body [...].

> From then on, he would grab me suddenly from behind as I was bent over working. Sometimes he used his hand, sometimes he tried to push his fist up, ram it up. [542]

At the fourth home she was hidden in, the sexual abuse continued.

> The father asked me to come to bed and lie next to him. I never said no. I still had hopes [...]. Then he was nice to me. And he squeezed, hugged and kissed, all the things I thought I would want. But of course, it was the same thing again. It started with my mouth [...] then my backside [...] he forced himself in there [...] I did want to die.[543]

> I did not know all this was wrong, because a child has to be told something is wrong to know it is wrong.[544]

Although Anne did not feel sexual arousal, she did crave touch and became a willing partner as is a common reaction under such circumstances.[545] Involuntary sexual arousal may also occur in a rape victim. This is then assumed to reflect her own desire. As a result, the rape victim is often blamed for the crime, frequently with the assertion that "She asked for it."

Anne went to school for the first time in her life while with this last family. But the youngest daughter told the others at school what Anne was doing with her father. "I still did not know it was wrong, except that it caused such agony."[546] The other children pointed at her, teasing her, and kept far away from her. After two weeks she had to leave and stay home. She cut her wrist with a pair of secateurs but fainted.

> He threated that if I told he would put my head into a large bucket of snails which he collected in the garden. Eventually he did. He turned me upside down and put my head in a bucket of water full of snails, with foam on the top. I screamed and screamed, until my head was submerged, and I swallowed the water. [...] He tried anything but I could never satisfy him, and then he bashed me. One day he poked a broom up. Another day he pushed the broom up my backside. And the rest of the time he would speak and behave nicely to me. The three months came [...] This must have been towards the end of the war because I was taken back to Paris and I was placed with a Jewish couple.[547]

As an adult she had nightmares about drowning in water and burning in fire. She remained embarrassed about these events all her life. "I do not think of the age I was then, or the force upon me, I think of the act of it. I feel as if I had just done it, because I can feel it, still feel the agony and the ugliness. I know that I am forced, but I am the one doing it. It is me who is there. I don't know, I have always taken the blame myself. I am ashamed of myself."[548]

Stories of sexual assault by the men in children's hidden families are also reported by Sara, [549] Astrid[550] and Lily.[551] Sara Spier was an adolescent when she was concealed in the home of a married couple who were in the coal business.

> Once he changed coal for a very nice velvet dress for me. I was very happy with it. I remember I had it on and I was upstairs and he came to me and I said, "I'm

so happy with my dress" and he embraced me and
took me close and close and close and I was suddenly
afraid. I thought, "What's he doing?" It happened
two more times that he came and said, "I'm so glad
because we have no children and you are a bit like
my daughter." He put his arms around me and he put
me against him and I didn't feel safe […] I started to
hate to be there because he always came upstairs, and
he never did it when his wife was there.[552]

Astrid Jakubowic was born in Belgium in 1937. At age five, she
and her brother, Paul, were hidden with a married couple in Antwerp.
One day, Astrid was alone with the husband and he took out his penis
and made her hold it. She was disgusted, but as a child, she did not dare
refuse or think of telling anyone. The couple eventually decided that it
was too dangerous to keep the children.

Lily Redner was hidden on a farm with a young couple who had a
fifteen-year-old-son. The mother was pregnant again. The father used
to take Lily for rides on his tractor while she posed as a Gentile child
visiting them. In the evenings he would come to her bed and fondle her.
She was about ten or eleven years old. She did not know what this
could lead to, but another worker on the farm observed the signs of
abuse and warned the local priest about what was happening to her. She
was moved to another farm shortly afterwards.[553]

One five-year-old boy, Noel, was sexually abused by his mother
while in hiding. Noel hid with his Jewish mother in a small basement in
Poland for two years. When he was five, his mother demanded that he
have sex with her and when he failed, she would hit his penis severely.
Later he was sent to Thereisenstadt and was separated from his mother;
he viewed that period as "the happiest years of my life."[554] He hated his
mother from the time of the abuse until the day she died at the age of
eighty-six.

SHELTERS

At the age of twelve, Simone Jameson endured sexual abuse by
French police officers while hiding in a dank basement in the national

library in Paris. She tried to forget about the daily rapes by police officers, the small food rations, the loneliness and the unwavering fear. Instead she focused on the books, which she says "kept my sanity and gave me a refuge from reality."[555]

Janina Bauman hid with five other family members and friends in a shelter. The Nazis discovered them and forced them out. One of the men forced her to go with him:

> He gently pressed my hand. "I'd like to make you an offer, my dear," he said softly. "I can see you are a nice girl, good-looking as well as brave. I have decided to help you. I'll take you with me to my own villa. You'll live safe with me there till [sic] the end of the war, or maybe for ever. Do you accept?" "No" I screamed spontaneously, but controlling myself, instantly changed my tone. "No" I repeated gently "I appreciate your offer but can't accept it. Never in my life would I part from my mother and sister." "Think first of yourself, my girl," insisted the man coming close and putting his arm, around my waist. "You can still change your mind." His face was now touching mine, his hands wondering over my unprotected body. He was trying to push me away from the hatch to the darkest corner of the room. I began to struggle wildly with him. In vain – he held me in a firm grip, pressing me down to the floor. Unexpected help came suddenly from the dark. "Leave the girl alone sir," said the old woman in the way peasants address their juniors. "Can't you see she's just a child?" The tall man jumped aside as if ashamed of being caught red-handed. [...] he came back to me. But the precious seconds of delay were all I needed to collect my wits. "Sir" I said gravely, "you were kind to me and that's why I feel obliged to warn you. I'm ill, you see, with this worst kind of disease ..." He stopped dead in his tracks [...] uncertain what to do next. I felt he did not believe me but was too cautious to take a risk. [...] he icily told me to go back to the shelter.[556]

UNDER THE BED

Some children were exposed to sexual activity at a very young age, but were saved rather than hurt by such actions. While being concealed under the bed of a sex worker would, in a peacetime setting, be regarded as sexually abusive, these hiding places served to save the children and were not intentionally traumatic, unlike most other abusive situations reported here.

Leszek Allerhand was hidden as a young boy under the bed of a whore serving the German army. He stayed there for some months and states that it was the safest of hiding places.[557] Aniko Berger, who, after being raped by the older brothers in her hiding family, and whose story is told above, was eventually sent to live with another woman, Jolàn, who worked from dawn until dusk every day, seven days a week, so Aniko was left alone. At night, men visited Jolàn, which earned her a little more money. During those visits, Aniko had to hide under the bed.[558] Although this exposed Aniko to sexual activity at a young age, it was, however, not sexually abusive and far better than being raped.

PARTISANS

Richard Rozen and his family were smuggled out of a ghetto to join the partisans as his father was a doctor, and the organization needed one. For his safety he had to pass as a girl – an unusual form of sexual suppression, although not specifically abuse. His hiding name was Marysia Ulecki […] his hair became long after years in hiding with no hair cuts. He was forced to learn a new language because, in Polish, when a boy says a certain word, it is said one way, but when a girl says the same word, one or two letters are changed. His mother taught him to speak, walk and act like a girl. His task was made easier by his mother saying he was a little bit "backward." They didn't risk taking him to school but they took him to church. He remembers that another child tried to flirt with him, but the lady they were living with told the child not to bother with him because he was retarded. After that the other children left him alone except to make fun of him.[559] Richard's mother was sexually abused by the men of the village under threat of betrayal as partisan sympathisers if they did not comply. Richard could hear this happening during the nights, which made his mother very unhappy, and she would often cry at night. Although he did not understand what was happening he heard the words, "Don't harm me, don't harm my child!" Sometimes he made noises from his mattress nearby that stopped the abuse. At other times he pretended to be asleep. He was never touched himself.[560]

Ultimately, twenty-three members of Richard's family perished, including his father. From approximately twenty-five thousand Jewish children from Radom and its surrounding areas – his birthplace – no more than thirty-five are known to have survived.[561]

PASSING FOR ARYAN

While Jewish children were assaulted in homes where they were concealed – and in some, if not most cases, were known to be Jewish – others, who tried to pass for Aryan, also faced sexual assault, not as Jewish children but simply as children. They were, however, Jewish children whose family settings had been destroyed forcing them to hide with family or friends often under conditions of severe restriction, such as never to set foot outside. Only a few incidents of sexual assault of Jewish children passing for Aryan are reported here although this may not reflect the true incidence of sexual assault of young girls prevalent in society at the time. For example, Zula escaped from a ghetto and went to live with her old nanny, passing for Aryan. She, however, refused to stay confined to her apartment and after a week she went out into the street. She was beautiful, with fiery red hair and it was impossible for her to not be noticed. She was seen by three Nazis who stopped her and then pulled her into a gateway. She emerged stark naked. The Germans, laughing, stopped a passing tram and forced her onto it, still naked. They jumped up onto the tram and waived the driver on. She never returned.[562]

Other girls were also raped or assaulted while passing for Aryan such as Izolda who tried to save a girl by helping her into the sewers where Izolda's husband would guide her out. Izolda collected her in the morning:

> they run into a policeman. He [...] grabs the girl by the plait and pushes her into an entrance. The girl pushes him away, the policeman jostles her against the wall and unbuttons her blouse. "Mister," Izolda says in her non-Jewish voice. "Who do you think you are? Why don't you go out and catch some Jews and leave decent people alone?" [...] The policeman turns away from the woman's bust [...] "Shut your mouth," he barks at the girl, but she has no intention of doing so. [...] she starts wailing louder and louder. "Let me go, I'm still a virgin" [...] Fortunately, the policeman is put off by the fact that the girl is still a virgin. So he turns to Izolda and she already knows what to do. She doesn't wail and doesn't struggle. The acquaintance looks discretely away. The policeman buttons his pants and the two women go home.[563]

Mona* was born in Hungary in 1928. She went to Budapest to try to get Aryan papers allowing her to live in a particular building, but was forced by the clerk to trade a sexual favour for the papers. She was carrying Christian papers and it is not known whether the clerk knew whether she was Jewish or not.[564]

Sewek Okonowski who together with thirteen members of his family was later killed, reports his experiences of hiding in Warsaw in his diary. In the summer of 1943, following an *aktion*, he saw the body of a naked, young, Jewish woman who had been raped and sexually tortured by sticking a walking stick up her vagina to the hilt: only the handle was showing out.[565] The torture occurred on the Aryan side of Warsaw to which Jews tried to escape through the tunnels in 1943.

Nechama Tec narrowly escaped being raped. She was sent to buy some oil at a nearby store one evening, while passing for Aryan in Kielce. She saw a man who looked like a German soldier near a street lamp. On her way home, she passed by this man again, who grabbed her, pushed her against a fence and forced himself on her in a sexually arousing manner. Nechama was able to escape, but lost her shawl, that belonged to Ziutka, a member of her family, in the process. She reached her house, still holding the bottle of oil. It took a long time before she could calm down enough to explain what had happened. Everybody was happy to see her alive. Everybody except Ziutka, who was furious that she had lost her shawl. Nechama was, however assaulted not specifically as a Jewish child but simply as a child, albeit one sent out in the evening on her own – a danger potentially faced by all children, especially in times of war.

Sara Avinum is the youngest child reporting sexual assault while living on the streets in Brody, Ukraine. Abandoned by the older girls who were looking after her, she roamed the streets until lured into a basement where she was sexually assaulted by an unknown man. She was five years old.[566]

Rural Areas

Children, often together with their families, hid on farms to escape Nazi capture. Sometimes these families were able to work on the farms, hiding in plain sight, while in other settings, the family was concealed in an underground bunker or a barn and assisted by the farmer. While they sometimes managed to stay safe from capture for lengthy periods, they were not always safe from sexual abuse by their rescuers.

Lula* was hidden by a Ukrainian farmer who first hid her and her father but then later abused her.[567] Julia* too, from the age of ten years, was hidden in a bunker with thirteen people in Poland between 1941 to 1944. It was dark all the time: it was seldom safe to talk, and all were hungry. There was nothing to do. Consequently, the group spent most of their days sleeping. When they could talk, they described their grandmother's food and could satiate themselves with such talk. Julia* lived on a slab of wood all day and night, and never undressed; they had no other clothes than those they wore. Once a week they could dip a *shmutter* (rag) in a single pail of water to be used by all thirteen of them to wipe themselves down. It was the same bowl used as a toilet to collect their feces. They took it in turns to go up to see the stars for five minutes in the evenings.

They were at the mercy of Mr. Kruper, the farmer. He only came down to the bunker once – when he was drunk – when he wanted Geika, who was sixteen or seventeen years old. She was sickly and would pass out all the time. They told Mr. Kruper that they would all leave if he slept with Geika. He left them alone as he was afraid that they would tell his wife why they all left.[568]

Carl,* who was also about ten years old, hid in the Netherlands on farms, in houses, in bunkers and in a barn near a boat. In one of these houses where he stayed for some months, there was little space and he had to share a bed with a girl from Amsterdam. She had scabies. He too got scabies. The maid had to rub a very bad smelling cream into his body. He has vague memories that she abused him. Recently, he asked his brother if that was possible. His brother said this was normal in those days on the farms.[569]

Petra* was born shortly before the war broke out in Warsaw. She and her mother were taken in by a farmer, who placed them in his attic. She reports her brother's birth, and then death from starvation as well as her (or perhaps her mother's) sexual abuse by the farmer – the limited available information on this testimony is unclear on this.[570]

Nona* was born in 1931. Her mother was murdered in the Warsaw ghetto and she was assisted by Polish workers to get papers. She was hidden by a Polish labourer who then sexually abused her. She was helped by nuns.[571]

Dunia's story reflects the horrific experiences that many Jews who fled to the countryside faced: starvation, hunger, poverty, disease, inhuman acts, betrayal, cruelty, death, and rape. When she was nine years old Dunia's family lost their home in Romania as well as everything they owned. They roamed the countryside and scavenged for pieces of torn clothing, sacks and newspapers to cover themselves and to protect their feet from snow. They took clothes off Jewish corpses: people who had died from murder, hunger or disease. She noted that local people would openly have sex with female corpses.[572]

Her family saw dogs eating parts of dead Jews. She saw a dog with a skull in his mouth that still had the scarf wrapped around it. It was like one that her mother's friend wore. Dunia saw a friend cut her wrists vigorously with an "iron" she had found. Her friend died in front of her.[573]

One day she and her grandfather were working on a farm cleaning out the pig pen. The family went to church. The farmer and his son left their family and returned to the farm. They hit her grandfather on the head and then the farmer grabbed her ten-year-old body and flung her to the floor.

> I still remember the smell from his mouth. As he violently raped me, he clamped my mouth shut. After he was through he turned me over to his son. The son bit into my inner thigh near my genitals ripping off a chunk of my flesh, leaving a scar that will remain with me until the day I die. They left quickly. I don't know whether they rejoined their family in church […]. I was so young that I didn't understand what had happened to me was rape.[574]

Her experiences led her to think that all Jewish females endured rape:

> The rest of my family and I witnessed my maternal aunt being gang raped by a group of Ukrainian youths who preyed on escaping Jews. When they were not participating in the rape, they stood guard with clubs and bats, ready to kill any family members who tried to help her. My aunt screamed all kinds of incomprehensible words before losing consciousness. The rape left her psychotic and her lower body was paralyzed. She would drag herself on the ground and became an easy target for flocks of rats that bit her. […]
>
> Next it was my mother who was raped. She never told us about it but the signs were all there. She had searched for menial day labor one morning and

returned that same day a very different person. She had had gold teeth and had returned that night toothless, with black and blue marks across her face. She was silent and rarely spoke after that day. The rape left her pregnant.[575]

Later, Dunia bled profusely with menstruation and often required transfusions. Under pressure from her family and to escape living under her dictatorial father she agreed to marry a thirty-seven-year-old man. He raped her vaginally and anally, abusing her like a psychopath. He made a point of letting her know that he betrayed her with high-society prostitutes. She got pregnant and gave birth to a healthy son. Her husband continued to rape her while ignoring his son. He had a mistress whom he also got pregnant. Dunia became pregnant again and had another son. She eventually held a knife to her husband when he came to her and after eleven years of marriage was able to divorce him. She lost everything except her two sons.[576]

While Dunia's story is filled with grief and horror, that of Molly and Helene, who were hidden in a bunker by a farmer for an extended period of time, and who also experienced sexual abuse, reveals a totally different experience. The earliest diary entries of Molly (Melania Weissenberg), written in 1942-1945, who was hidden with her older cousin Helene (Helcia) in an underground box, provides one of the most unusual accounts of child sexual abuse perpetrated by a rescuer.[577] Sometime in late 1943 or early 1944, thirteen-year-old Molly's diary reveals that she started to have sex with the forty-year-old farmer who hid her and who was already engaging sexually with her much older cousin Helene. Both girls were half starved, afraid and totally dependent on the farmer, Wiktor Wojcik (Victor in the diary) – whom they called Ciuruniu – and his sister Eugenia Kulaga.[578] The two girls were hidden in a box underground for two years. The box was the size of a double bed and just too short for them to stretch their legs. It was too shallow for them to sit up – they could only rest on their elbows. They only had a small hole through which to get air from outside, although they could crawl into the stable at night for their "natural functions" and to glimpse the outside world through cracks in the stable door. They had an old curtain, used to cover the straw they lay on and shared one pillow and a feather-filled comforter. They also had a small jug to hold water, a knife for cutting bread, and two spoons that they licked clean.[579]

At times the girls were fearful of being betrayed by Victor. To encourage Victor, they schemed that offering him sex might keep him from betraying them. Molly's diary entry reveals the start of this relationship:

Sunday October 10: Sex[580]

[...]

December [no date specified]: We talk a lot about having sex and Kitten [Molly's name for Helen] shows me exactly how it is done. I convince her to provoke Ciuruniu to let him know that she was also willing despite the cold. She listened to me and she approached him and it happened. And we have such a pleasant topic for another couple of days.[581]

[...]

Sunday, December 26: Sex again[582]

January 12 1944: Kitten wrote the following letter to Ciuruniu:

"I am embarrassed to write to you again, fearing that you might think ill of me. But the last time left me with such a terrible yearning. I bet that you think that I have had enough? It only provoked my desire. Afterward I relive it all night long, every nerve trembling in me at the very memory. I felt a particularly overwhelming need after the last time because I had not played enough and I wanted some more ... Honey, my dearest, your every touch feels like an electric current, everything vibrates in me and begs for more ... Honey, come caress me a little but this time you need to lay me down, because I must feel all of you on me and pressing down on me. Honey on the tip and with your finger. And that [sweet?] hole with an edge. My baby, hold me and quench my thirst, because I want to faint in your strong virile arms ...".[583]

[…]

April: Kitten was suffering from weakness of the heart so I convinced her to invite Ciuruniu over to strengthen it. And she wrote the following note: "If you want to, come over for a while in the evening, because I am lonely and sad." And he did. And there was some [sex]. And her heart became stronger right away because she needed it as medicine.[584]

On May 16 and June 1st and 2nd she again reports that they had sex with Ciuruniu.[585]

July: That Rascal [Ciururniu] came to me on July 3 and on the 5th to Kitten. On the 10th to me again and on 12th Kitten got so angry and said she had to have some. She wrote a letter: "if you want me to, I will come later in the evening to the barn through the plank, because I cannot stand you lying so close under your eiderdown. I'm dying of desire for you because I have become possessed. I want to play with you for a moment, naked. I want to have all of you to myself. I am dying of lust. I need to have it as medicine. To hell with the war! Let us enjoy ourselves for a moment. You are my whole world. I will give it to you on the tip … Is it going to get hard? For I become wet at the very thought. My love for you is so strong."

He came over, but he did not want to take Kitten to his place, so they did it at our place. But Kitten was glad anyway.[586]

Her diary entries report that he had sex with her on July 23rd and on August 9th and 29th and with Kitten on 25th and 30th.[587] As she recounts, Melania (Molly) started to write her diary as a precocious twelve-year-old and finished as a fourteen-year-old woman.[588]

During the late 1980's Melania made an appeal to Yad Vashem in Jerusalem to recognise the wartime sacrifice of Ciuruniu and his sister and in 1992, Wiktor Wojcik and Eugenia Kulaga were awarded the medals of *Righteous Among Nations*. The sanitized version of events submitted to Yad Vashem is markedly different from what is in Melania's diary. Molly today remembers her saviours, Wojcik and Eugenia, and she is still in regular correspondence with their children and grandchildren. Every few weeks she sends them an envelope enclosing a fifty dollar note.[589] She has done so for the last fifty years. Many years later, in the 1990's Molly rewrote her memories of hiding, this time for her children and grandchildren; in this version, understandably, she again makes no mention of sexual abuse.[590] The full diary, including all reports of sexual activity, was published in 2017.

This story, like many of those who rescued children, raises difficult issues. For one, rescuers who denounced their hidden guests stood to be charged themselves: keeping them hidden saved their own lives as well as those of their wards. Further, Yad Vashem does not recognize rescuers who were paid to hide Jews. Could Molly and Helene's sexual activities be regarded as an alternate form of currency, invalidating their worthiness for recognition? The fact that Molly did not reveal the sexual abuse to Yad Vashem lends some support to this possibility, although modesty or embarrassment may have led to this concealment. What can we make of Molly and Helene's apparent enjoyment of their sexual encounters? Hidden in isolation for two years, totally dependent on their rescuer/rapist, and grateful to him and his sister for their protection, with little or nothing else to occupy their minds, is it so surprising that they might have gained some pleasure from these sexual encounters? Although Wiktor did not forcibly restrain Molly and Helene in their underground bunker, could their affection or identification with him be viewed as a version of the Stockholm Syndrome? It is not possible, to judge their emotional reactions both during their period of hiding or in the years following. Nor is it easy to judge whether Victor was abusing the girls for his own pleasure, being a humanitarian rescuer, or maintaining their hidden presence to avoid being found out by the Nazis or by his neighbours who might betray him to the Nazis – or all of the above? While there are others, who, like Molly and Helene, were hidden in bunkers, or in concealed places for years, there are, to date, no other extant diaries that so explicitly reveal the sexual acts and dreams of a young adolescent girl, living in such impossible circumstances, during the Holocaust.

SEXUAL ABUSE BY RUSSIAN LIBERATORS

Jewish children, like their mothers, were not spared exposure to the notorious rapes committed by the advancing troops of the Russian army as they liberated camps and conquered German territory. Brigitte Medvin (a Polish twelve-year-old) watched as Russian soldiers attempted to rape her mother. Luckily an officer pulled him off her. She did, however watch from her window as the liberating Russians raped girls in her garden.[591] Hanna Mishna in Lodz Poland, was liberated by Russian troops who were "wild" with five men raping any one girl. In response to their protests that they were Jews who had been oppressed by the Germans, she reports the Russians as saying: "You are Jews! You must have survived by sleeping with the Germans, so now you can sleep with us."[592] She was saved by the owner of the house she was in by being hidden under the floorboards, where the potatoes were stored. A month later the advancing rear troops stopped such rapes by threatening to, and actually, hanging Russian soldiers for raping women.[593] Irene Kempfner was in Vienna when the Russians raped her mother in the bed they shared. She was eight years old. Her mother pleaded for the other women in the room to take Irene from her bed but none of them wanted to attract the attention of the Russians to themselves. Irene stayed in the bed and from then onwards hid her mother in the bed when more Russians arrived seeking women to rape.[594]

DISPLACED PERSONS (DP) CAMPS

Judy Abrams was in a DP camp together with her parents. Her parents were grateful that Mr. N took her for walks and entertained her for hours during the long afternoons, and had no suspicion that he might have been 'grooming' Judy as is a familiar pattern of child sex abusers who are family friends.

Mr. N educated me about "love." He described with precision how to kiss in different ways, and related in detail the role of the man and the woman when making love.

"How long does it take?" I asked

"That all depends, could be minutes, could be hours."

"What does it depend on?" I wanted to know.

I began to wonder whether, given an appropriate time and place we would progress to demonstrations."[595]

Shortly afterwards, the family set sail for Canada. She turned twelve on the boat, and her periods started.[596] After arriving in Montreal, Mr. and Mrs. N came to visit their family. Mr. N cornered her in the kitchen and touched her breasts commenting "You're really getting bigger, aren't you?"[597] She squirmed and escaped. Later, she told her parents. Mr. and Mrs. N were never invited over again.

Both Dovid* and Eric* experienced sexual abuse while in DP camps after the war ended. Dovid* was in a British refugee camp in Poland, Klausheider, from 1945-1949. He was seven years old. He recalls that when the Poles came into the garrison for one week of every month, all the women were raped. When the British ran the camp for the other three weeks of each month, things were better controlled. He was, however, the only Jewish DP in the camp. He used to hide his genitals and managed to avoid being exposed as a Jew: this was possible as it was not unusual for a boy to hide his genitals when women were around.[598] Sadly, antisemitism was still prevalent in some DP camps, possibly explaining why Dovid* hid his Jewishness. For example, one of the British officers in charge of a British run DP camp in Austria said about the thousands of displaced persons in the camp "It is too bad the war didn't last another two or three months…They'd all have been done away with by then. We'd have had no problem."[599]

Similarly, two priests who met with the Anglo/American commission into the DP camps and the Palestine/Jewish question after the war - a bishop of Vienna and the head of an Austrian Catholic Charity organization - informed the commission that "We believe that the best solution to the Jewish problem would be to change this Jewish spirit to a Christian spirit. The Jews should become Christians."[600]

They claimed that the Jewish community had collaborated with the Nazis during the war and had discriminated against baptised Jews in favour of Jews of the Jewish faith. They claimed that when asked to provide lists of those to go to the camps, the Jews/*Judenrat* had chosen the baptised Jews rather than those of Jewish faith. In reality, however, of the 152,000 Jewish people in Vienna in 1942, only 4,000 (2.6%) remained alive after the war while of the 8,000 Catholic Jews in Vienna at the start of the war, 7,200 (90%) remained alive.[601] Such antisemitic attitudes did not make life for Jews and Jewish children any easier at the end of hostilities. Nor did the restrictions on supplies such as food, clothing and medical services to Jews in DP camps. For example, in some camps, such as the American run DP camp in Austria, the only conditions under which the American Military Police would release these supplies was if the women in the camp had sex with them.[602]

Eric* was only five when he arrived in an Italian DP/reception camp, Bari, in 1945. An incident occurred there that he does not usually share and did not tell his mother about. He needed to use the bathroom. While there, a soldier tried to molest him – it was painful so he ran away. Eric* does not know who it was. Fear of exposing his Jewishness haunted Eric* for some years. He went to a Catholic school as it was the only school around. He was afraid to tell the nuns he was Jewish, as Italy had also been on the side of Germany. Eric* came to believe he was Catholic. His mother took him out of school as a consequence. He loved the new school he went to: being with the children, having ice cream, seeing his first movie – *Tarzan*. But it was difficult for him to reconcile his Judaism with his Catholic schooling. Instead he turned to Buddhism for many years. In addition, he turned inward and refused to speak for years either as a part of his commitment to Buddhism, or out of psychological distress. He became a silent child, hidden again.[603]

Katrina*, aged eleven, was in a DP camp in Germany from May 1945 to May 1949. She stored her belongings under her bed. There was a man sleeping in the bunk next to her. Once, when she was the only one in the room, he grabbed her as she bent over to look for a sweater. She knew nothing about sex. His hand was around her waist then around her neck. She bit him hard. He slapped her, and she ran away. She was scared and hid behind the barracks. Her mother couldn't find her for hours. She thought she'd done something wrong. She was afraid to tell her mother. The man said that if she told, he would beat her up. She continued to sleep in the bunk next to him, just six inches away – he never said anything else to her. She never told her mother. In her testimony, she explained his behaviour was just a reaction to the situation in which they found themselves.[604] In many ways, many, if not most, of the stories of rape or assault were also reactions to the opportunities for assault created by the Nazi era.

Child sex was also used as leverage by people in power after the war. Bella* was twelve years old and living in Heidelberg after liberation. Her parents met with Judge Kramer to try to get reparations. The judge was most accommodating but said that his daughter needed a friend. Bella's* parents agreed she could go with him to the Black Forest to meet his daughter. The meeting was a ploy; his daughter never turned up at the Black Forest. Instead, Judge Kramer raped Bella and threatened her to ensure her silence. She was too embarrassed to tell her parents. She refused to ever meet with Judge Kramer again, despite the judge's unilateral power over her parents' reparations case, and his frequent requests for her to do so. Her parents' case dragged on. When Bella* learned she was pregnant, she told Judge Kramer; he claimed the baby was not his, accusing her of having another boyfriend. With no other choices, Bella* got help from an older friend to get an abortion. She was admitted to a Catholic hospital and was made to feel guilty.

Bella* spent years feeling angry, depressed, and guilty; she felt as though she were the reason her parents did not receive reparations and, consequently, that her brothers could not obtain higher educations or better employment. She also felt betrayed. She tried to make the best of it. She moved from Heidelberg to Munich and then Paris. Bella* eventually had three daughters while living in the United States of America.

ABUSE OF HIDDEN CHILDREN WAS FACILITATED BY NAZI IDEOLOGY

It is almost incomprehensible that some rescuers abused children, physically, emotionally and especially sexually. It appears that while some of these assaults were, perhaps, stimulated by erotic desires, many if not most, were facilitated by the contempt and disrespect that Jews were held in because of long-held antisemitic views and widespread Nazi ideology. In addition, such antisemitism did not disappear when Germany was defeated and abuse, including some instances of forced sexual exchange for food, clothing or medicines, were experienced by survivors in, at least, some American run DP camps in Europe.[605]

The secrecy surrounding hidden children, both for their own safety and for the safety of their rescuers who would have been punished, condemned or killed for hiding Jews, would clearly have provided opportunities for sexual assault to be implemented and to go unreported and undetected. Their vulnerability as children, and usually as Jews, alone in a strange environment, afraid, miserable, and separated from their families, culture, language, traditions, and friends, made such children easy targets for cruelty. That such people became victims of sexual and other abuse is not surprising. It is their abusers, so called "rescuers," who should be condemned for their actions. Instead, scholars, for the most part, have chosen not to reveal the children's experiences, hidden them in shame, and allowed the perpetrators to remain unrecognised and unpunished. While most rescuers deserve the highest praise for their willingness to help save Jewish children, others, such as many of those described in the testimonies reported here, should be named, shamed and prosecuted.

CHAPTER 8: UK, USA AND CANADA

During WWII, non-Jewish children, were moved away from war zones for their safety.[606] Major mass migrations of children occurred in the UK, to escape London during the Blitz, or flee from coastal towns when invasion from Europe became possible. A few Europeans were able to send their offspring to homes in the USA or Canada. What was distinctive about these transfers was that the children were moved to places where the prevailing ideologies, while sometimes retaining some antisemitic sentiments, did not depict the children as enemies, unlike the prevailing European Nazi ideology that condemned Jews as "vermin to be eradicated." Children who moved to the UK, USA and Canada, were not "hidden children." While emotional, physical and sexual abuse also occurred in these settings, there are no reports of children being killed or dying while being sheltered in these countries, unlike children hidden from Nazis in Europe, where the hiding places of many were revealed, betrayed or discovered, with disastrous and often fatal consequences. The dangers and horrors faced by the children in Nazi occupied Europe were aggravated by the immediacy of the genocide in their midst. Those abused in the UK, USA and Canada also suffered the horrors of separation from their families, at great risk, and being forced to live with strangers, but their chances of survival, albeit accompanied by significant emotional trauma, were significantly greater.[607]

ATTEMPTS TO EVACUATE JEWISH CHILDREN FROM EUROPE

Token attempts were made to seek refuge for Jews in other countries. The Evian Conference attended by delegates from thirty-two countries and thirty-nine private relief agencies met in France at Evian-les-Bains to seek a solution to Jewish emigration. Attendees made few offers to take in Jews while expressing sympathy for these Jewish refugees. Possible destinations such as Madagascar, the Dominican Republic (which ultimately took in about 500 Jews[608]) and the American Virgin Islands fell through for various reasons, though a lack of support was the primary cause.

Limited but significant attempts were made to rescue Jewish children from Germany and occupied Europe before and during WWII.[609] Most of these attempts were made by Jewish organizations such as Youth Aliya which succeeded in getting 5,000 children to Palestine before war broke out, 9,000 more during the war and afterwards, while 15,000 were sent to Western European countries. In the prewar years, the German Children's Jewish Aid group established in New York in 1934 managed to bring several hundred children into the United States despite that government's restrictive immigration rules. Other networks that assisted Jewish children in Europe included Zegota (the Council of Aid to Jews) in Poland which helped place Jewish children in non-Jewish homes. In France, about 7,000 children were saved by the *Oevre de Secours aux Enfants* which set up an underground children's rescue network known as *Circuit Garel* as well as by a number of local groups, Catholic and Protestant church leaders, ordinary citizens, and underground groups that placed children in safe Christian homes and institutions or smuggled them into neutral Switzerland or Spain. Over 6,000 children were saved in Hungary by Zionist activists who established homes under the protection of the Red Cross International as well as by members of the Protestant and Catholic Churches. In the Netherlands and Belgium, resistance movements managed to hide thousands of Jewish children in monasteries, hospitals and boarding schools.[610] A plan by the Bulgarian Government to allow emigration of 4,000 Jewish children failed. On June 5 1943, the Grand Mufti of Jerusalem successfully protested to the Prime Minister of Bulgaria against this, preferring that all Jews should be exterminated rather than ghettoized or saved.[611] Most of the children sent overseas never saw their parents again and many were converted to Christianity.

At least, between December 1938 and September 1939, the British Cabinet allowed some 10,000 unaccompanied children into Britain – including 7,500 Jewish children - in an action called the *Kinder-transport*.[612] Those rescued came from Germany, Austria, Poland and Czechoslovakia with the help of British, Jewish and Quaker welfare organizations. The British did, however refuse to allow a further 21,000 Jewish children into Palestine. Similarly, from February to June 1939, in the USA, a proposal to allow 20,000 Jewish children into America over a two year period (the Wagner-Rogers Bill) failed to gain support, largely due to the antisemitic attitudes rife in public and in Congress, as well as the lack of support for the Bill from President Franklin Roosevelt.[613] Laura Delano Houghteling, President Roosevelt's cousin and James Houghteling's (the Commissioner of Immigration) wife, commented that the problem with the Bill was "that 20,000 ugly [Jewish] children would all too soon grow up into 20,000 ugly adults." [614] Ultimately, the USA offered refuge to fewer Jewish children - about 1,000 between 1934 to 1945 – than Belgium, France, Holland or Sweden, despite the fact that USA immigration quotas for Jews remained unfilled for almost all of this period.[615] Despite this lack of formal support for saving Jewish lives, illegal immigration during the 1930's and continuing after the outbreak of war, saved more than 3,000 Jewish children. After the war, another 15,000 were brought to kibbutzim in Palestine before the establishment of the State of Israel in 1948. The Youth Aliya, responsible for this activity was a German-Jewish organization.[616] Canada too, was hostile to Jewish immigration with their attitude being summed up by a senior Canadian official – Frederick Blair, Director of the Government of Canada's Immigration Branch of the Department of Mines and Resources from 1936 to 1943 – saying, when asked how many Jews would be allowed into Canada after the war replied, "None is too many."[617]

THE UK

Over three million mainly Gentile British children were affected by evacuation to safer housing during WW2.[618] There were three waves of evacuation: the first was in September 1939 when one and a half million women and children were officially moved from major cities to the countryside in three days. In addition, an estimated two million children were sent away privately and were not part of the official system. The evacuation was carefully planned, but on arrival in the districts it became disorganised.

> [...] the scene which ensued was more akin to a cattle- or slave-market than anything else. The prospective foster mothers, who should not have been allowed on the field at all, just invaded us and walked about the field picking out what they considered to be the most presentable specimens, and then harassed the poor billeting officers for the registration slips which were essential to get the necessary cash for food and lodging from the government.[619]

The second wave occurred in 1940 when 213,000 children were removed from coastal towns, of which some 20,000 were sent to live abroad. The third wave, involving about one million people, was in March 1944 when bombs were dropped on London and south-east England. The government did not organize this evacuation, although it did provide financial support for travel out of London.[620]

Children placed in homes were offered safety but, in some cases, faced negative experiences. Many were abused physically by having to "earn their keep" by helping with daily chores, sometimes arduous, in the home and on farms, sometimes to the exclusion of attendance at school. For example, fourteen children were sent to Mount Pleasant farm. Four-year-old Pat was one of the youngest and Dennis, nine-years-old, was the oldest. Life was cruel for these children as Denis recalls:

> [...] with the children being used for slave labour, nothing more. We had to work the farm in the absence of any farmhands. Aunt Nancy made us pick potatoes by moonlight, we did backbreaking field work and even the little ones like Pat had jobs. She had to do the chickens, you know, feed them, clean them out and collect the eggs and things. We were only allowed to go to school if there was no work on the farm, and that did not happen very often.[621]

Aunt Nancy instilled terror into the children with her leather strap. She would beat them for any misdemeanour including beating the little ones publicly for wetting their beds. Dennis remembers one boy being so badly beaten that his legs bled.

Many children suffered public humiliations imposed by their foster families. Six-year-old Lilian was one of these.[622] She was picked by a great burly Welsh farmer who chose her and another girl to return to his cottage. There they had to strip naked and get into a bath of green disinfectant:

> he told us to get in it and we got in smelling awful and she [the farmer's wife] was pouring the jug over our heads and the dog came in from the back and went to sniff our clothes and she screamed and kicked the clothes out the back door. These clothes were new, my mother had bought new things for us. They were thrown out the back and she was washing us and then when we got washed she put a big towel around us and sat us on a chair and he got a razor and he was shaving our heads and if he cut you with the razor she put gentian violet on the cut so that you had a bald head with purple dots on your head which used to burn when they cut us.[623]

They were sent to school but were not allowed to wear hats to cover their heads. The farmer had burned all their clothes so that they were dressed in whatever could be found for them. At school they were teased and bullied for being "nit-ridden townies." They were not the only ones. Lilian stayed with this farmer for five years. She recalled that once a week, on Friday evenings, the farmer would smoke his pipe while watching the children having a bath in front of the fire. "The lady used to say to us – oh God, I'll never forget it – she used to say 'Here's the flannel, I'll put soap on it, stand up and do between your legs' and we had to do that and he used to be sitting with his pipe, watching."[624]

Sexual abuse also occurred in Swanage and, unusually during this period, was punished. In October 1943, a man was jailed for twelve months for indecently assaulting three evacuees in his care. The claim he made, that he was using the children as "human hot-water-bottles," was not accepted by the jury.[625] This is one of the few occurrences of child sexual abuse that occurred where the perpetrator was punished.

Thirteen-year-old Rose Clarke was treated as unpaid help and was expected to look after the younger son and clean the shoes of the older boy. The other children soon began to treat her as a maid, although she shared a room and bed with the remaining girl of her own age. She was called names and was bullied.

> [...] each week, M and I went to the church youth group. The club leader kept the room in virtual darkness and then proceeded to sexually abuse us to differing degrees. Looking back, I suppose I was fortunate personally as I was not subject to too much, other than the man fondling me. But some of the others experienced much more.[626]

Jen also experienced sexual abuse:

> One night when I had gone to bed, my foster father came into my bedroom and sat on my bed, which he had never done before, and then he kissed me. I was absolutely terrified because it wasn't an ordinary kiss, it hurt my lips against my teeth and I couldn't move to escape from it. He left but I didn't move for hours and hours. I was completely and utterly immobile. I was paralysed with fear. The next time he came back I can't remember if he kissed me first but he started moving his hands across my body and holding my breasts in his hands. He never raped me but he just used to handle and kiss me. I could never tell anyone.[627]

She developed insomnia for fear he would come to her. She also concluded that her foster mother knew what was happening, but chose not to, or did not know how to stop it. Later she said: "the betrayal was the thing that came to me through it all. The deep sense of betrayal by my foster father, of course, and somehow by many others, including the authorities responsible for our welfare. I was left with this deep sense of betrayal, abandonment and disillusion."[628]

One family of three girls nine, seven and five, were taken to live on an isolated farm in South Yorkshire in 1939 where they stayed for some years. The couple, who were, scandalously for that time, unmarried, abused them emotionally by telling them that they had been abandoned by their parents because they were unwanted. The girls had to work on the farm as free labourers, being fed bread and dripping (roasted animal fat) with little other comfort or affection. Some years later, the farmer came to their bedroom and made advances to the middle daughter, Marie, (the only child who is named in this narrative) who, at that stage, was about ten. She screamed, and the mistress came running. The farmer left Marie alone from then on but made her life miserable. He then approached the older girl who was twelve. Marie, the middle child, became aware that her older sister had developed a new smell about her – a smell that she later realised was the smell of sex. The youngest sister, who was eight, saw the farmer having sex with her oldest sister but did not know what she was witnessing. She sensed it was wrong so kept quiet about it.

A teacher at school noticed the eldest sister's changing shape. She was removed from the farm to have her baby, which was then given up for adoption: the eldest sister refused to name the father out of fear. No explanation was given to the other two girls; she was just taken to the doctor and never came back. The police questioned the girls but Marie had seen nothing and the youngest girl was too afraid to say anything.

The farmer was a swindler, a bully, and a black marketeer who supplied the police. The villagers knew that the farmer and his "wife" were mistreating the girls but because the farmer was so influential with the police, they knew the police would turn a blind-eye; they did not think they would be believed if they spoke out and might even have feared to report him. So the girls remained at the farm. Marie felt guilty and had a great sense of bitterness and distrust of people for the remainder of her life.[629]

While stories of sex abuse are the exception rather than the rule, the reluctance, guilt, shame and fear of repercussions result in the suppression of such experiences. In recent years, however, an increasing number of ex-evacuees have revealed that they were emotionally, physically or sexually abused. It was more prevalent than had ever been imagined.[630]

SEXUAL ABUSE OF JEWISH CHILDREN BY RESCUERS IN THE USA AND CANADA

Joan Zilva's parents (her father was Jewish although not her mother) who lived in England, but feared the possibility of a Nazi invasion of the UK, decided that she should be evacuated to Toronto through an agreement between the Universities of Cambridge and Toronto. She was sent to live with a wealthy family in Toronto in August 1940. The couple were childless. Joan was fourteen, timid, shy and unhappy. Her relationship with the man of the house became difficult. He would play games with her in the evenings, take her for drives, tell her funny stories. But he never missed a chance to kiss her at night.

> "Kiss me" hides a multitude of sins! In fact, he came up after I was in bed every evening, felt me all over and French kissed me at length. I was physically mature but knew nothing about the sexual act. I only knew there was something wrong but thought it was just me. The fact that I didn't mention it in my letters shows that I was confused and I said I liked him because I had to like someone and he, at least, was kind to me, whatever the motives. I think that Mrs. H knew and thought I was leading him on.[631]

Joan wrote to the person in charge of the rescue program and was moved to another family. But Mr. H wrote to her parents to complain that their daughter was cold and unresponsive. Her parents, who were unaware of Mr. H's attempts to seduce Joan, reproached her for upsetting her Canadian hosts. Joan was left with the feeling that she was somehow to blame. She was also left with discomfort about physical intimacy. She never married although she desperately wanted to have children.[632]

As with the current scandals surrounding the sexual abuse of children by clergy, sexual abuse by Rabbis is equally repulsive as it reflects not only child sexual abuse but abuse by those who set themselves up as spiritual leaders and models for their community. Yet it happened. For example, after the war, following two years of living in foster homes, Marie Claire Rakowski, born in 1943, and her sister, were sent to the United States, without their mother, and placed in a Hasidic family headed by a Rabbi. Her sister fought with her awfully and foster families could not tolerate this. They were moved from the home of one Rabbi to another: the second Rabbi sexually abused Marie-Claire.[633]

Also, at eight-years-old, Hanna, after surviving the war in eastern Europe, was taken in by a Satmar Hasidic family in New York. She was assaulted by the man of the house who fondled her and tried to enter her manually, although she says he did not succeed. She has had difficulty relating to men ever since, has been afraid of sex, and has been in therapy for most of her life.[634]

Maya was hidden with a family, and in orphanages in and around Paris, before being sent to the USA. After being hidden with a woman who starved and beat her, Maya was sent to an orphanage that had two parts, one of which was a government funded reform school for juvenile delinquents and the children of prostitutes and criminals. The other part was for orphans and children abandoned by their parents. Without government funding, the nuns were not interested in them, providing them with exceptionally inadequate diets: no breakfast, a watery soup made of potato peels for lunch, a slice of bread, two boiled potatoes or some noodles, a small bowl of beans and a teaspoon or two of jam. Nor was the convent heated, resulting in Maya being unable to hold a pencil with her frozen and swollen fingers. When she outgrew her shoes, she was forced to go barefoot despite the cold. "Although the nuns provided neither adequate food nor heat for their young wards, they managed to give them a uniform for weekdays and another fancier one for Sundays and religious holidays."[635]

Maya was moved to another Jewish orphanage in Paris, and was well cared for by a young couple. When they disappeared one day, they were replaced by people who were "mean and greedy."[636] They were caught embezzling the assets of the orphanage and selling the gifts that had been sent to the children from the USA. One day, in 1945, she was visited by two Americans who offered to help get her to her aunt in the USA, who they reported, would "love to have her." At fifteen she moved to the USA to find that her aunt and uncle and their baby lived in poverty. Her uncle was a gambler and a drinker and every time he got drunk, he tried to rape her. She was helped to move to a more affluent family, but they expected her to take care of the entire family. They also starved her.[637]

Many orphans who were cared for in orphanages tell similar stories. Their "rescuers" knew that the children had nobody to stand up for their rights; they were extremely vulnerable to exploitation by those who appeared to be altruists but were some of the worst exploiters of children.[638]

Jewish *Kindertransport* Children in the UK

While most children who were rescued by the *Kindertransport* were probably well cared for, some were not. Clare G was a Polish girl sent on the *Kindertransport* to England:

> I met these people in their liquor store. They looked like nice people. [...] The [man] came in and started to touch me all over. [...] I couldn't speak to anybody. That was a household that was helter-skelter. One day I said to him, "Aren't you ashamed? You are old enough to be my father? You have a daughter." He said "I don't want my daughter I want you." I said "I was raised Orthodox! I don't know such things." Clare's protests came to no avail. She was raped repeatedly by the man. "He came to the bedroom, put a hand over my mouth. "If you say a word, I have people in big places. I will send you, your sister, and your brother back to Germany." I said, "What did we do to you?" He didn't care. He raped me. I was up all night. I took a

bath. My God, what has happened to me? What can I do? This happened for quite a while. I was destroyed, totally destroyed.[639]

Clare enlisted the help of a local Rabbi, who confronted her rapist, but Clare was accused of coming on to her assailant. Unable to tolerate this any longer, Clare escaped one night, accompanied by the man's daughter.

Stella*, a child on the *Kindertransport*, reports sexual abuse and rape, although it is not certain whether this took place before or after her transfer to the UK.[640] Two other *Kindertransport* children report sexual harassment or abuse: Bertha Leverton and Mira Blaustein. Bertha was fifteen when she was sent to live with "Uncle Billy" and "Aunt Vera" for five years, where she served as a maid. She was later joined by her much younger sister Inge and brother Theo. She endured, and repulsed, the advances made by "Uncle Billy" over the five years and only refrained from leaving the household to protect her sister (six years her junior) from becoming the target of his attentions.[641]

Mira Blaustein was twelve when she was sent to the UK where she was cared for in multiple foster homes. In one of these she was included into the family but in others she was exploited for her labour and abused both emotionally and sexually.[642]

Another devastating story of the sexual abuse of a *Kindertransport* child is told by Susi, called Grace by her rescue family. Susi/Grace and her twin sister were adopted by Baptist minister Reverend Mann and his wife as part of the *Kindertransport* program.[643] The Reverend became sexually attracted to her and, from nine-years-old, he emotionally manipulated her and forced her to have sex with him. She was terrified and unable to refuse him. The abuse usually occurred in his study and occurred both at night and during the day. In her teens she asked him why she had to do this:

He replied:

"Because if you do this to me, Grace, [...] it makes me feel that you are my own child. You know that

the greatest tragedy in my life has been that I
haven't been able to have children of my own. So, if
you do this for me, it just makes me feel that much
closer to you."

She obeyed, but loathed him for it.[644]

The Reverend Mann treated her ailing sister badly and Grace was
afraid that if she reported his abuse to the police there would be nobody
at all to care for her sick sister. He never allowed other boys to get close
to her as he wanted her for himself.[645] On a number of occasions,
Irene, his wife, walked in on father and daughter in compromising
moments resulting in confusion and embarrassment. Grace was then
severely berated by Irene.[646]

At the age of twenty-four, her foster father suggested they get
married: "You know I would love it if we could be together [...] You
know, I mean married. Why don't we just drive off somewhere now?"
She replied, "But you know that's impossible, Daddy."[647] She eventually dated a man secretly and married without telling her parents
until just before the wedding. After the birth of her own son, she
became seriously emotionally disturbed wondering about her own real
parents and the stories that she had been told that her birth papers had
been burned at the Munich orphanage in which she had lived for a few
years before coming to the UK.[648]

In 1988, while searching for her real family, she entered therapy.
She was encouraged to write about any negative feelings that were still
troubling her. She did:

> 19.10.88: I was asked to express how I feel about
> you E.J. Mann – you were given a gift – a child to
> love – what you did was DESTROY – I FEEL
> DEEP BITTERNESS, RESENTMENT AND
> ANGER – the latter I am scared of. It might ERUPT
> and destroy all I have bravely fought to build. And
> so I bury this emotion knowing that as I do this I am
> partly immobilized.

How did you DESTROY me? You abused me mentally and physically. A LEECH sucking my life blood. You chained my whole being. You are a DIRTY UNCLEAN HYPOCRITE PREACHING TO OTHERS – abusing me by ACTS OF CRUELTY.

How were these MANIFESTED? I will tell you – you bastard. You would creep into my bed at 10 years and insert your filthy p into my v. I WOULD HAVE FEELINGS OF HATE FOR YOU, but also FEELINGS OF INSECURITY LEST I DENY you what you wanted under the pseudo-excuse of THIS ACT MAKING ME YOUR FLESH AND BLOOD. YOU ARE SICK – YOU WOULD MAKE ME HOLD YOUR FILTHY P FOR A THRILL. I GUESS and as I developed you would the life blood from me (sic) denying me rightful relationships. WHY? I guess you were SCARED I would talk. I didn't then but I will now. I WOULD LIKE TO SAY "MAY YOU ROT IN HELL" BUT NO, I CAN'T LIVE WITH SUCH DESTRUCTION. YOU MUST PAY THE PRICE AS "GOD" CHOOSES. FIRST THOUGH THERE IS DEBRIS TO THROW AWAY. I MUST FREE MYSELF FROM YOUR BONDAGE – YOU ARE A SNAKE ENCROACHING me with your sting[649] [emphasis in original].

Much later she wrote directly to her rescue father accusing him of three major injustices: (1) His sexual abuse of her, and his anger when his wishes were denied. (2) The psychological abuse she had experienced – the reverend's obsession with her which had prevented her from forming a mother-daughter bond with his wife/her mother but also from getting to know other men. (3) His denial of the truth about her and her sister's origins. The family had known of her Jewish origins but had not told her. "In a final bitter attack Susi [her real name] added that the Reverend had saved her from Nazi persecution only to become her persecutor himself."[650] Her father admitted his wrongdoing and asked for his daughter's forgiveness.[651] While the Reverend and Irene were not legally prosecuted, Susi's story was filmed and aired on BBC2 and in other countries. The couple were clearly identifiable from the film. Interestingly, many defended the Reverend as a highly respected member of the Baptist Church whose overprotectiveness of the girls was simply seen as genuine care. While Irene was vocal in her feeling of indignation and hurt aroused by the film, the Reverend became silent.[652]

These stories of emotional and sexual abuse of children who believed they were to find safety in the homes of volunteer foster parents are shocking and contemptible. The abuses expose the perpetrators as opportunistic, manipulative, authoritarian and with distorted sexual personalities. They also reveal the well-known finding that child sexual abuse occurs in the home, and is perpetrated by someone known to the child, more often than not. The power imbalance between a child and his/her parent/caretaker may make any resistance on the part of the child seem futile.

In 1953, the Israeli government passed a *Martyrs and Heroes Remembrance Law* that recognized and honoured Gentiles "who risked their lives to save Jews" by placing plaques naming them at Yad Vashem.[653] This law delineates only a small group of rescuers that have been proposed by survivors or their families, within a larger group who helped Jews in ways that did not necessarily involve danger to the rescuer and which might have been motivated by financial or other gain. As of January 1 2017, the exact number of recognized Righteous Among Nations was 26,513 from fifty-one countries.[654] Today, the American Jewish Foundation for the Righteous and the Anti-Defamation League send monthly stipends to needy and elderly rescuers to make their lives easier.[655] Until recently there has been no formal recognition of Jews who saved other Jews during the Holocaust: Yad Vashem's award is specifically limited to Gentile rescuers. More recently, in 2011, the Jewish Rescuers Citation was established by the B'nai B'rith World Center-Jerusalem—and the Committee to Recognize the Heroism of Jews who Rescued Fellow Jews During the Holocaust (JRJ). Many who could have fled chose to remain behind to rescue others such as Miriam Gillis-Carlebach's father, Chief Rabbi Joseph Carlebach of Hamburg[656] who paid for it with their lives. Jews in every country in occupied Europe employed subterfuge, forgery of documents, smuggling, concealment and other methods to ensure that Jews survived the Holocaust, or assisted them in escaping to a safe haven. As of 2019, 270 such heroes have been honored with citations for rescue activities in Germany, France, Hungary, Greece, Slovakia, Yugoslavia, Russia, Poland, Ukraine, Belarus, Lithuania, Italy and Holland.[657]

CHAPTER 9: EMOTIONAL IMPACT

In Auschwitz-Birkenau, Rena remembers watching a young teenage girl eat a lemon while her mother begged for a bite. The girl glared angrily at her mother and devoured the already squeezed pulp and rind. She ate the whole thing without sharing it. Rena asked herself: "What have they done to us?"[658]

The inhumanity experienced during the Holocaust with its violence, emotional trauma, physically devastating hardships, and betrayal of faith in humanity had long lasting effects. In particular, the effects on those who experienced child sex abuse took many forms including fear of sex, inability to enjoy sex, problems establishing relationships, marital difficulties, reluctance to become pregnant, and inadequate feelings of self-worth. Many never revealed their humiliation to others. For example, Inge F was interned in Theresienstadt and describes the lasting effects of being raped by a German officer.

> I was very hungry. Someone in Terezin gave me a piece of bread and a German saw it. He took me and raped me and said if I wanted the bread I had to earn it. I didn't want it anymore. Then I started to grow up and see that I am nothing. They can do whatever they want. I never told anyone. I didn't want my brother to know. I am so very ashamed. I am 70 and still ashamed. It shouldn't have happened that way [...] I never married. I used to like men. Now I tolerate them. I couldn't stand the thought of going to bed with them.[659]

Similarly, Lidia Brown-Abramson who was raped by a partisan as a teenager, reported that even though she did have children, she never enjoyed sex, but had to agree to it. "I never experience pleasure from sex, never. I waited for my husband not to want it, not to be able to perform. I am always in control during the sexual act. I never relax, I never let myself go. I also don't know how to love."[660] Similarly, another fourteen-year-old Jewish teenager who ran away from the ghetto was raped by a man with a rifle who stopped her. She had resulting long-lasting sexual difficulties. At the time of her interview with Nechama Tec, many years later, she said that something inside her broke and that she could not look at men and was conflicted about sex. She was excited about sex but was scared and turned inward. She never liked the physical aspect of sex and did not place sex as an important part of her life. She said, later, that she was glad that she did not need it.[661]

Abused children were trapped, leading often to dissociation from their feelings, thoughts or actions – resulting in a lifetime of psychological disorder for many.[662] Others were conflicted about their rescuers/abusers, feeling both a desire to approach and avoid them simultaneously. Another survivor who was violently molested by his foster father said "regardless of what he had done to me, I can't hate him [...] I wonder if he ever loved me [...] after all, he saved my life."[663] Many child survivors are still tormented by the memories of being physically or sexually abused by the same people who rescued them.[664]

Survivors report multiple emotional horrors including fear, horror, physical and emotional pain and profound loneliness during the war as well as anxiety, numbness, emptiness, or depression afterwards. At night they are tormented with fearful dreams while during the day they feel sad and empty.[665] They suffer from more health problems than others who were not sexually abused including more chronic pelvic pain, greater sexual dysfunction, painful menstruation and vaginal discharge. Their self-loathing may result in self-destructive behaviour, self mutilation and riskier sex.[666]

Children's feelings towards their sexual perpetrators differed depending on the perpetrators' religious background. Strong negative feelings were evoked by the few Jewish perpetrators that are reported; Jews were supposed to help other Jews, not to harm them. Gentile abusers, on the other hand, evoked both positive and negative feelings – both hate and love, resentment and longing, gratitude and anger, as so clearly expressed in Molly and Helene's account of their years buried underground by their sexually exploitative rescuer.[667]

Some interpreted their abuse experiences within a cultural framework of being Jewish.

> Being sexually abused (whether by Jewish or non-Jewish strangers, biological parents, or caretakers) was perceived as part of the targeted massive barbarity against them as Jews. Some even thought that they deserved the abuse, both physical and sexual, because of their Jewish origin (that it was somehow God's punishment for having being born a Jew or for Jews allegedly having murdered Jesus). Some explained that the perpetrators used abuse as a means of "educating" the Jews about their suitable social status. They, the Jewish children, were expected to serve and satisfy their "saviours" in any way they could.[668]

Such an interpretation is typical of the ideologically and religiously strict world in which many of the survivors were hidden. As with children in many of the Christian, and primarily Catholic, run schools during the 20th century, children of poor or dysfunctional families were perceived and treated as though they were being punished for the supposed sins of their parents (or in the case of Jews, the alleged sins of their ancestors). As Shimon Cohen testified about his four or five-year-old hidden sibling:

> My younger sister was born with a shortened forearm. She was hidden with a Calvinist family in Holland. They regarded the deformity as "a punishment from God for doing bad things." As a consequence, she could not go to Church with the rich people but only with the poor people (who were also being punished by God). If you were rich God was blessing you.[669]

Age and cumulative trauma influenced outcomes; the younger the child, and the more stressful the events experienced, the worse the outcome. The support that children might benefit from in normal settings was absent for Holocaust survivor children: family members, teachers, and extended family were not present.[670] Sexually abused hidden children remained with a lasting sense of horror, terror, vulnerability, betrayal and problematic adult relationships.[671] Recovery from such trauma is difficult.[672]

Some children's experiences of multiple, violent, abusive events – physical, emotional and sexual – were so extreme as to make recovery almost impossible. Judith,[673] for example, was sent to a labour camp (not identified) with her mother and other family members when she was about six or seven. She was put to work in a reclusive, smelly warehouse without windows. On the table were many teeth of people who had died, full of mould and blood. She refused to sort them and the manager slammed her hand with a pole, breaking one of her fingers. When she was eight, a new manager arrived, who selected girls of sixteen or seventeen and would take them into a room sometimes together and sometimes alone. The girls would be gang-raped by him and other soldiers. When they emerged from the room they were injured and sick. Some died. One day, Judith was sitting drawing in the sand when a tall man wearing a black suit and high boots approached her. She was not wearing her patch and when she said she was Jewish he swung a big stick in her face breaking her nose and several teeth. He ordered his dog to attack her: the dog bit her and ripped her clothes off. Then the man burned his cigarette into her face. Next, he put his penis into her mouth and urinated. She started choking and vomiting. He shot her in her leg and left her there. Later, the same guard accused her mother of stealing Judith from some Christians because she looked Aryan. Her mother showed him Judith's birth certificate but he ripped it up, yelling "You Jews are all liars! You ruin the world!"[674] Then he forcefully grabbed her little sister, slammed her on a rock, took an ax and chopped her into two pieces. Her grandmother jumped to help her granddaughter and the guard shot her in the head. Her mother passed out and when her aunt went to help her mother, the guard shot her aunt in the head too.

In 1946 she was reunited with her father who had joined the partisans. She was eleven. She refused to speak to her father, accusing him of being a bad man because he had abandoned them. After her father learned what had happened to his family, he went insane and was hospitalized.

Judith struggled after the war. Whenever she saw a dog, she assumed a fetal position on the floor and wouldn't move until someone came to help her. She couldn't read or write at twelve. She went to school and was teased unmercifully because of her scars and disfigurement: the children called her Frankenstein. She stayed away from boys because of the image of the penis in her mouth. Judith's struggles continued. Her father became alcoholic and physically abused her and her mother. She married someone she didn't love at seventeen, just to get out of her home. She had a seizure on their wedding night; she panicked when she saw her new husband's penis. She was hospitalized and divorced her husband. She eventually married a man when she was twenty-seven but had never had sex and was too frightened to do so on their wedding night. He was gentle and treated her kindly. She was never able to enjoy sex although she did have both a son and a daughter. Thereafter, she became very depressed: her husband hired a helper to care for her and perform household chores. One day she found her husband in bed with this helper. She did not allow her husband into her heart again. He died of a heart attack at forty-five, when she was fifty-one. She remained a widow for the remainder of her life.[675] Judith's story incorporates some of the most extreme incidents of physical, emotional and sexual abuse that children reported including betrayal by Nazis as well as by both her father and her second husband.

Despite any achievements in life, including their raising functioning families and success in their lives or careers, survivors report that they are plagued by painful childhood memories. Many struggle with spousal intimacy or interpersonal intimacy with their children. As many as three-quarters of the survivors of child sexual abuse interviewed by Lev-Wiesel and Amir generally consider life itself to be meaningless and painful. "One participant sums this up by saying 'Yes, I did well in business. I also have a loving wife: without her I could not have survived...But is my life worth living? No. [...] Life is not worth living!' "[676]

SILENCE AND DENIAL

About 715,000 Jewish men and women who survived the camps were liberated by Allied forces – but only a bare 4,000 orphaned Jewish children. Many were on the verge of dying.[677] Most of the children who survived had been hiding. Hidden youth learned to be silent about their identities, whereabouts, feelings, worries, and fears. As Abba Kobner described at the Eichmann trial:

> When we broke into the ghetto, suddenly a woman ran towards us. She held a little girl in her arms [...] When she ascertained that we were Jews, she broke out sobbing hysterically and told us what had happened to her. I gathered that she and her little girl, who was probably four but looked three-years-old, had hidden in a pit for more than eleven months. She poured forth her tale of agony in a torrent of words. [...] at the end she wept bitterly and without stop.
>
> At that moment the little girl in her arms, looked and behaved as if she were mute, opened her mouth and said, "Mama, may I cry now?"
>
> Later we learned that the mother had drilled into the child that she should not cry out under any circumstances because she would be heard and endanger their lives.[678]

Hidden children learned never to speak and, least of all, about any sexual abuse they had experienced. When they did speak of sexual assaults, their stories were denied. " 'What could you know?' they were asked, 'What could you possibly remember or understand?' "[679] Their memories were almost always discredited by their adult counterparts, who were regarded as the "real" survivors. Many regarded such stories as fabrications or false, ignoring children's reports; they were crazy, too young to remember, or they were wrong.[680] Not only were children's reports of sexual encounters, harassment or assault discounted, but so too were all their experiences during the Nazi era. "You were just a child! What did you know about such things?" was a common response to children's stories, compounding the anguish and confusion of their lives during the Holocaust.[681] As children themselves said at the end of the war, their voices were not heard. Parents, counsellors, caregivers, and other authorities simply did not want to listen to their stories, or if they did, listeners most often denied the veracity and validity of their accounts, experiences, and emotions. Some children expressed the feeling that they faced Holocaust denial.[682]

Children who survived the Holocaust remained silent about sexual abuse even when this occurred after the war. For example, Irina*, at the age of eleven, emigrated to America after the war.[683] She attended a school where the man in charge of the horses at the school tried to sexually assault her, touching her before allowing her to ride the horses. She never told anyone about this until providing her testimony many decades later. During the war she was told never to talk to anyone about anything and then later, when she did start to tell people her stories, they never believed her.[684]

Social services in multiple countries after the war, such as in Canada, paid little attention to the psychological needs of child immigrants, presuming that they were too young to have been affected by wartime trauma; they were not given any special care.[685] Many child Holocaust survivors have expressed strong feelings of anger about the ways in which their feelings were dismissed.[686] Maya Schwartz, for example, testified:

> When I think about all the experts who claim that children faced the assault on their lives with resilience and that they did not mind the bombings if they were with their parents and got a lot of reassurance, I get pissed off. We were terrified. When your life is at gunpoint and the bombs are falling towards your head, what do you mean by resilience? With each explosion you die a little, even if you survive it. With each explosion your heart stops beating […] With each bomb you feel more certain that the next one has to be for you.[687]

Sabine Heller confirms such reactions:

On the surface I looked like a happy child, but underneath was a very frightened little girl. Now when I read about it, I am infuriated. I was never given a chance or encouraged to talk about my feelings. I was just expected to go on with life as if nothing had happened.[688]

It was not only social services who failed to encourage children to recount their stories or to respect them when they did. Such neglect occurred in families as well. Similarly, Clem Loew, living in Poland writes that his mother was never able to help him deal with his experiences emotionally. Although he wished she had, she never asked him such questions as "How do you feel about not having a father?" Or, "how is it for you?" As he writes, "Children were ignored, and as a result a lot of us pushed our feelings under the rug. Maybe this is one reason why it's taken so long to 'come out' with those feelings in a public way."[689]

Twelve-year-old Dirk Van der Heidde who escaped to America in 1941 struggled with his fear and his memories and recorded in his diary that his Uncle Klaus had been angry when he learned that he was writing about the war in Holland in his English class at school. His Uncle would have preferred that he forget about what happened. In his diary he notes "I know I'll never forget about it anyway, or forget the Germans and how Mother died."[690] Nevertheless, at that time, like Uncle Klaus, "the universal wisdom was that it was best to leave the past behind and forget the traumas."[691] Even when surviving Jewish children were sent away to holiday camps in the immediate post-war years, they never talked to each other about the Holocaust or the relatives they had lost.[692]

Often, no one was willing to listen to their stories; many thought that since the war was over it was time to move on.[693] Polack writes powerfully about children's reactions to being denied their Holocaust experiences:

The 1950's, the decade of nocturnal screaming, the decade of total silence. The decade of everyone presuming the Holocaust was behind us, that horror and evil could be put behind us. Two child survivors that I know had their parents shot in front of them when they were ten years old, each in different Polish ghettos. How could anyone imagine that these children would *get over it*? [Italics original]

We the child survivors, were told by our surviving parents if we had any, or by their friends, if they had any – what do you know about the Holocaust? You were just a child.

"To say to us "what do you know, you were just a child" was to tell us we were not who we thought we were, we were not survivors like those grown-ups. We experienced, in this way, the Jewish version of Holocaust denial.[694]

He writes further:

"Do you really know, child", they would ask, "do you really know what it is to have your parents shot before your eyes, do you really know what it is to have your grandparents thrown out of the upstairs window during a liquidation?"

Did I know? I would put my hands in my pockets […] Did I know? The question was an accusation. You do not understand, they were saying, you were too young to make sense of it. The carnage and death, the murder by fever and hunger – all of which I witnessed, some of which I experienced – were not valid to them because I could not have made sense of such experiences as they occurred. […]

"You say you were there." They argued, "But you really weren't."

Then they would appear astonished at the pain that came over my face from such invalidation and would hastily take pity.

"Bist geven a yingeleh," they would say. It's not
your fault, you were just a kid. Children, they
meant, are frivolous; let's not take their experiences
seriously.[695]

Children were clearly distressed and disturbed by what they had
experienced. Opdyke's memories provide further support for this: After
the war she eventually went to a DP camp at Hessich-Lichtenau where
she reports children became introverted, and sedated like sleepwalkers.
They played only quiet games and moved silently in groups. She writes
that they mistrusted any tenderness.[696]

Mark Mazower confirms these observations saying that children
were depressed and serious beyond their years. He writes that "They
seemed cynical, despondent and distrustful of authority. [...] They
were suspicious of signs of affection and prone to violence, often
dangerous."[697] They appeared to expect no support from adults.

Children's experiences were even occasionally denied by psychiatrists. When Josie Martin was seeing a psychiatrist after the war, he
related his story. Afterwards, the psychiatrist looked at him and said,
"Gee, that's very interesting, but nothing major happened. You weren't
abused, and your parents lived."[698]

As Steinfeldt writes, "In the period immediately after the war, the
universal wisdom was that it was best to leave the past behind and
forget the traumas."[699] There are some, such as a few archivists at
Holocaust research centres in Israel as well as audience members at
conferences where I have presented some of this information, who,
despite such accounts by children, remain adamantly opposed to
addressing the question of sexual abuse of boys and girls during this
dark period of history. The emergence of child survivors' groups and
their testimonies in recent decades that have clearly illustrated the
psychological trauma and lifestyle consequences ensuing from such
denial of children's experiences, lends credence to the children's
anguish, and anger, incurred by this betrayal of, and disrespect for, their
realities. [700]

Society in general still does not give credence to the voices of children. The old maxim – that children should be seen but not heard – survives in many ways, if not in its rigidly and literally imposed controls over children in the 20th century. Yet there are few societal systems that give sincere credit to children's voices. The United Nations' focus on children's rights and needs, including the establishment of the Declaration on the Rights of the Child, and the two subsequent conferences in 1990 and 2001 at which teenagers' voices were heard, is still focused on educating children about the United Nations as well as learning of their perceptions of world issues.[701] Yet power to act on these issues remains in the hands of (adult) United Nations employees.[702] There are few individuals or organizations that, like Janusz Korczak[703] in the Warsaw ghetto orphanage that he established, give any authority for the implementation of solutions to their concerns to the children themselves. Yet children have demonstrated, repeatedly, that they are capable of acting on their own behalf. After the Parkland school shootings in the USA, masses of teenagers actively engaged in the political fight for stronger gun laws in the United States and actually made some headway in this highly politicised and polarising issue, despite the fact that few of the teenagers were old enough to vote and they live in a country that gives little or no political agency to teenagers. In South Africa too, under Apartheid, youth action against Apartheid policies was a significant obstacle to the regime.

REUNIFICATION WITH PARENTS AFTER THE WAR

On liberation, many if not most survivors found themselves in Displaced Persons (DP) Camps sometimes situated in the same concentration camps from which they had just been freed. Wanting to seek out their lost families, many traversed Europe looking for close or even distant relatives, often with little or no success. Destitute, emotionally and physically battered, and traumatized beyond belief, these remaining few Jews began their long struggle back to society, family, community and the creation of new homes and lives. Children were usually orphaned. Many found themselves alone on the streets, having been thrown out of the homes in which they had been hidden.

Fear of exposure by the families for having hidden the children led to their eviction.

In November 1945, between two and three thousand Jewish children were living in Christian homes in Poland, not out of compassion, but as a source of income for the family.[704] Most hidden children – except perhaps those who remained with their foster families if, indeed, these were happy families – faced traumatic adaptations after the end of World War II. Those few who were returned to their surviving parents experienced the initial loss of their families, adjustment to their hiding families, and then readjustment back to their now, often, largely forgotten original family. This final change involved not only changes in caregivers, but further changes in language, religion, and identity. These children were not only survivors themselves, but now became the children of survivors with all the challenging connotations that second generation children experienced added to their own. Nor were these children always immune from sexual abuse. For example, in 1945, Max, aged nine, was returned to his father and his newly married wife. He learned, by accident at the age of thirteen, that the woman he regarded as his mother was in reality, his stepmother and also, that he was Jewish – facts that his father had decided to keep from him after the war. His stepmother was emotionally and physically abusive, behaviours that culminated, when he was fourteen, in sexual abuse as well. After four years of forced sexual activity with her, usually following beatings, he left home at the age of eighteen.[705] Max was a postwar sexual abuse victim.[706] Although not sexually abused during the Holocaust, the resulting upheavals in his family life, led to his living in an abusive family relationship.

Some hidden children were placed in orphanages from where they were occasionally claimed by distant relatives, again requiring multiple adjustments to differing family environments and interpersonal relationships. Some foster families considered it in the best interests of the children for them to return to their Jewish heritage and willingly relinquished them to the orphanages, asking for no compensation.[707] Some families that had hidden children handed them over but asked for compensation for the costs of their care: as this information spread, commerce in rescued children grew.[708] Many children were "ransomed" back to Jewish rescue organizations who offered to compensate the family for some of the expenses they had incurred by caring for the children over the years, in exchange for handing them over to the care homes established for Jewish child survivors. While the original amount of compensation offered was low – in Poland, 14,000 zlotys per child (approximately US \$200) in April 1946 – the amount escalated rapidly as families realised that they could bargain to exchange the child – rising to 140,000 zlotys per child in April 1947.[709] In 1947, the amount required rose to between 200,000 and 400,000 zlotys (approximately US \$5,500).[710] At today's rates, these amounts increased from approximately US \$3,500 to over US\$ 100,000 in the one year period. Some families that ransomed their children returned a few days later and took them back by fraudulent means, albeit with the child's cooperation.[711] Sara Avinum's gentile rescue mother, Julia, was one who had bargained for payment to relinquish Sara to a Jewish orphanage and had then enticed Sara to run away from the orphanage and return to her.[712]

Other children were not identified by their foster families as Jews, or were not relinquished by them. Many of these were very young children who knew nothing of their Jewish origins, were unclaimed orphans, and could not have returned to their Jewish roots on their own. There were children who resisted moving from their foster families into the arms of their relatively unknown relatives and there were cases when the adoptive families refused to relinquish them. Some foster families declared that the children had been left in their care by the parents with the understanding that if the parents did not return, the family would have the right to adopt the child and to inherit the families' assets. If distant relatives claimed a child, negotiations were sometimes entered into in the hope of receiving remuneration as well as the assets of the child's parents.[713] Some foster families only agreed to relinquish the child to distant relatives if they could accompany the child.[714]

In many convents, the Jewish children in their care had been baptised – often to hide them so that they blended in with other non-Jewish children in their care by their full participation in Catholic rituals. As a result, the nuns and priests no longer considered them to be Jewish, and, consequently, had no intention of handing them over into Jewish hands.[715] According to Halakha (Jewish law), however, a Jew remains a

Jew even if baptised.[716] Furthermore, according to Jewish law, death is to be preferred to idolatry or conversion.[717] Convents, however, viewed the children as Christian and did not encourage them, no matter how young, to leave and rejoin their families. In cases when they did relinquish the child, they informed the parents and the child that s/he had been baptised and that they expected the child to continue practicing their Christian faith.[718] In some convents, toddlers and infants, in particular, were baptised and then placed with adoptive Christian families as the convents did not have the facilities to care for such young babies. According to the Franciscan Sisters, who rescued many children but who were also ardent missionaries with proselytizing intentions, eighty such children survived in this way although their fate is not known.[719] Records were haphazardly kept regarding these infants, and the nuns did not check to see if the children had parents or other relatives; all traces of the children were deliberately obscured.[720] The nuns kept the names of adoptive parents secret. At the war's end, when the children's parents or relatives came to collect them, the nuns refused to reveal the adoptive parents' identities,[721] a similar scenario to that played out in numerous Catholic orphanages and women's homes in Ireland at about the same time.[722] Desperate parents of the *Kindertransport* children often agreed to their children being hosted by Christian families in the UK, in an attempt to ensure they might be rescued. At least twenty-five children were brought out by the Barbican Mission, an explicitly conversionist organization. These children were rescued on the clear understanding that they would be baptised.[723]

The convents have never disclosed how many Jewish children were placed in their institutions.[724] The difficulties of removing Jewish children from convents occurred across Europe. Some estimate that dozens, if not hundreds of Jewish children remained in convents in Poland alone and could not be restored to their Jewish heritage.[725] There is only one known instance in which nuns handed over the children they had hidden to a Jewish children's home. The Convent of the Sacred Hearts in Przemyśl, Galicia, handed over thirteen children they had rescued. This convent was also unusual in that it did not baptise the children, objecting to the practice on principle. One older child from this convent refused to move to a Jewish children's home and later converted to Christianity.[726] Some of the children rescued by convents (a handful) decided as a gesture of gratitude and in identification with the sisters to take their religious vows.[727] Many who were relinquished from the convents emerged with feelings of alienation and inferiority compounded by their frequent exposure in the convents to abusive epithets in Christian antisemitic tradition. Convent education included negative imagery of Jews related to their supposed act of deicide and torture of the Son of God. These children felt torn between the devoted care given to them by the nuns and their remarks about Jews, contributing to guilt on account of their alleged sins.[728] Repeated visits and appeals (towards the end of the war, in April 1945, in September 1945, in March 1946),[729] by Rabbis to Pope Pius XII during and after the war, to issue an unequivocal statement that Catholic Clergy were to refrain from pressuring those Jews whom they saved to convert, were ignored. Similarly, in the UK, a significant number of *Kindertransport* children who had been hosted by Christian families abandoned their Jewish faith in adulthood. There are claims that although many Jewish families had offered to take the children in, the Government had mandated that the children be dispersed widely across Britain to avoid antisemitic backlash against the program if a large contingent of Jewish children had been placed in any one community. The lack of emphasis on maintaining the children's Jewish affiliation led to complications in later years.[730]

In some countries, parents who survived the Holocaust and, by some miracle, located their surviving offspring, were denied access to their children on the grounds that they were so traumatised by their experiences that the children would be better off staying with their adoptive families. As Polak writes:

> If a Jewish child had been separated from its parents during the war, and these parents had survived, it was not given in Dutch law that parent and child would be reconciled. On matters of family reconciliation, Dutch law seemed to have been written to protect the children from their parents, especially if the parents were Jewish, and Dutch courts soon became clogged with hysterical mothers and fathers who just wanted their kids back.

[...] You came back from Bergen-Belsen, and Theresienstadt, physically and emotionally devastated, having no certainty that anyone in your family is alive – not even your children. You then engage in what must be history's most desperate, harrowing manhunt for your missing child, and when in some moment of divine grace, you locate your child, the authorities tell you your child is no longer yours – that the child's adoptive parents, who have hidden them all these months and years, are more competent than you are in your laughingly humiliated, compromised and shaken condition, and that these adoptive parents now get to keep your son, your daughter. Such a parent is left feeling that where the Nazis did not ultimately succeed in separating parent and child, the Dutch did.

Even in those cases where the adoptive family is more competent than the hapless returning concentration camp survivors, the cruelty involved in refusing these parents their children, to me, overrides any consideration of "what's best for the children."[731]

In contrast, those who dedicated themselves to returning Jewish children to their parents, Jewish relatives or Jewish communities after the war struggled with the ethical dilemmas that this created. At the time, the predominant feeling was that, after the decimation of the Jewish population in Europe, Jewish children who survived in hiding – usually while converting or identifying as Christians – must return to Judaism. In Poland, around six hundred of the 2,000 to 3,000 Jewish children that were living in Christian homes were retrieved by a Zionist organization – the *Koordynacja* [Coordination Committee] together with the support of Rabbi David Kahane and Yeshayahu Drucker working on behalf of the Committee of Jewish Communities.[732] Arye Sarid, the founder of the *Koordynacja* who, along with others involved, agonized about the heartache caused by such rescues,[733] wrote:

There are those who ask me if it would not have been better to leave the children with their adoptive families and not shatter their tranquility, particularly

177

if coercion was used [...] And there are some who ask whether I have no pangs of conscience for thrusting these children into a fate of suffering, calamities, and new experiences. The truth is, that such thoughts did cross my mind [...] especially in the complex case of redeeming children who were lovingly cared for by a Christian family. But at that very moment I lacerated myself for such bursts of weakness. In the final analysis we are fulfilling the last request of their parents: to leave them descendants. We are ensuring that their child will remain Jewish and not become one of those who attack and murder Jews.[734]

Sara (Shner) Neshamit expressed similar feelings:

Sometimes we had serious qualms about whether we had the right to remove a child from the home of his adoptive parents and thrust him into a psychological crisis. It was hard to be a witness to the tears shed by children when they parted from their Christian adopters, in whose home they had been so warmly treated. It was also hard to be a witness to the tears in the eyes of the adoptive mother when she handed over the child she had nurtured. Frequently we were apprehensive about the wrong that we were doing to both the children and to their 'parents'.[735]

Given that, at that time, views of children's experiences in the Holocaust were discounted, and that it was believed that they would not remember their traumas, it was likely that these rescuers also believed that the children would adapt to another relocation and disruption in their lives with little or no lasting adverse psychological effects. With the benefit of hindsight, we now know that these tumultuous experiences did have lasting effects. The children suddenly found themselves back in a Jewish world from which they had barely managed to escape and because of which they had suffered so cruelly. They were again traumatized.[736] Even children who had been taken to the UK on the *Kindertransport* and who have been, until recently, regarded as the lucky ones who escaped from the horrors of the Holocaust by being rescued by apparently loving foster parents, experienced considerable traumas including loss of their families, changes in language, culture, religion, lifestyle, and social status. Like hidden children in Europe, many were unhappy and were abused emotionally, physically and occasionally sexually, and were generally fairly helpless to avoid such misuse. Few were reunited with their families and most had to make their own way in life with little educational training to support them. Loss of family remained a severe source of trauma for these children from which many, if not most, hardly ever recovered.[737] Mental illness and subjects such as sexual abuse among the children have often been ignored, glossed over, or minimized making their exposure, though uncomfortable, an important corrective to commonly held redemptive images of this program.[738]

Despite the qualms expressed by rescue agencies that sought to return Jewish children brought up as Christians to their religion, some, today, would assert that removing an orphaned child from a loving adoptive family and re-traumatizing a child through this separation from virtually the only family s/he has known, simply to ensure they followed their religious heritage, is unconscionable.[739] These view the wishes of the (deceased) parents to save their child as of paramount importance and not their wish to ensure the child's adherence to Judaism. As with many issues raised by the Holocaust, this ethical dilemma is a most challenging one. After the decimation of Jews by the Nazis, the importance of saving Jewish lives was undeniable. In addition, post war relations between Jews and Christians in Europe and particularly in Poland were acrimonious; the antisemitic climate of the times was not a safe society for the children to return to.[740] On the other hand, causing even further distress to the children is horrifying given the traumas they had already endured. Also, removing a child from a loving family would have been heartbreaking for the foster parents, despite their probable prior knowledge that the child was only temporarily entrusted to them. While some hid the knowledge that their fostered child was Jewish from both the child and/or authorities, others planned for this eventual relinquishment and gave up the child, along with a narrative account of his/her life to the rescuing parents or agencies.[741]

Some of those who were raised as Catholic even became priests or nuns, and one, Cardinal Lustiger, a Cardinal.[742] Additionally, while Christian religious institutions did not necessarily accept Jewish children in order to convert them, many Christian educators and members of religious orders saw it as their vocation to encourage those under their care to become pious Christians. Assessments indicate that most of the Jewish children hidden in Christian institutions in Poland and Ukraine converted to Christianity. At times, such conversion was a condition for offering shelter.[743] The Catholic Church in France, at least, forbad Jewish children who had been baptised from being told they were born Jewish or from being handed over to non-Catholic rescuers.[744] "Saving" their souls became as, if not more, important than saving their lives.

CHAPTER 10: OBSTRUCTING STUDY

This book is intended to honour the memory of the Holocaust and its child victims by recognising the realities that they faced and by placing the blame for these actions, not on the children – who frequently feel guilty or shamed by their experiences – but on the perpetrators of such horrors. Our reluctance to face the truth of child sexual abuse in the Holocaust and to examine it in the light of the 21st century is concerning. With regard to the writing of this history, we need to reiterate the goals outlined by Emannuel Ringelblum when compiling the Warsaw ghetto diaries, of the need to: "Compile dozens of individual voices into a multilayered portrait" [and] "to present the whole truth as bitter as it may be."[745]

OBJECTIONS TO STUDYING CHILD SEXUAL ABUSE IN THE HOLOCAUST

Child sex abuse in the Holocaust has yet to be systematically examined. Although a number of Holocaust texts briefly mention child sex abuse,[746] some of the most significant histories of children in the Holocaust do not.[747] What little scholarship exists has primarily been reported by therapists who have treated survivors of such abuse and who have reported on a select few case studies.[748] Reasons for this may include (a) historians' reluctance to examine a taboo subject; (b) sensitivity regarding exposing intimate and personal experiences; (c) a desire to prevent re-traumatizing the victims by forcing them to re-visit their abuse or by exposing it to the public; (d) horror that we could even consider that such things happened to or were observed by children; (e) disbelief of children's reports of sexual abuse in the same way as children's experiences of any horrors during this time were discounted after the war; (f) a belief that such details about the Holocaust are not necessary to study, or are degrading to the memory of the victims; (g) concern that such material might be mis-used by Holocaust deniers or revisionists; (h) testimonies that survivors specifically requested not be shown to others; and, significantly, (i) a dearth of recorded testimonies or writings from children describing such events. Even when this information is acknowledged to be available – multiple testimonies include reports of sexual abuse of children – archivists are unwilling to allow access to them, primarily on the grounds that privacy must be preserved. For example, on May 18, 2017, I received the following email from the archivist at The Massuah Institute for the Study of the Holocaust in Israel, who willingly assisted me to find a number of testimonies that reported on child sexual abuse during the Holocaust:

> "In that matter – the testimonies – I have unfortunately some bad news. During a routine meeting with Massuah's Director General, […] she prohibited any use of the testimonies we discussed. So you <u>cannot</u> use them in your study. I'm terribly sorry.
>
> In the year working here I didn't know there is a total prohibition on these testimonies when researching those issues. […] doesn't allow any use of the witnesses of these testimonies in this research not even in their initials. [sic] She regards this [sic] testimonies on these issues as being on the highest privacy level."[749] [edited solely to remove Director's name]

Even with strong academic credentials and my assurances that privacy would be protected by whatever method was requested by the archive, no access was allowed to these testimonies. It is theoretically possible that when providing these testimonies to the Massuah institute, these survivors specifically requested that they not be shown to anyone, although this was not given to me as an explanation for their restriction. Archivists might also fear that – in our digital age – hackers might gain access to the names and stories of abused victims, although with what purpose in mind is not clear. In any event, the latter argument is largely fallacious, as privacy can be respected by changing names and removing all biographical information from the testimony, in the interest of reporting the event rather than specifying the source. This is commonplace in academic research in the humanities and health sciences at least, and is a recognized and effective means of preserving privacy. While this is contrary to traditional, historical reporting that requires citing names, places, dates, and surrounding circumstances, these can be omitted if a focus on issues – child sex abuse for example – is demanded, and not precise historical specificity. The very fact that these children have recorded their experiences for posterity in testimonies, memoirs, biographies and interviews and have sometimes, like Anna,* who was sexually abused but also told her story,[750] explicitly stated the importance of doing this, is evidence that they do wish their experiences to be recorded and acknowledged even if some might want their identity to be concealed.

Moral indignation about revealing disturbing information about Jewish experiences, or behaviours, that leads to concealment of information is misplaced. For years, many Holocaust scholars have criticized the Catholic Church for maintaining closed archives regarding the Church's role during the Holocaust,[751] yet, as my experiences, noted above, indicate, some archivists are similarly reluctant to share details about child sex abuse in the Holocaust. Moreover, those few scholars, like myself, who choose to study these issues, are often reprimanded at academic conferences for discussing such topics. Is this not hypocritical? Is this equivalent to "bystander behaviour;" we know it happened but we won't expose or admit to it?

Moreover, victims of sexual assault often suffer fragmented memories – they know they have been abused, but many are unable to provide the precise dates, times and places (or even names, in the cases where multiple abusers assaulted a child) required by traditional historiography. Children, in particular, may have incomplete memories of such details. Preventing study of these events, which is tantamount to suggesting they never occurred, due to the sensibilities of an archivist whose role is not that of arbiter of historical truths, but simply to

183

maintain the collection under their care, itself is a form of re-victimization. More simply, if a victim wrote or told about their experience, that very act implies they wanted their story shared (at least in the moment it was revealed), and if the record of that experience is stored in an archive, it is because an archivist deemed it informative and therefore valuable. Preventing legitimate access due to personal (or modern political) sensitivities reduces the importance of historical records to curiosities on a shelf, items to be occasionally dusted, but otherwise generally ignored.[752] As Langer writes, "Testimonies resting unseen in archives are like books locked in vaults: they might as well not exist."[753]

It is also remarkable that some Holocaust scholars, in addition to archivists, do not wish anyone to address the subject of sexual abuse of women, men, and particularly children during the Holocaust as experienced by both myself and Father Patrick Desbois when presenting papers on this topic at conferences.[754]

Despite my own commitment to discussing such issues, the question, as Desbois asks, remains and warrants closer analysis: "Do we need to talk about this? Do we need to write on this subject? [...] How many people must have stayed quiet out of respect for their daughter, their mother, and their sister? Do we need to talk about this now?"[755] Desbois reports that one member of his team participated in a seminar in Los Angeles organized by the Shoah Foundation focused on violence against women. The invitation reiterated several times that the seminar would be confidential.[756] Sixty years after the Holocaust, Desbois asked "should we say it, or keep it quiet?"[757] Desbois' answer to his rhetorical question is powerful and worthy of noting here:

> My sense is that it's essential to recognise that the Germans who marched in front of their insane leader through Nuremberg Square with robotic expressions on their faces were – once they were far from Berlin and in the Russian towns they believed they were colonizing – nothing more than criminals, murderers freed from any moral obligation. Theft and rape were of a piece with the genocidal crime. Of course, in the *Einsatzgruppen* reports they'll

> count the number of Jews murdered. Of course,
> before the courts, they'll try to minimize their
> responsibility. They did nothing but obey orders!
> They surely would never admit that they were also
> thieves. That they were also rapists.[758]

He also notes that testimonies, such as that of Alfred Metzner, provided to his team, reports "The night before, [a mass murder of Jews by the *Einsatzgruppen*] the women had been raped by the police and then shot. The police bragged about the number of women they had abused in this manner."[759] Desbois questions whether this was one of the reasons for the silence of witnesses that he and his team encountered when exploring the role of the *Einsatzgruppen* in the nighttime requisitions of Jews in preparation for their slaughter the following day. Not only were the women at the mercy of the Germans but also of the local police.[760] Today, we hope and expect that witnesses to such crimes will reveal what they saw, or even did. This expectation applies to all crimes against children as well, and not just their murder, for as Desbois notes, rape is also a form of murder.[761] Unfortunately this expectation is often unfulfilled as evidenced by the current day exposé of multiple and repeated sexual crimes committed against American gymnasts that were covered up and hidden for decades,[762] as well as the globally occurring sexual abuse of children in Catholic schools and institutions by priests, brothers and nuns that was systematically and deliberately concealed for almost a century.[763] Similarly, while these cover-ups were instigated to protect the abusers from discovery, the concealment of Holocaust child sex abuse testimonies from study does not protect the children, only the abusers.

DENYING JEWISH EXPERIENCES

Failing to acknowledge the sexual abuse of Jewish children that was facilitated by the Nazis is a denial of an aspect of the Jewish experience of the Holocaust. This is, however, not the first instance of failing to acknowledge aspects of the Holocaust. Early post-war historians and politicians throughout the past seventy years, frequently failed to acknowledge that Jews were the primary target of Hitler's genocidal regime. Holocaust scholars have decried the denial by others of the Jewish experience under the Nazis for decades. Denial of any aspect of the Holocaust including child sexual abuse is unacceptable.

It took many years for the Jews to be acknowledged as the primary target of the Nazis for elimination and even today, knowledge about the Holocaust is dismal. Knowledge of the atrocities against Jews was not immediately apparent at the close of the war, but only began to be revealed during the Nuremberg Trials. For example, at the first Nazi war crimes trials held in Kharkov in 1943, the word Jew was not even used, even though most of the victims were Jewish.[764] Newsreels showing the liberation of some extermination camps, and the horrific scenes that these depicted, were screened for a few months after the war and then shelved.[765] Also, it was psychologically easier to believe (erroneously as it later emerged) that these atrocities were committed not by a multitude of the citizens of civilized nations, but by a small group of insane or perverted persons, and therefore did not apply – or ascribe blame to – much of humanity.[766] The truth of these reports was also denied by the German government as horror propaganda or *Greuelpropaganda.*[767] These films did not acknowledge that the majority of the victims depicted in films showing the liberation of the camps were Jews. The public only became aware of the mass murders of Jews as a genocide rather than a war crime or a crime against all humanity many decades after the end of the war.[768] While the word "holocaust" predates the war, it was used to describe a tragedy, natural or manmade, the term Holocaust (with a capital H) began to be used to refer to the tragedy of the Jews at the hands of the German and Austrian Nazis and their collaborators in the 1960's, following the Eichmann trial.[769] In itself, the term Holocaust was a form of psychological denial, as it replaced the use of everyday language that evoked revulsion, to describe the mass murder of individual people, men, women and children, with a rarely used technical term that was only understood intellectually and without the visceral implications of the inhumane catastrophe that had been imposed on innocent people.[770] Using technically or specially created terms instead of simpler words in our vocabulary is a widely used and well known means of separating our emotional experience from our intellectual understanding.[771] After the Eichmann trial in Israel in 1961, world interest and knowledge were re-awakened, resulting in significant TV and other films, like Marvin Chomsky's TV miniseries *Holocaust* in 1978, Claude Lantzman's nine-hour long epic *Shoah* made in 1985, and Steven Spielberg's *Schindler's List* in 1993, that have directed attention to the Jewish Holocaust experience. These productions, with their visually impactful and emotionally evocative imagery, have spread the knowledge of Jewish experiences more widely and have now spawned a plethora of Holocaust related films, although the concurrent fate of Roma and Sinti, homosexuals and others targeted by the Nazis have not yet received similar attention. Yad Vashem's drive to encourage, support and facilitate education about the Holocaust in schools and universities is only recently beginning to take effect, although it is not surprising that knowledge of the Holocaust remains dismal among young people. For example, a recent (2018) demographically representative survey of Americans' knowledge about the Holocaust implemented by the Claims Conference on Jewish Material Claims Against Germany revealed that nearly one-third of all Americans (31%) and 41% of millennials believe that substantially less than 6 million Jews were killed (two million or fewer) during the Holocaust. Also, while there were over 42,000 concentration camps, ghettos, transit camps and other types of detention centres in Europe during the Holocaust,[772] about half of Americans surveyed (53%) cannot name a single one.[773] Similar findings have emerged from surveys in Germany, the UK and Canada: in Germany 47% of fourteen to sixteen-year-olds did not know what Auschwitz-Birkenau was,[774] and in the UK, 5% of adults do not believe the Holocaust happened, one in twelve (8%) believe its scale has been exaggerated and 19% believe that fewer than two million Jews were murdered.[775] In Canada, nearly half of those surveyed by the Conference on Jewish Material Claims Against Germany in association with the Azrieli Foundation, could not name a single concentration camp or ghetto, with millennials being particularly uninformed.[776] In Canada too, 32% of respondents thought that Canada had an open-door policy for Jewish refugees during the war. In, reality, official Canadian policy towards immigration of Jews was "none is too many" with only 5,000 Jews allowed into the country – fewer than any other Western country. In these surveys, findings reveal that both intellectual (facts) and emotional knowledge (the extent of the horror) of the Holocaust is still lacking,

Many countries occupied by the Nazis suppressed, and continue to suppress, knowledge about the Jewish experience under the Nazis, and even more relevant, their own country's role in contributing to these events, perhaps because it is embarrassing to do so and also, possibly to avoid potential economic compensation that might then ensue. For example, Russian authorities refused to allow discussion of the mass murder of Soviet Jews both during the war and after its end. Even the term Holocaust was unknown in Soviet literature until 1997. Jews were mentioned only as "Soviet Citizens" for decades. The Soviet slogan "Do not divide the dead" was used to justify this.[777] Neither do some memorials constructed at the death camps in Poland encompass the killing of Jews; rather they remember these deaths under the broader theme of Polish National Remembrance. Neither the memorial that was established at Majdanek by the Soviet liberators, where 360,000 Jews were murdered,[778] nor the state memorial that was built at Auschwitz, emphasize Jewish victimization even though 90% of the more than one million deaths that occurred at Auschwitz were Jews.[779] Rather they memorialize all victims of National Socialism partially on the grounds that as Communism did not acknowledge religion, only nationality would be recognized.[780] Renovation of the Auschwitz-Birkenau Museum, to acknowledge the extent of its Jewish murder rate started in the 1990s and took a dozen or more years to implement.[781] Some sites of *Einsatzgruppen* mass killings still remain unacknowledged as sites of Jewish burial grounds; some major ones still acknowledge them as sites of Ukrainian citizen burials. Only after the collapse of the Soviet Union in 1989 was any reference to Jews incorporated into some memorials for murdered Jews, such as at Babi Yar in Ukraine in 1991. The first and only public Holocaust museum in Ukraine opened in 1996.[782] Poland and Lithuania are still under Jewish fire for denying full, national recognition of atrocities committed against Jews by collaborators in those countries.[783] In Poland, 2,900,000 Jews died and in Lithuania, 220,000 Jews were killed, representing 88% and 94% of these countries' Jews respectively. Austria has for decades tried to present itself as a victim of Nazism, neglecting that it welcomed Hitler's annexation of their country.

Speaking publicly about work in concentration camps became a taboo subject in both Austria and Germany immediately following Germany's surrender; a taboo that continues to this day.[784] Even the use of unobstructed photographs of female Nazi guards enjoying a birthday party, or standing outside their barracks during their leisure time in Majdanek, were not permitted in a recent (2015) English translation of a German text on the pretext that these were "private settings" but more likely to avoid revealing their happy expressions in such a setting.[785] The unedited pictures were published in the original 2009 German language book.[786] The first commemoration of the Holocaust by the Vatican only occurred in 1994.[787] It also took until 1994 for France to first officially remember the wartime deportations of 76,000 French Jews who were sent to the death camps with French collaboration: over 8,000 – 11,000 (estimates vary) were children under thirteen years old. Only 2,500 Jews returned.[788] It took until 1995 for Bayer, a subsidiary of I.G. Farben, to apologise for the pain, suffering and exploitation the company perpetrated through their use of concentration camp slave labour.[789] The Prime Minister of the Netherlands only apologised for his country's role in implementing the Shoah in 2020 although previous apologies for the way Jews who returned after the war were treated in the Netherlands had been issued in 2000.[790] Clearly, denial of the Holocaust is still a major concern.

Given these larger concerns regarding even the most simplistic understanding of the Holocaust in many countries, exposing the sexual horrors undergone by Jewish children is easily relegated to the periphery of study. There is no way to judge the seriousness of Nazi atrocities or to pass judgement as to which should be highlighted and which neglected. For the children who were abused, however, there can be little that is more important than this. This book adds their voices to the list of denied Holocaust experiences.

DENIAL OF INDISCRIMINATE BEHAVIOUR BY JEWS

Holocaust denial is a readily acknowledged phenomenon as it applies to those who would discount the occurrence of the Holocaust at all, or at least, the extent of its horrors, often referred to as Holocaust revisionists. There are however, perhaps other levels of Holocaust "denial," sometimes expressed by serious Holocaust scholars who, with regard to most other aspects of the Holocaust, do not hesitate to expand on the horrors inflicted on Jews. These scholars tend to avoid study of, or accounting of, those aspects of behaviour by Jews or imposed on Jews, that are less admirable to admit – perhaps describable as less politically correct. These include acts of selfishness, or moments of dishonour, that may even include sexual transgression committed against Jews, or against non-Jews, or even more embarrassingly, by Jews. In this book, of the 160 individual stories reporting sexual abuse of Jewish children, only a handful reflect abuse committed by Jews. It is not surprising that such dishonourable actions are downplayed or hidden in Holocaust writings. Fear of admitting that some Jews behaved inappropriately during the Holocaust or perpetrated wrongs against other Jews and that these actions might be misinterpreted to reflect that Jews were the victims of other Jews' cruelty and not only that of Nazis, is, however, a real concern that must be addressed. Notwithstanding this concern, such behaviour must be acknowledged, examined and understood in the context of Nazi policies and actions.

Suppressing discussion of immoral behaviour of Jews during the Holocaust has been an issue since the end of WWII in relation to all scholarship and not specifically that focused on women, children or sexual behaviour. In 1945, Mark Dworzecki called for Holocaust studies to examine the cases of "degeneracy and pollution caused by the insane conditions of a sort never previously known by any people"[791] in an article titled *To Ignore or to Tell the Truth*.[792] His original article in Yiddish includes a long catalogue of "immoral behaviours" of Jews in the ghetto, which was omitted when the article was published a few weeks later in Hebrew.[793] Ben-Zion Dinur, an academic, agreed with Dworzecki, calling for "collecting material about the traitors and degenerates, too, those who were weak in mind and feeble in spirit" [794] as well as focusing on the human side of the Holocaust.While Dworzecki notes that insensitive or even immoral behaviour occurred in response to the inhumane conditions imposed by the Nazis, Dinur's comments are more judgemental, regarding such persons as "weak in mind and feeble in spirit." [795] His later talks, however, no longer mentioned this.[796] According to Mendel Piekarz, as time passed, historians increasingly presented a sanitized picture of Jewish behaviour during the Holocaust.[797]

Lawrence Langer warned against "sweetening the Holocaust"[798] many decades ago, although this approach to Holocaust study still prevails today through our emphasis on heroes rather than victims. For example, the formal name of Israel's Holocaust Museum in Jerusalem is *Yad Vashem: The Heroes and Martyrs Remembrance Authority,* and their educational programs emphasize focusing on the courageous lives of survivors of the Holocaust rather than the deaths of victims.[799] In the early days of the Israeli state, survivors who immigrated to Israel in their emotionally, physically and economically devastated state were criticized for not opposing the Nazis and were condemned for having gone to their deaths as sheep to the slaughter – a form of victim blaming. Naming Yad Vashem as a commemoration of heroes and martyrs may well have contributed to uplifting this perception of their fellow Jews. In reality, however, most people are neither heroes nor martyrs. Under stressful conditions, such as in the Holocaust, some will become heroes, but many if not most will be downbeaten rapidly.[800] Just as some Nazis were occasionally reported to save Jews, some Jews could have behaved inhumanely to their fellow Jews. Failing to mention indiscriminate behaviour of Jews or embarrassing or degrading experiences – such as child sexual abuse – may be perceived as a further symptom of sweetening the Holocaust or its memory.

AVOIDING VICTIM BLAMING

Victim blaming, particularly with regard to sexual abuse, is rampant and is evidenced by blaming women for inciting their predators to abuse them by, for example, their dress, their behaviour, their previous sexual experiences, their attractiveness etc. In Nazi Germany, as this book reveals, girls who were sexually assaulted by *Wehrmacht* soldiers were, more often than not, blamed for the actions of the perpetrators. Even today, in a trial in 2014, a Canadian judge, Robin

Camp – who was, as a result, removed from office – indulged in victim blaming for the rape of a girl by asking her why she "did not keep her knees together"[801] and why she did not move her pelvis to avoid penetration.[802] Victim blaming with regard to sexual abuse clearly does happen and writings reflecting on sexual atrocities are not exempt from such discredited myths regarding rape of women, as well as stereo-typical accusations.

Another example of victim blaming emerges from a review of my own book, *Birth, Sex and Abuse: Women's Voices under Nazi Rule*. All the published reviews of the book were most positive[803] and it won a dozen awards including the most prestigious American and Canadian Jewish literary awards,[804] but one review, carried by the message board *H-German*, stated, in response to my reporting two assaults of young Jewish girls by Jewish community leaders in two ghettos, that "While most of the violence and inhumane behaviours perpetrated against women can be attributed to Nazis some of the blame also falls on the *kapo* (Nazi appointed Jewish prisoners in concentration camps) and ordinary Jewish men."[805] Only two assaults out of many hundreds reported in the book were perpetrated by Jews, both of them in ghettos and not camps. In addition, *kapos* in camps were not all Jewish, with many being drawn from the ranks of political prisoners, criminals, or those who did not live up to Nazi social ideals, so blaming Jews and Jewish *kapos* for the inhumane behaviours and violence women experienced that were reported in the book, is inappropriate. This is a clear realisation of the fear expressed by scholars that admitting to the wrongdoings of some Jews against other Jews might negate the seriousness of the crimes committed against Jews in general; the idea that: "the Nazis were not so bad: the Jews did this to themselves as well."

The particular case of crimes committed by Jewish *kapos* against other Jewish prisoners is a decidedly controversial and difficult question that is considered further. As Moshe Silberg, an Israeli Supreme Court Justice said:

> It is hard for us, the judges of Israel, to free ourselves
> from the feeling that, in punishing a worm of this

sort [referring to any *kapo* suspected of criminal acts towards Jews], we are diminishing, even if by only a trace, the abysmal guilt of the Nazis themselves. [806]

As Bazyler states, "The perfidy of the Nazi regime was in forcing Jewish victims to be instruments of their own destruction [...] Jewish *kapos* were just one rung above the miserable existence of the ordinary Jewish prisoner."[807] Primo Levi refers to the murky area between victim and perpetrator occupied by the Jewish *kapos* as the "grey zone."[808] While in some cases collaboration with the Germans could be readily ascertained as wrongdoing, in the case of Jewish *kapos* this is not easily decided. The choices made by these *kapos* were what Lawrence Langer calls "choiceless choices [...] imposed by a situation that was in no way of the victim's own choosing."[809] Becoming a *kapo* meant choosing between the possibility of life and almost certain death.[810] After the war, Jewish *kapos* came under particular fire for their perceived collaboration with Nazis against their fellow Jews – as did members of the *Judenrat* in ghettos, and the ghetto police. In Israel a controversial law was promulgated in 1950, soon after the State came into being, to charge Nazis and Nazi collaborators – both Jewish and non-Jewish – in Israel.[811] This law emerged in a society consisting of a majority of non-survivors, that regarded all Holocaust survivors as possible collaborators as otherwise, how could they have gone like "sheep to the slaughter" as was a common narrative after the war. As one parliamentarian of the time said, "Had there been the slightest sign of physical resistance, it would not have been possible to murder six million Jews."[812] Survivors were scornfully referred to as *sabonim* (soap), reflecting a widely held belief at that time that the Nazis had made soap out of the remains of murdered Jews.[813] Among female survivors it was claimed that some Jewish women, especially young and pretty ones, had survived because they had been prostitutes in the brothels of the German forces.[814] As Ruth Bondy wrote, "In Israel Jews wanted to know: "How did you stay alive? What did you have to do in order to survive? And in their eyes, a glimmer of suspicion: Kapo? Prostitute?"[815] Helen Lewis, an Auschwitz survivor who returned to Prague, reports that in 1946, while travelling on a crowded tram, her sleeves fell back while she was holding on to the overhead straps. A nearby man said loudly and distinctly, "Isn't it funny how only the young and pretty ones have come back?" The implications were clear. She reported that this comment "Hurt as much as anything we had survived. More."[816] Israeli films such as *Tel Aviv-Berlin* (1987), *Eretz Hadasha* (1994) and *Henrik's Sister* (1997) released between 1987 and 1997 continued to present the image of the whore-survivor.[817] As Ayala H. Emmett, the daughter of Holocaust survivors growing up in the new Israel related:

> What I hated and dreaded most when I was a child was summertime. It was a time when the numbers on my mother's arm would be there for all to see and people would know that she was a survivor and was one of the despised people. People like my parents were despised in Israel, and I was ashamed of them.[818]

If most survivors were disrespected then possible collaborator survivors were even more so. Exact numbers of trials held against *kapos* are not known as some records have only recently been released [trial records are embargoed until seventy years after the conclusion of each trial that was held]. Scholars indicate that only about forty were held between 1951 and 1972 following public complaints about these individuals – emerging from about 200,000 survivors living in Israel at the time.[819] Available records indicate that fifteen of about forty cases ended in convictions with sentences tending to be light, and only rarely was a *kapo* sentenced to longer than the time period spent awaiting a trail outcome. None were found to have directly or indirectly caused the death of another person.[820]

Bazyler posits that:

> kapos cannot be judged under commonly understood standards of decency that translate themselves into secular legal norms [...] International law, in setting out conduct that binds all states and individuals, speaks of 'civilized legal systems' as the basis for these universal norms. The

most notable characteristic of the world of Nazi camps, however, is the very absence of this 'civilization.'[821]

Bazyler himself experienced challenges to including a chapter on the Israeli *kapo* trials in *Forgotten Trials of the Holocaust*. He writes:

> The sensitivity of the subject was also demonstrated to the author of this chapter (Michael Bazyler) in the course of its writing. Survivors I spoke to urged me to avoid examining this 'grey zone," and surprisingly, in contrast to the other chapters, my co-author [Frank Tuerkheimer] and I could not agree on a joint conclusion. Therefore, I take full responsibility for the analysis and conclusions in this essay.[822]

As Primo Levy says, moral judgements in the Nazi created, grey zones cannot be made.[823] Italian philosopher Giorgio Agamben, examining the camps a half-century later, comes to the same conclusion: "Every question concerning the legality or illegality of what happened there simply makes no sense."[824]

No wonder that Holocaust scholars are reluctant to promote even a careful and precise exposure of inappropriate Jewish behaviours. I believe, however, that by exposing the horrors faced by Jews especially when they were forced by the Nazis and their followers into the most outrageous moral and ethical dilemmas and choices, exposes their deeds in a more positive light than implying guilt by hiding their indiscretions. Holocaust scholars examining these activities, and contextualizing them clearly within a full understanding of the Holocaust and the ethical and moral tribulations it imposed on Jews, provide a more nuanced exposure, and greater clarity of understanding, than might be expressed by others who could be less knowledgeable than those steeped in Holocaust study. In many ways, suppressing the less morally or ethically acceptable aspects of Jewish behaviour during the Holocaust, such as the experience of sexual abuse of men, women and children, does a disservice to its study, particularly if the disastrous experiences of Jews is to be remembered and respected.

"Sweetening the Holocaust"

It is not clear whether the lack of analysis of child sex abuse in the Holocaust to date results from a need to deny such sexual behaviours during this time, to "sweeten the Holocaust" or whether the subject has simply not yet been studied as other topics have taken priority over the past seventy years.[825]

We, as a society, need to emphasize the positive rather than the negative in life. Such thinking helps us to cope with a world that is sometimes fraught with anguish and terror. This Pollyanna-like view of the world, and especially of the Holocaust, would tempt us to downplay the negative experiences of children and seek more uplifting conclusions from the nightmare of the Nazi era. By playing Pollyanna's so-called "glad game" we – as indirectly advocated by Yad Vashem[826] – emphasize the martyrdom of Jews in the Holocaust, remember the heroes who survived, or the Gentiles who served as rescuers and righteous among nations. We highlight the stories of courage and resilience of those who resisted the Nazis, and while acknowledging the injustices, humiliations and cruelty that were imposed on Jews and others, we seek rather to focus on the strength and honour of those who overcame the horrors inflicted on them. For example, the Yad Vashem memorial exhibition in Jerusalem does not mention the *kapo* trials even once.[827] As of 2019, their archive did not refer to any of the documents it holds regarding the kapo trials on their public computers.[828] As Porat writes:

> With a few exceptions, a taboo developed with regard to discussing instances in which Jews acted harshly during the Holocaust.[829]

Children's stories of sexual abuse, however, leave the reader horrified, and may be viewed as creating demeaning images of victimhood: they may be framed by some as, possibly, desecration of the children's memory by exposing intimate and extremely sensitive personal information, and therefore, warrant their banishment from academic and public view. In contrast, given what we know today about the immense difficulty that victims of child sexual abuse experience when ultimately revealing their abusive experiences – even in a liberal and sexually more aware and open world – examination of the children's reports indicates that these Holocaust testimonies are evidence of remarkable heroism, worthy of recognition and respect. Having recorded these experiences in testimonies or memoirs, their stories need to be acknowledged and understood, and not hidden from view.

HIDING THE EXPERIENCES OF CHILDREN

It was not until 1991, more than four decades after the war ended, that hidden children were able to admit to and consider their experiences of concealment. Survivors themselves could not expose their own sexually abusive experiences for a further decade until a climate of acceptance and support for them was established, confirming the difficulty experienced by children who are sexually abused to reveal their experiences. Nate Leipciger, once abused as a *piepel*, only revealed this after his tenth visit to Auschwitz-Birkenau as a Holocaust survivor-educator. He noted "The sexual abuse was something that bothered me all my life. At first I was ashamed to admit it to anyone, except my wife, and thought it was my fault. […] it took me years to get up the courage to talk about it. […] This was the last secret."[830]

In all likelihood, the majority of survivors of child sexual abuse have still not revealed their experiences; it is simply too psychologically difficult for them to do so, and our world is clearly still not all that accepting of such experiences. Suppressing women's abusive sexual experiences has been a feature of global narrative for centuries. The #metoo hashtag, initiated in 2006 by Tarana Burke, an American social activist, went viral when used by actress Alyssa Milano in 2017. This publicised a medium where people could both share their experiences of sexual abuse and support each other. This movement is changing our world, at least with regard to removing the stigma and shame of rape from victims and placing the blame for this where it belongs, on the abusers. Since then, there has been an ongoing outpouring of revelation regarding sexual abuse of, primarily girls, but also boys, in multiple walks of life, including the arts, sport and business, that is revolutionizing global society, albeit more gradually in more repressive societies. Such a sharing medium for child sex abuse victims of the Holocaust has not yet come to light, except through the supportive conferences where child survivors have found some solace. These survivors are now well into their seventies and eighties, if not older, and have lived with far more restrictive mores and norms regarding sexual behaviour than are now prevalent in society. As censure for such revelations continues among some Holocaust scholars, it is unlikely that we will ever uncover the full extent of the sexually abusive horrors – over and above the nightmare world of the Nazi era – that these children experienced. There is increasing concern regarding the challenge facing Holocaust scholars of how to remember the Holocaust once the few remaining survivors are no longer with us to testify in person about their experiences. Multiple conferences today are addressing this issue. We urgently need to incorporate the challenge of how best to identify those who experienced sexual abuse, to explore, record and analyse their experiences respectfully, and to report them for perpetuity, into the agendas of these meetings. Hopefully the rapidly narrowing window of opportunity will remain open for long enough for us to do so.

Chapter 11: Why?

It is hard to understand the mentality of those who abuse children, let alone those who do so when the children are simultaneously living through the genocidal murder of their parents, siblings, friends, families, communities and societies, and whom they, the rescuers, have (frequently) volunteered to save. Most of the perpetrators are likely no longer living, and few would ever admit to their actions even if still alive so that we cannot ask them about their motivations. Before analysing this further, however, we need to acknowledge that tens of thousands of people, families, and institutions assisted children during the Holocaust and saved their lives.[831] Many rescuers gave children loving homes and relinquished them safely to their parents – in the rare cases when these survived – or to their relatives or communities after the war. For example, one Dutch, non-Jewish woman kept a diary, *Het Boek van Wim* (*The Book of Wim*), about the development of the Jewish toddler, Wim, that she cared for, in case the mother was able to return. The mother did survive and the woman handed back both the boy and the diary to her.[832] Another similar incident reporting the care of Abraham Packter who was seven weeks old when entrusted to his rescuer, is also recorded.[833] Others saved children's lives but sometimes with less amicable outcomes, as occurred in Holland where Dutch officials did not always recognize the child's own surviving parents, or even the Jewish community to be the legal heir to deceased Jewish parents, and refused to relinquish the rescued children to them after the war.[834] While acknowledging the tremendous service of those who rescued children, this book focuses on the experiences of children who were abused, often by those who cared for them, and this chapter proposes some theories explaining how such abuse could take place.

PEDOPHILIA

Some might be tempted to discount the multiple cases of child sexual abuse in the Holocaust as the actions of pedophiles, implying that the perpetrators were not normal, everyday people but those who were clinically diagnosable as pedophiles. Such a categorization allows the reader to distance him- or herself from such behaviour, as attributing these perversions to arising in a person of unsound mind. The sexual abuse of children during the Holocaust is not, however, simply pedophilia. Pedophiles, whether they act on their sexual impulses or not, are sexually aroused by children. Some are exclusively excited by children, either prepubescent (pedophilia) or pubescent (hebephilia), or both (pedohebephilia); others are aroused by adults as well.[835] It is hard to appreciate any explanation that allows every case of sexual abuse, particularly of Jewish children during the Nazi era described in this compendium of horrors as the result of clinically diagnosable pedophilic urges, although the sexual abuse that occurred among German schoolboys is more typical of abuse perpetrated by a pedophilic predator. Pedophiles seek out situations where they have unsupervised access to, and power over, young children (usually boys) such as in schools, youth groups, or clerical settings,[836] or in the Holocaust setting, as rescuers of children who cannot escape from them. They are more likely to groom their victims over a period of time and to win their trust before assaulting them, often repeatedly. Studies suggest that about 40% – 50% of men who sexually offend against children are clinically diagnosable as pedophiles. [837] Many have multiple victims and are resistant to either treatment or punishment, with resulting high rates of recidivism.[838] There are no estimates as to how extensively pedophilic urges occur in the general population.[839] While some of the sexual crimes committed against Jewish children reported in this book may be explained by this, such as those of Rumkowski,[840] most are likely to result from, or be facilitated by, such motives as opportunity, autocracy and authoritarianism, little fear of exposure, or of any punitive consequences, ideological hatred and fear, and presumably, sometimes, sexual arousal or frustration. Regardless of whether the abusers could be clinically classified as pedophiles, or men taking advantage of opportunities created by war conditions, the end result of

sexual abuse for the victim is similar; a lifetime of challenging adjustment to the experience.

OPPORTUNISTIC CRIMES

Most of the child sex abuse reported in this book is likely to have
been opportunistic and resulting from the Nazi manipulation of the
children's lives. Under few other circumstances would children who
were loved deeply be separated from their families, or left alone, or
sent to live with strange families, or be so isolated from all sources of
support and care, with no ability to, or means of, escape. Yet because of
the treacherous situation faced by Jewish parents because of Nazi
persecution, loving parents sought such situations for their children in
their hopes of saving their lives. Jewish children – passing for Aryan or
hidden in plain sight with rescuers during the Holocaust – provided
opportunities for the fathers/men (or very occasionally mothers/aunts)
to abuse the newcomer to the family without fear of retribution, as
occurred with a number of children in this book including David,[841]
Sara,[842] Anne,[843] Astrid[844] and Lily. [845] Often seen by neighbours as
doing good deeds by sheltering a "cousin" or "family relative from
afar" or "saving a soul by conversion to a Christian faith," such as
David's foster father, they had free reign to abuse the children within
the confines of the family home without fear of being exposed. As
children like David reported, their hiding families sometimes abused
them as slaves. In these cases, they were treated far from equally to
other children in the family and were often only rescued because slave
labour was desired. As most men were involved in World War II, there
were severe shortages of household and farm workers. By necessity,
children took over these jobs. While this was probably the norm in
many war-time rural families, in some instances this resulted in the
hidden children being exploited to the detriment of their education,
health and happiness. Wives, or women in the household, were often
subjugated by the dominant male roles – more acceptable in the mid
20th century – and did not oppose their husband's sexually inappropriate
actions; some facilitated their husband's activities and may even have
benefitted from them. Others may not have been able to admit to

themselves (or the children), or may not have wanted to believe, that someone they loved could commit such an act. Older boys in a family, perhaps spurred on by opportunity, power needs, and by their family's derisive attitudes and behaviours towards the hidden children, were also sometimes tempted to take advantage of younger hidden children as happened to Sabine,[846] Esther,[847] Condolisa[848] and five-year-old Aniko.[849] It is well acknowledged today that child sex abuse in today's world takes place in or close to the home more often than not and is usually perpetrated by someone known to the child. The Holocaust provided even greater opportunities for such abuse as so many children were placed into foster homes and, separated from those who might otherwise have prevented such abuse, such as their parents, teachers, siblings or friends.

Families who offered shelter were not selected by rescue services on the basis of any other criterion than that they were willing to provide shelter for a child. There was, understandably, simply no way to check whether the household consisted of a happy family offering safety. Couples in these rescue families were often elderly, where perhaps the sexual relations in the hard-working lifestyles of the day, meant that a young child or early adolescent entering the home provided an arousing alternative to the existing marital relationship. We can never know exactly what happened, other than that sexual abuse of the child was attempted or implemented. Children who did report abuse were, whenever possible, moved to a different place of shelter as happened to Esther,[850] but this was not often possible or reported. In other instances, such reports were simply not believed, or, on occasion, the children were blamed for being provocative. Threats used against the children to prevent them from revealing the abusive acts could include their betrayal to the Nazis, or the exposure of their sibling/s or other family members, or even their own murder.

Conditions in homes were not always conducive to preventing child sexual abuse. A few children, such as Ruth,[851] reported having to have their weekly baths in the family living space – often together with any other children in the family – as was common in homes without extensive indoor plumbing and separate washrooms, with the male head of the household, and perhaps other male siblings, "enjoying" these "erotic" moments. Apparently excluding the father or foster brother(s) from this space on these occasions was regarded as unnecessary.

Children who were hidden out of sight, such as in cavities dug underground, or in attics, or other concealed places were even more dependent on their rescuers for their survival. They were totally dependent on their rescuer for their day-to-day subsistence, including disposal of waste, news, and continued safety and secrecy. Providing sexual favours under such conditions may well have been the price extracted for these services or may have been perceived to be a means to maintain their secrecy and their rescuer's assistance as was the case of Molly Applebaum and her cousin Helene.[852] Others, such as those living on farms, were sometimes raped by the farmers who hid them, as happened to Dunia.[853]

Yet other children encountered sexual abuse while passing for Aryan, such as Nechama,[854] Izolda,[855] Sara[856] and Zula.[857] In these cases, it is not clear whether these children were abused as Jewish children or just as children.

Child sex abuse imposed by the SS or Nazi allies took place in ghettos and camps and was perpetrated by the *Einsatzgruppen* and some members of the *Wehrmacht* as well, such as occurred to Tova,[858] Nina[859] and Gusta.[860] These instances are frequently associated with *Aktions* where large numbers of Jews were rounded up to be sent to their deaths. Sexual abuse before their murder or transportation was an opportunity that allowed for sexual indulgence without fear of repercussion.

Notwithstanding the need of many to murder their sexually abused victims, others were quite comfortable turning their sexually abusive actions into a public spectacle of Jewish humiliation or punishment. This provided an opportunity to reveal just how superior Germans were compared to the "inferior" Jews and was often designed to serve as a deterrent to Jewish resistance. Remarkably, descending into being a rapist was perceived as evidence of such superiority. Interestingly, as far as we know, onlookers did not object. We do not know if they too were cowed into submission by the perpetrators, were aroused by the spectacle and enjoyed it, or endorsed such actions as congruent with their own ideological/ Nazi framework.

RELIGIOUS IDEOLOGY

Sexual abuse of children was sometimes undertaken under the guise of errant religious righteousness, as a means of redeeming the children's souls. As seen by these perpetrators, it was an act inspired by religious ideology; such abuse was seen as a means of paying the price for the sins of their ancestors. These children, such as David,[861] were "getting their just deserts" for the crime of killing Christ or for the belief that their ancestors used Gentile children's blood in the making of matzo.[862] Their emotional, physical and sexual abuse was therefore justified, in the name of religion, belief and ideologically inspired "justice." It is not known whether those who expressed such sentiments truly believed them, or whether this justification provided an excuse for more base motives.

ANTISEMITISM

We do not know the extent to which antisemitic ideology towards Jews contributed to the abuse of children. Certainly, antisemitism has been rife in Europe for centuries, and remains so. Nazi policy that excluded Jews from society and that led to the total breakdown of Jewish family life was based on antisemitic thinking masquerading as racial superiority; the need to create a Master Race and eliminate non-Aryans. Such antisemitic views certainly resulted in creating multiple opportunities for sexual abuse as exposed in this text. Some children's testimonies, such as David's,[863] reveal they were denigrated as Jews in the home, regardless of how respectfully they were presented outside this environment to neighbours. Did this dehumanized image of Jews make them easy targets in the home, as "racially inferior peoples," not worthy of the respect usually given to those of one's own kind? Certainly, Nazi ideology reviled Jews, and depicted them as sexual predators and "race defilers" in addition to being filthy vermin, lice, and sources of racial contamination not fit for anything other than extermination.[864] In this ideological view, Jews were the sources of sexual abuse of Aryan children in particular, as so clearly depicted in such publications as the children's book *The Poisonous Mushroom*[865] and the widely screened Nazi propaganda movie, *Jud Süß*.[866] Despite these stereotypically degrading images of the sexually perverted and contaminating Jewish man, the Nazis and their followers, as well as some rescuers of children, were, whenever abuse occurred, almost always, the instigators of child sexual abuse.[867]

"MACHISMO"

Differing standards of appropriate sexual behaviour among girls and boys – and women and men – still pervade society today. Glorifying strength, dominance and so-called "macho" masculinity still characterizes some societies which then also emphasise the subservient role of women. Men are expected to be "experienced" although the women with whom they gain this experience are devalued as whores, prostitutes or sluts. Even the growing strength of the feminist movement over past decades in some countries, now combined with the #metoo movement, is not always enough to counter the apparently predominant view that men who make aggressive sexual demands on women are acceptable while female resistance to their advances is discredited. Blaming the victim of rape for her own rape remains a concern today just as it did in Nazi times. As in the Nazi era, such stereotypes are pervasive among the military and in times of war, but not exclusively so; civilian society follows similar philosophies.[868]

Instances of group rape, such as of the French village children,[869] suggest that some aspects of child rape are also instances of male swagger and audacity, performances that glorify the perpetrator as a dominant audacious male. Such instances of male bluster and cruelty in front of compatriots, such as the beating of Sala Pawlowics,[870] support suggestions that these acts are intended to promote a dominant masculine bravado.

RAPE AS A REWARD

Rape is not just a sexual act, it is an act of violence and power,[871] widely used as a weapon of war. Abusing Jewish children was one further way of defeating the enemy. Even more so, and in addition to being a horrendously cruel attack on the children, it was a way of emasculating the men who were unable to protect their women or children from such degradation, injury and humiliation. Killing women and children was one weapon hurled against men; degrading them first, often in front of their eyes, was a cruel addition.

Russians too, who raped women and children as they conquered German forces at the end of the war, regarded rape as a spoil of war. Russians regarded this as their due reward for saving the women.[872] In their view, German women owed it to them in retaliation for German forces' equally atrocious treatment of Russian women. Until such acts became punishable within their own ranks after the first few days of the liberation of camps, rape was part of their ideological justification and imposed through authoritarian, and brutal, actions. It was a rampant sport, implemented by many if not most, and regarded as justified, unbridled, and desirable.

An explanation of the sexual abuse of youth by Nazi followers, collaborators and even rescuers of children, needs to incorporate additional variables. Rape can be seen as a spoil of war, but also as an act of cruelty against those deemed vastly inferior and not worthy of recognition as human and sentient beings. Rape of boys was viewed as a right of *kapos* and others in positions of power in camps. It was also a crime of opportunity, and could have served to satisfy sexual urges outside of the normal constraints of peace-time life. Added to this is the frequently reported enjoyment of lurid acts of sexual cruelty, female and male reproductive organ torture in medical experiments involving both Jewish and non-Jewish children, and vicious murders with or without their prior sexual abuse. As revealed in this book, these actions were not limited to a few, rare, pathological sadists, although these did exist as well.[873]

TOTALITARIANISM, INDIVIDUALISM, TECHNOLOGY AND CRUELTY

Totalitarian societies tend to demand that the individual serves the state rather than the state serve the individual. Much of mankind both in the Nazi era, and today, is ruled by totalitarian governments, even democratic societies tend to have some totalitarian tendencies.[874] Dominant world societies also tend to focus on technological advancements rather than our human dimension. Such technology puts incredible power in the hands of the state – such as the ability of the Nazis to impose such a remarkably well organized national and international killing machine, or the American development of nuclear power that brought an end to World War II. The individual fades into insignificance against such power.[875] Humanity, caring, and sensitivity to the feelings of others, become of lesser importance than controlling them. Inspired by the apparently magnificent dominance of Hitler, followers were encouraged to, and probably became, insensitive to the humanity in people, and perhaps, even more so to those who lacked any power at all, the children. Against this background, perpetrating acts of cruelty on them, whether this was physical, emotional or sexual abuse, became a psychological possibility.

CHILD SEXUAL ABUSE EVEN WHEN NOT UNDER GENOCIDAL CONDITIONS

In addition, one must consider the abominable occurrence of sexual abuse of children sent for safety to countries that were not under Nazi occupation or rule and where families were not constrained by the need for secrecy about, or fear of punishment for, hiding Jewish children. In these settings sexual abuse appears to have been a crime of opportunity perpetrated by people in positions of authority. These crimes probably bear closer association to the worldwide problems of child sexual abuse that are prevalent today, particularly among pedophiles or in some religiously inspired and sometimes extreme communities,[876] than they do to the specific conditions of child sexual abuse during the genocide of the Jews in Nazi Germany and Europe.

CHILD SEXUAL ABUSE GLOBALLY

Although by no means excusing this behaviour, it is worth noting that child sexual abuse, especially, but not only, in times of war or genocide is not exceptional; other situations in our recent history – and in our daily lives – reveal similar atrocities. Some of these result in the murder of the children as well as their sexual abuse. Peace-time examples include the physical and sexual abuse of children in religiously run schools in Ireland, Australia, Canada, and other countries where the Christian brothers and other, largely Irish, religious orders moved.[877] These include the physical, emotional and sexual abuse of aboriginal children forced into residential schools in Canada;[878] children trafficked for sexual slavery globally;[879] child marriage practices still prevalent in some societies;[880] abduction and rape of young girls as a means of obtaining them as wives as occurs in some Central Asian countries;[881] and the continuation of forced or coerced sterilization of girls reportedly ongoing, occasionally, among aboriginal women in Canada even today.[882]

Children in all countries are at risk of sexual abuse. Children are at even greater risk of sexual abuse during times of war. Rape and sexual abuse are reported in war torn regions across the globe including Burundi, Sierra Leone, Somalia, Northern Uganda, Sudan and others. In Northern Uganda, for example, 26,000 children were abducted and forced to become "child soldiers" often used for sexual exploitation and serving as weapons of war.[883] World War II provided opportunities for child rape and abuse including the Russian rape of women, children and the elderly in Berlin and in territories overtaken by Russian forces, as well as that of the violent and gruesome rapes and torture of so-called "comfort women" and children by soldiers of the Imperial Japanese Army in all the Asian countries they occupied, including what is now termed the Rape of Nanking.[884]

Psychologists and psychiatrists consider both Holocaust atrocities and child sexual abuse as two of the most serious childhood traumas that can be faced.[885] In society, we are able to accept the realities of physical violence more readily than that of sexual violence, at any age. Among children, our reactions of horror, disbelief, and aversion to sexual violence are compounded. Both survivors and therapists find it difficult to explore these events.[886] The dearth of writing and information about this aspect of the Holocaust reflects our academic hesitancy and unwillingness to explore this subject as well.

As UNICEF notes, sexual violence against children, particularly against girls, is universally condemned but much more frequent than people realise.[887] It not only occurs under conditions of war, or genocide, but on a day-to-day basis, in families, schools, churches, hospitals, and in foster care settings. It is clear that we still have much to understand about human nature's ability to commit unspeakable crimes, particularly when driven by ideologically inspired fear, hatred, or greed, even in everyday settings.

SEXUAL ABUSE OF CHILDREN AND NAZI IDEOLOGY

More puzzling, however, is that rape and sexual exploitation of Jewish women in particular, were not condoned as part of Nazi ideology, precluding these actions from being considered as a simple distortion of evil into ideological good. Sexual contact with Jewish women was forbidden by Nazi ideology. Child sexual abuse was also explicitly condemned in German law.[888] The fact that all Jewish children were to be killed, however, might have made them an even more appealing target as their "justified" murder might have made their prior rape unlikely to ever be disclosed or reported. Jewish children might well have been regarded as fair (sexual) game alongside their mothers, sisters and aunts. Their rape in these instances was likely, predominantly, a crime of fear, violence, hate, anger, bravado, superiority, as well as sexual arousal, release or satisfaction.[889] From a Nazi perspective, it demonstrated the dominance of the ideologically superior Aryan race. It was also a way of devaluing, dehumanizing and demeaning their victims, in congruence with Nazi ideology, before killing them.

Nazi policy, while condemning sexual contact with Jews and with children, also served to provide multiple opportunities for such abuse. Examination of Appendices 1 and 2 reveals that of the 177 incidents of sexual abuse reported, 160 were of Jewish children, nine of gentile children in the UK, and eight of German gentile children. The majority of Jewish children were sexually assaulted in camps (20.0%), while hiding (18.1%), by the *Wehrmacht* or the *Einsatzgruppen* (16.3%) or in ghettos (13.9%), while a few were abused as part of medical experimentation in camps (5.1%), by Russian soldiers towards the end of the war (1.9%), while in prisons (1.3%), in partisan groups (0.8%), or while on transport trains (0.6%). Some were abused after being sent to the UK, the USA, or elsewhere for safety (5.1%) and in post-war Displaced Persons camps (3.2%). The details of the sexual abuse experienced by eight other children remain concealed in archives (5.0%). A further 3.1% were abused while passing for Aryan and not as Jewish children, although the fact that they were forced to hide in this manner was also determined by the Nazi regime's determination to kill Jews. Almost none of these sexual abuses would have occurred if the Nazi regime had not destroyed the family life of Jews and created these incomprehensible and inhumane conditions for children.

Given the extreme difficulty that sexual abuse survivors have in telling their stories, the reports included in this book are likely a vast under-representation. Telling such stories seventy-five years ago, when discussion of sexual activity was far more restricted than it is today, and when children were simply not believed when they did come forward with these encounters, suggests that there were many who did not reveal their experiences or, when they did, these were not believed, acted on, or recorded. In addition, there is no record of the sexual abuse of children who were then murdered to prevent them from ever telling their stories. This book, therefore, reflects just the tip of the iceberg of this aspect of the Holocaust.

In this book, rather than analysing one or two case studies as examples of Jewish child sexual abuse, I have compiled 160 individual voices into a multilayered portrait – an initial picture reflecting the tragic, but realistic and expansive issue of child sexual abuse during the Holocaust. I have drawn from the writings of as many people who could be traced, including the voices of children, their caregivers, their rescuers, their teachers, their parents, siblings and family in an effort to expose the variety and extent of sexual offenses against children. Obviously, the majority of children who were abused in this way were not likely to have survived the Holocaust and their stories can never be told. It is, however, hoped that the value of this initial examination of the subject will be acknowledged by future generations who might gain a clearer understanding of the children's experiences of sexual abuse and who might be able to delve even deeper into the subject.

There will, no doubt, be some who take comfort from, and reflect on, the relative paucity of reports about these horrors, taking this as an indication that this rarely occurred. Hard though it is to accept, we need to recognise that this occurrence is a hidden horror that was far more prevalent than we would ever like to acknowledge.

BETRAYAL

The Holocaust served as an opportunity to abuse children both physically and sexually, not only as conquered enemies – as occurs in such wars – but as victims of their rescuers. This double assault – sexual and psychological – as both figures in authority offering to help, and as perpetrators of sexual violence against them, parallels the deepest level of Dante's *Inferno*,[890] that of betrayal or treachery. Jewish children during the Nazi era were betrayed on many levels: by their parents who – in the children's eyes – abandoned them to strangers; by Nazis, soldiers, guards and other Nazi allies who occupied their lands, cities, villages and homes; by rescuers who, while professing to save their lives, sexually, physically and emotionally abused them; by their peers and friends who ridiculed them as well as abused them at times; by their families, communities, and countries of safe haven after the war who discounted their experiences, disbelieved their stories, and suppressed their emotional pain by not listening to them or acknowledging their truths; and in later years by Holocaust scholars, archivists, and conference attendees, who refuse to acknowledge or study child sexual abuse during the Holocaust. With credit to Shakespeare's Julius

Caesar, this betrayal by those who should be their friends is, perhaps, "the unkindest cut of all."[891]

I accept Father Patrick Desbois' statement, that I belong to a race that kills children.[892] I must add, however, that we may also abuse them physically, emotionally and sexually first. Worse still, we sometimes believe that we are justified in doing so by ideological or even religious righteousness. By concealing these cruel, criminal acts perpetrated against children, we have shamed the children even further by not honouring their inhumane experiences. Instead, we have been quite comfortable allowing the perpetrators to go unnamed, unprosecuted and unpunished.

APPENDIX 1: SUMMARY

SEXUALLY ABUSED CHILDREN IN THE HOLOCAUST			
Jewish Children Abused Sexually (N=160)	**Perpetrator**	**Age**	**Type of assault**
Sexual abuse prior to WWII			**Subtotal 8 (5.0%)**
1	Janina Bauman[893]	Youth at party	14	Teenagers having sex around her
2	Pnina Granirer[894]	Male in alley	10	Male flashing of penis
3	Erika*[895]	SS officer	10	Witnessed assault of mother
4	Akiza Barouch[896]	Forced marriage	15	To avoid separation
5	Shari Braun[897]	32-year-old man	14	Breasts grabbed
6	Anna*[898]	German man	8	Raped in her home
7	Dalia*[899]	Nazi man	8	Sexually assaulted
8	Regine[900]	Gang of boys	12	Chased by boys/ clothes pulled off
Sexual abuse by Soldiers and *Einsatzgruppen*			**Subtotal 26 (16.3%)**
9	Susan[901]	Storm Troopers *Kristallnacht*	Young girl	Nightgown ripped to shreds

10	Liza Silbert[902]	Ukrainian guards	Young girl	Witnessed rape of women on transport trains
11	Marion Lowe[903]	Ustashi guards	10	Witnessed gang rape
12	Dana S[904]	German soldier	Small child	Fondled or raped
13	Maria Scheffer[905]	German soldier	11	Manually assaulted
14	Tova [906]	Guards /German soldiers/Jewish foreman	13	Raped repeatedly/ witnessed rapes
15	French school children[907]	German soldiers	Young boys and girls	Forced oral sex
16	Szeina.[908]	German and Polish soldiers	11	Attempted rape
17	Nina Rusman[909]	German officer	13	Raped
18	Jezechiel F[910]	Germans	?	Witnessed rape/ women and girls
19	Vivi*[911]	SS	13	Witnessed rape and murder
20	G[912]	SS officer	15	Witnessed rapes/ murders of girls
21	Aron*[913]	Romanians	10	Raped with bayonets/breasts cut off
22	Carla*[914]	Ukrainian soldiers	10	16-year-old cousin raped by 40 soldiers
23	Petrivna[915]	Hummel, head of local Gestapo	School girl	Witnessed classmates taken/raped
24	Sonia Palty[916]	Ukrainian farmer	14	Witnessed rape and torture
25	L I Melchukova.[917]	Hummer, German officer	16	Raped and breast cut off

26	Gusta Glozman[918]	German soldiers	14	Raped and killed
27	In Distomo[919]	SS battalion	Little girls	Raped
28	Lilya S Gleizer[920]	Germans/ Policemen	Young girls	Raped/sexually mutilated girls
29	Kulski[921]	Ukrainians	Young girl	Gang rape of dead girl's body
30	Survivor[922]	Two SS men	16	Raped
31	Nechama Tec[923]	German soldier	Teen	Sexual assault
32	Desbois[924]	German soldiers	15/16 girl	Raped
33	Desbois[925]	German soldiers	Young girls	Raped
34	Desbois[926]	German soldiers	16 girl	Gang raped

Sexual abuse in ghettos			Subtotal 22 (13.8%)	
35	"Coal minors"[927]	Sexual activities	10-14	Ghetto coal pickers
36	Luba M[928]	Germans	15 and under	Rape of 20 girls
37	Jacob*[929]	unknown	14	Witnessed rapes
38	Mary Berg[930]	Germans	15	Sexual voyeurism
39	Noam*[931]	Gendarmes	Girl and female child	'Fur' in exchange for survival
40	Two sisters[932]	Policemen	Young girls	Sexual exchange for survival
41	Rita*[933]	Policeman	14	Sexual exchange for survival
42	Sala Pawlowicz[934]	Polish-German	Young teen	Breasts beaten repeatedly
43	Izolda[935]	Policeman	'little Jew girl'	Sexually abused/raped
44	Sia Herzberg[936]	Latvian police	child	Sexual assault

45	Daughter Sima Mandels[937]	Biebow German head of Lodz ghetto	16	Attempted rape
46	Esther H[938]	Biebow	Young girl	Raped Rita
47	Bina W [939]	Biebow	?	Raped
48	Rita H[940]	Rubenstein *Judenrat*	child	Molested when coming for milk
49	Chaya[941]	Jewish policeman	child	Caught raping children
50	Andre Stein[942]	Ghetto man	8	Raped
51	Lucille Eichengreen[943]	Rumkowski (*Judenrat*)	17	Forced masturbation
52	Luba[944]	Rumkowski (*Judenrat*)	16	Manually assaulted
53	Bronia[945]	Rumkowski (*Judenrat*)	11	Manually assaulted
54	Yulek[946]	Rumkowski (*Judenrat*)	13	Manually assaulted and forced masturbation
55	Mania Zylberstajn[947]	Rumkowski (*Judenrat*)	8	Manually assaulted
56	Fishman[948]	German/ Lithuanian police	8-year-olds	Raped in front of their mothers
Sexual abuse on transports			**Subtotal 1 (0.6%)**	
57	Eva Grinston[949]	Man on train	13	Fondling
Sexual abuse of girls in camps			**Subtotal 15 (9.4%)**	
58	Gabis[950]	Stutthof Camp SS	Young virgin	Gynaecological check
59	Freda*[951]	Russian women	12	Witnessed lesbian sexuality

60	Rachal Hanan[952]	Dogs	16	Rape of girl by dogs
61	George Reinitz[953]	Ukrainian guard	Young boy	Dogs attacked 'private parts'
62	Dora Goldstein Roth[954]	SS	11	Witnessed 3 prisoners being raped by guards
63	Hana Bruml [955]	Guard in camp	Young women	Voyeurism in showers
64	Marina[956]	Ukrainian guard	11	Fondling
65	Jehuda Bacon[957]	Young boys	8	Witnessed pimping of girls
66	Lily Wolf[958]	30-year-old guard	Young girl	Sex exchange to help imprisoned mother
67	Bernard Z[959]	Hungarian guards	Young girls	Sexual abuse
68	Sara B[960]	SS officers	5	Gang raped
69	Eliahu Rosenberg[961]	Demjanjuk	?	Raped women and young girls
70	Regina[962]	Prisoner in Auschwitz possibly Jewish	13	Attempted rape
71	Hannah*[963]	Prisoner in Theresienstadt	9	Sexually assaulted
72	Judith[964]	Camp official	8	Raped, tortured
Sexual abuse of boys in camps			**Subtotal 17 (10.6%)**	
73	Leon*[965]	Kapo	About 15	Sexual slavery
74	Julian Reuter[966]	Jewish *Kapo*	14	Sexual slavery
75	Eisenberg report[967]	SS	12	Sexual slavery
76	Greenman report[968]	Schiller *Kapo*	16	Sexual slavery
77	Heger report[969]	Kapo	Young boys	Sexual slavery

78	Frans*[970]	German	Young boy	Sexual slavery
79	Gunter*[971]	SS officer	Young boy	Sexual slavery
80	Harry*[972]	Hendrik Homosexual	10-14	Sexual slavery
81	Branko Lustig[973]	*Kapos*/senior prisoners	Young boys	Sexual slavery
82	Kenneth Rowan[974]	*Kapos*/senior prisoners	Young boys	Sexual slavery
83	Sam Steinberg[975]	*Kapos*/senior prisoners	Young boys	Sexual slavery
84	Peter[976]	Guards/Family Camp Birkenau	8	Sexually abused
85	Paul Molnar [977]	Kapo	15	Sexual slavery
86	Rudolf Satovitz[978]	Kapo	15	Sexual slavery
87	Gilbert[979]	Kapo	15	Sexual slavery
88	Abraham Malach[980]	Female Kapo	9	Attempted sexual abuse
89	Nate Leitciger[981]	Kapo	15	Sexual slavery
Sexual abuse in prisons			**Subtotal 2 (1.3%)**	
90	Aliza Barak-Ressler[982]	Prison guard	14	Sexually harassed
91	Irene Binzer[983]	Cetnici prison guard	15	Raped daily in prison
Sexual abuse in medical experiments			**Subtotal 8 (5.0%)**	
92	Eva Moses Kor[984]	Mengele	Twins	Experimentation to change sex
93	Isaac*[985]	Buchenwald	About 15	Sodomized/ sexual experiments

94	Moti Alon[986]	Mengele	9	Forced witnessing of sex
95	Efraim Reichenberg[987]	Mengele	About 16	Forced witnessing of sex
96	Moshe Offer. [988]	Mengele	?	Sex organs of twin brother removed
97	Lilliput dwarf family[989]	Mengele	Infant to adult	Sexual humiliation/ Lilliput dwarfs
98	Cornelia[990]	Mauthausen	8	Sexual medical experimentation
99	Peter Shenk [991]	Buchenwald: Ding or Hoven	17	Sexually assaulted twice
Sexual abuse of children in hiding			**Subtotal 29 (18.1%)**	
100	Agi Stein-Carlton[992]	Superintendent of hiding cellar	13	Fondling
101	Eva Heyman[993]	Hidden child	13	Fear of sexual assault
102	Ruth[994]	Hiding mother	11	Massaged by hiding mother
103	Boris*[995]	Hiding brother	7-8	Attempted rape by brother. Witnessed rape of sister
104	Aniko Berger[996]	Hiding brothers	5	Raped by hiding brothers
105	Sabine Wagschal[997]	Older boy	Child	Raped by 11/12- year-old boy
106	Lucy[998]	Teenage boy	About 9	Sexual assault
107	Esther[999]	Older hiding brother	Child	Sexual abuse

108	Condolisa[1000]	15-year-old hiding brother	7-8	Sexual abuse
109	Pauline[1001]	Male relatives of hiding family	11-12	Sexual abuse
110	David[1002]	Hiding father	14	Fondled / voyeurism
111	Anne[1003]	Hiding father	8	Sexual abuse
112	Sara Spier[1004]	Hiding father	Teen	Sexual abuse
113	Astrid Jakubowicz[1005]	Hiding father	5	Forced manual sexual abuse
114	Lily Redner[1006]	Hiding father	11	Fondling
115	Noel[1007]	Jewish mother hiding	5	Attempted forced sexual activity
116	Leszek Allerhand[1008]	Whore serving German army	Young boy	Hidden under bed
117	Simone Jameson[1009]	French police officers	12	Hiding National Library of Paris
118	Janina Bauman[1010]	Man in shelter	Child	Sexual harassment
119	Julia[1011]	Farmer	10	Witnessed sexual harassment
120	Carl.[1012]	Maid	10	Abused by maid while in hiding
121	Lula[1013]	Ukrainian farmer	Child	Abused by farmer who hid her
122	Petra*[1014]	Farmer	Child	Witnessed rape of mother/was raped
123	Nona*[1015]	Polish labourer	About 12	Raped
124	Dunia[1016]	Farmer and son	10	Raped by farmer and son. Witnessed rape of aunt, mother Raped by husband

125	Molly Applebaum[1017]	Farmer	13	Sexual abuse in hiding
126	Helene[1018]	Farmer	Teen	Sexual abuse in hiding
127	Ora*[1019]	Hiding family	Child	Possible sexual assault
128	Lien de Jong[1020]	Uncle and Father	11	Rape and harassment
Sexual abuse while passing as Aryan			**Subtotal 5 (3.1%)**	
129	Sewek Okonowski *[1021]	Aryan side Warsaw ghetto	?	Witnessed sexual torture of girl
130	Zula[1022]	3 Nazis	Young girl	Raped while passing for Aryan
131	Izolda[1023]	Policeman	Young woman	Raped to save another girl
132	Mona*[1024]	Clerk	About 14	Raped while passing for Aryan
133	Sara Avinum[1025]	Unknown man	5	Sexually assaulted in basement
Sexual abuse in partisan group			**Subtotal 1 (0.6%)**	
134	Garfunk[1026]	Witnessing sex	Small boy	Bielski partisan group
Sexual abuse by Russian soldiers			**Subtotal 3 (1.9%)**	
135	Brigitte Medvin[1027]	Russian soldiers	12	Witnessed attempted rape of mother and rapes of girls

| 136 | Hanna Mishna[1028] | Russian soldiers | Young girl | Witnessed rapes |
| 137 | Irene Kempfner[1029] | Russian soldiers | 8 | Raped her mother in Irene's bed |

Sexual abuse in the postwar period			Subtotal 5 (3.1%)
138	Judy Abrams[1030]	Friend in DP camp	11	Groomed for sex and fondled
139	Dovid*[1031]	Polish DP camp guards	7	Witnessed women being raped
140	Erin*[1032]	Italian DP camp	5	Sexual assault by soldier
141	Katrina*[1033]	Man in DP camp	11	Grabbed by man in next bunk
142	Max[1034]	Gentile Stepmother	14	Forced sexual relations

Sexual abuse in UK, USA, Canada, postwar Europe			Subtotal 10 (6.3%)
143	Marie Claire Rakowski[1035]	Hasidic Rabbi Post war rescuer in USA	About 5	Sexually abused by Hasidic Rabbi
144	Hanna[1036]	Hasidic family post war rescuer father in New York	8	Fondled and digitally raped
145	Maya[1037]	USA post-war rescue family	15	Frequent attempted rape by man of the house
146	Joan Zilva[1038]	Toronto war-time rescue family father	14	Sexually harassed
147	Clare G[1039]	Rescuer family father	Young girl	Raped repeatedly

148	Stella*[1040]	Kindertransport child	Child	Sexual abuse and rape
149	Susi/Grace[1041]	Baptist Minister rescuer father *Kindertransport* child	9	Raped repeatedly for years
150	Bella*[1042]	Post war reparations officer	12	Raped and used for blackmail
151	Bertha Leverten[1043]	Foster father	15	Sexual advances over five years
152	Mira Blaustein[1044]	Foster family abuse	12	Abused emotionally and sexually

Undisclosed archives			Subtotal 8 (5.0%)	
153-160	8 children	Born 1930 or later	Yad Vashem undisclosed archives	

Sexual abuse of Gentile children moved to safety in UK			Subtotal 9	
1	Lilian[1045]	Rescuer father	6	Voyeurism
2	Rose Clarke[1046]	Church youth group leader	13	Fondling
3	Jen[1047]	Rescuer father	Young girl	Fondled
4	Marie[1048]	Rescuer farmer	10	Sexual assault
5	Older sister[1049]	Rescuer farmer	12	Sexually abused and pregnant
6	Younger sister[1050]	Rescuer farmer	8	Witnessed sex
7-9	Three evacuee children[1051]	Rescue father	unknown	Sexual abuse

Sexual abuse of German children				Subtotal 8
1	Hans-Georg Behr[1052]	German child in Catholic school	11	Masturbation of boys, oral sex with Catholic father, and farmer
2	Anni Nagel[1053]	Older boys, aunt's husband	8	Accused of sexual abuse but raped
3	Jost Hermand[1054]	KLV camp boys	10	Forced masturbation of older boys
4-5	Two girls [1055]	5 Hitler Youth boys 14-16	Under 14	Raped girls
6-8	Three girls[1056]	Two boys 13,16	9	Raped girls
				Jewish children total 160
				German children total 8
				British children total 9

APPENDIX 2: OVERVIEW

Jewish children sexually abused	Number of children (160)	% of Jewish children	Average age (when known) (101)
Prior to WWII	8	5.1	11.4
By Soldiers and *Einsatzgruppen*	26	16.3	13.1
In ghettos	22	13.9	12.7
On transports	1	0.6	13.0
Of girls in camps	15	9.5	10.3
Of boys in camps	17	10.6	13.1
In prisons	2	1.3	14.5
In medical experiments	8	5.1	13.0
Of children in hiding	29	18.1	9.9
While passing as Aryan	5	3.1	9.5
In partisan group	1	0.8	--
By Russian soldiers	3	1.9	10.0
In post-war period	5	3.2	9.6
In USA, Canada, postwar Europe	10	5.1	11.3
Undisclosed archives	8	5.1	--
Total	160	--	11.3

Sexual abuse of gentile children (17)			
Children moved to safety in UK	9	--	9.8
German children	8	--	9.5

NOTES

1   R D Rosen, *Such Good Girls: The Journey of the Holocaust's Hidden Child Survivors* (New York: Harper Perenial, 2014), 226.
2   V Dadrian, "Armenian Children Victims of Genocide," http://www.genocide-museum.am/eng/online_exhibition_3.php.
3   Emmanuel Sehene Ruvugiro, "Rwanda: The Gruesome Plight of Children During the Tutsi Genocide.," Justiceinfo.net, www.justiceinfo.net/en/tribunals/ictr/34925-online-exhibition-pays-gruesome-tribute-to-child-suffering-in-rwandan-genocide.html.
4   United to End Genocide, "The Cambodian Genocide," United to End Genocide, http://endgenocide.org/learn/past-genocides/the-cambodian-genocide/.
5   The History Place, "Stalin's Forced Famine: 1932-9133: 7,000,000 Deaths," The History Place, http://www.historyplace.com/worldhistory/genocide/stalin.htm.
6   United States Holocaust Memorial Museum, "Plight of Jewish Children," USHMM, www.ushmm.org/wic/en/article.php?ModuleId=10006124.
7   Ruvugiro, "Rwanda: The Gruesome Plight of Children During the Tutsi Genocide.".
8   Musa Wakhungu Olaka, "Living a Genocide: Rape," USF Tampa Library, http://exhibits.lib.usf.edu/exhibits/show/darfur-genocide/modeof destruction/rape.
9   Monika J Flaschka, "Race, Rape and Gender in Nazi-Occupied Territories" (Kent State University, USA, 2009), 177-204.
10 Mike Milotte, Banished Babies: The Secret History of Ireland's Baby Export Business (Dublin: New Island, 2012); John S Milloy, A National Crime: The Canadian Government and the Residential School System 1879-1986 (Manitoba: University of Manitoba Press, 1999); Mary Raftery and Eoin O'Sullivan, Suffer the Little Children: The inside Story of Ireland's Industrial Schools (Dublin, Ireland: New Island Books, 1999).
11 Father Patrick Desbois, *In Broad Daylight: The Secret Procedures Behind the Holocaust by Bullets* (New York: Arcade Publishing, 2015), 72.
12 135633 Ka-Tzetnik, *Atrocity* (New York: Lyle Stuart, 1963); *Phoenix over the Galilee* (New York: Harper and Rowe, 1966); *Shivitti: A Vision*

(Gateways, 1989); *Piepel* (London: The New English Library, 1961); *House of Dolls* (London: Granada, 1973).

[13] Miryam Sivan, "Stoning the Messenger: Yehiel Dinur's House of Dolls and Piepel," in *Sexual Violence against Jewish Women During the Holocaust*, ed. Sonja M Hedgepeth and Rochelle G Saidel (Waltham, Massachusetts: Brandeis University Press, 2010), 203.

[14] Elie Wiesel, *Night* (New York: Hill and Wang, 1958), 62-3.

[15] United States Holocaust Memorial Museum, "Children During the Holocaust," USHMM, https://encyclopedia.ushmm.org/content/en/article/children-during-the-holocaust.

[16] Ibid.

[17] Deborah Dwork, *Children with a Star: Jewish Youth in Nazi Europe* (New Haven: Yale University Press, 1991), 69-83; Judy Abrams and Evi Blaikie, *Remember Us: A Collection of Memories Form Hungarian Hidden Children of the Holocaust* (Bloomington, Indiana: Authorhouse, 2010), 259; Rosen, *Such Good Girls: The Journey of the Holocaust's Hidden Child Survivors*, xxii; United States Holocaust Memorial Museum, "Plight of Jewish Children".

[18] "Plight of Jewish Children".

[19] Ibid.

[20] Ibid.

[21] Jane Marks, *The Hidden Children: The Secret Survivors of the Holocaust* (Great Britain: Bantam Books, 1995), 281-3.

[22] Susanne Vromen, *Hidden Children of the Holocaust: Belgian Nuns and Their Daring Rescue of Young Jews from the Nazis* (New York: Oxford University Press, 2008), 134; United States Holocaust Memorial Museum, "Plight of Jewish Children" xxii; Rosen, *Such Good Girls: The Journey of the Holocaust's Hidden Child Survivors*.

[23] Maria Hochberg-Marianska and Noe Gruss, *The Children Accuse* (London: Vallentine Mitchell, 1996), 45.

[24] United States Holocaust Memorial Museum, "Children During the Holocaust".

[25] Patricia Heberer, *Children During the Holocaust* (Lanham, USA: Rowman and Littlefield, 2011), xxv.

[26] Dwork, *Children with a Star: Jewish Youth in Nazi Europe*, xx.

[27] Deborah Lipstadt, "Introduction," in *Auschwitz: A Doctor's Story*, ed. Lucie Adelsberger (Boston: Northeastern University Press, 1995); Bradley E Smith and Agnes F Peterson, *Heinrich Himmler: Geheimreden 1933 Bis 1945* (Frankfort1974).

[28] Dwork, *Children with a Star: Jewish Youth in Nazi Europe*, xxi.

[29] Ibid., xvii.

[30] Alexandra Zapruder, *Salvaged Papers: Young Writers' Diaries of the Holocaust* (USA: Yale University Press, 2002), 1.

[31] Dwork, *Children with a Star: Jewish Youth in Nazi Europe*, xxiii.

[32] Zapruder, *Salvaged Papers: Young Writers' Diaries of the Holocaust*, 428-29.

[33] Ibid., 429-30.

[34] Ibid., 433.

[35] Ibid., 438.

[36] Ibid.

[37] Hochberg-Marianska and Gruss, *The Children Accuse*; Boaz Cohen, "The Children's Voice: Postwar Collection of Testimonies from Child Survivors of the Holocaust," *Holocaust and Genocide Studies* 21, no. 1 (2007).

[38] Lucjan Dobroszycki, ed. *The Chronicle of the Lodz Ghetto 1942-1943* (New Haven: Yale University Press 1984).

[39] Dwork, *Children with a Star: Jewish Youth in Nazi Europe*, xxiv, xxxii.

[40] Anonymous (Ora*), 2017.

[41] Dwork, *Children with a Star: Jewish Youth in Nazi Europe*, xlii.

[42] Ibid., 22.

[43] Julie Heifetz, *Too Young to Remember* (Detroit: Wayne State University Press, 1989), 19.

[44] Etien G Klug et al., "Child Abuse and Neglect by Parents and Other Caregivers," in *World Report on Violence and Health* (Geneva: World Health Organization, 2002).

[45] Ibid., 149.

[46] Rachel Lev-Wiesel and Susan Weinger, *Hell within Hell: Sexually Abused Child Holocaust Survivors* (Lanham, Maryland: University Press of America, 2011), 13.

[47] Ibid., 16.

[48] Dwork, *Children with a Star: Jewish Youth in Nazi Europe*, 256.

[49] Joanna Beata Michlic, "The Aftermath and After: Memories of Child Survivors of the Holocaust," in *Lessons and Legacies X: Back to the Sources: Reexamining Perpetrators, Victims and Bystanders*, ed. Sara Horowitz (Evanston, Illinois: Northwestern University Press, 2012), 143.

[50] Ibid., 144.

[51] Ibid., 143.

[52] Ibid., 148.

[53] Omer Bartov, *Anatomy of a Genocide: The Life and Death of a Town Called Buczacz* (New York: Simon and Schuster, 2018).

[54] Christopher Browning, *Ordinary Men: Reserve Police Battalion 101 and the Final Solution in Poland* (New York: Harper Perennial, 1992).

[55] Lawrence Langer, *Holocaust Testimonies: The Ruins of Memory* (New Haven and London: Yale University Press, 1991).

[56] Jan T Gross, *Neighbours: The Destruction of the Jewish Community in Jedwabne, Poland, 1941* (London: Random House, 2003).

[57] Dwork, *Children with a Star: Jewish Youth in Nazi Europe*.

[58] Nicholas Stargardt, *Witnesses of War: Children's Lives under the Nazis.* (London: Jonathan Cape, 2005).

[59] Jacob Boas, *We Are Witnesses: Five Diaries of Teenagers Who Died in the Holocaust* (New York: Scholastic Inc, 1996).

[60] Laurel Holliday, *Children's Wartime Diaries: Secret Writings from the Holocaust and World War II* (London: BCA, 1995).

[61] Marks, *The Hidden Children: The Secret Survivors of the Holocaust.*

[62] Andre Stein, *Hidden Children: Forgotten Survivors of the Holocaust* (Canada: Penguin Books, 1993).

[63] Alex Woolf, *Children of the Holocaust* (London: Franklin Wwatts, 2014).

[64] Zapruder, *Salvaged Papers: Young Writers' Diaries of the Holocaust.*

[65] Heberer, *Children During the Holocaust.*

[66] Nahum Bogner, *At the Mercy of Strangers: The Rescue of Jewish Children with Assumed Identities in Poland* (Jerusalem: Yad Vashem, 2009).

[67] Jennifer Craig- Norton, *The Kindertransport: Contesting Memory* (Bloomington, Indiana: Indiana University Press, 2019), 104, 321.

[68] Michlic, "The Aftermath and After: Memories of Child Survivors of the Holocaust," 148.

[69] Lev-Wiesel and Weinger, *Hell within Hell: Sexually Abused Child Holocaust Survivors*, 24.

[70] Michlic, "The Aftermath and After: Memories of Child Survivors of the Holocaust," 175.

[71] Dwork, *Children with a Star: Jewish Youth in Nazi Europe*, xl.

[72] Ibid.

[73] Stargardt, *Witnesses of War: Children's Lives under the Nazis.*, 324.

[74] Ibid.

[75] Dwork, *Children with a Star: Jewish Youth in Nazi Europe*, 270.

[76] Romeo Vitelli, "Angel-Makers, Baby-Killers - Take Your Pick," *Quaill Bell Magazine* (2013).

[77] Ibid.; Lloyd deMuse, "The Childhood Origins of the Holocaust," (Klagenfurth University, Austria2005).

[78] "The Childhood Origins of the Holocaust."

[79] Charles Dickens, *Dombey and Son* (UK: Wordsworth Classics, 1995).

[80] deMuse, "The Childhood Origins of the Holocaust."

[81] Ibid.

[82] Alison Owings, *Frauen: German Women Recall the Third Reich* (London: Penguin Books, 1993), 342.

[83] deMuse, "The Childhood Origins of the Holocaust."

[84] Anna Bikont, *The Crime and the Silence: Confronting the Massacre of Jews in Wartime Jedwabne* (New York: Farrar, Straus and giroux, 2004), 270.

[85] Ibid.

[86] Ibid., 253.

[87] In the late 1990s, while working in Lithuania, I purchased a Baba Jaga witch doll to take home to my children. In the era of Harry Potter and the wizarding world, this became a favourite and still graces a child's room.

[88] Krystyna Chiger and Daniel Paisner, *The Girl in the Green Sweater* (New York: St Martin's Griffin, 2008), 15.

[89] Lucille Eichengreen, *Haunted Memories: Portraits of Women in the Holocaust* (Exeter, New Haven: Publishing Works Inc, 2011), 71.

[90] Hans-Georg Behr, *Almost a Childhood: Growing up among the Nazis* (London: Granta Books, 2005), 1.

[91] Ibid., 8.

[92] J Llewellyn, J Southey, and S Thompson, "Children in Nazi Germany," Alpha History, alphahistory.com/nazigermany/children-in-nazi-germany; Peter Sichrovsky, *Born Guilty: Children of Nazi Families* (London: I.B.Tauris and Co Ltd, 1988), 169.

[93] Peter Longerich, *Goebbels: A Biography* (New York: Random house, 2015), 302.

[94] Ibid., 362.

[95] E T Gershoff and A Grogan-Kaylor, "Spanking and Child Outcomes: Old Controversies and New Meta-Analyses," *Journal of Family Psychology* 30 (2016).

[96] Sichrovsky, *Born Guilty: Children of Nazi Families*, 88.

[97] Ibid., 90.

[98] Uwe Timm, *In My Brother's Shadow* (London: Bloomsbury, 2005), 135.

[99] Ibid.

[100] Behr, *Almost a Childhood: Growing up among the Nazis*, 223.

[101] Ibid., 220.

[102] Ibid., 279.

[103] Caroline Pukall, ed. *Human Sexuality: A Contemporary Introduction* (Don Mills, Ontario, Canada: Oxford University Press, 2014), 13.

[104] Ibid.

[105] Behr, *Almost a Childhood: Growing up among the Nazis*, 39-40.

[106] Ibid., 285.

[107] Ibid., 42-3.

[108] Ibid., 44.

[109] Ibid., 55.

[110] Ibid., 58.

[111] Ibid., 81.

[112] Ibid., 92.

[113] Sichrovsky, *Born Guilty: Children of Nazi Families*, 143.

[114] Stargardt, *Witnesses of War: Children's Lives under the Nazis.*, 70-2.

[115] Ibid., 60-1.

[116] A handwritten Post-It note was inserted into my copy of this book at this point. It read: "This fear applied to British delinquents in 'care' too. I know … I was always convinced Mam and Dad knew I was getting my just

deserts" (Second hand book purchased from and formerly the property of Baysgarth School Library, UK.)

[117] Dagmar Herzog, "Hubris and Hypocrisy, Incitement and Disavowal: Sexuality and German Fascism.," *Journal of the History of Sexuality* 11, no. 1/2 (2002): 13.

[118] Ibid.

[119] Ursula Mahlendorf, *The Shame of Survival; Working through a Nazi Childhood* (Pennysylvania: The Pennsylvania State University Press, 2009), 94; Pauk Roland, *Life in the Third Reich: Daily Life in Nazi Germany 1933-1945* (London: Arcturus, 2016), 56.

[120] Elizabeth Heineman, "Sexuality and Nazism: The Doubly Unspeakable?," *Journal of the History of Sexuality* 11, no. 1/2 (Jan-Apr 2002): 31.

[121] Ibid., 50.

[122] A Krüger, F Krüger, and S Treptau, "Nudism in Nazi Germany: Indecent Behaviour or Physical Culture for the Well-Being of the Nation," *The International Journal of the History of Sport* 19, no. 4 (2002): 34-8.

[123] Richard J Evans, *The Third Reich in Power* (USA: Penguin Books, 2006), 280.

[124] The History Place, "Hitler's Boy Soldiers," The History Place, www.historyplace.com/worldwar2/hitleryouth/hj-boy-soldiers.htm.

[125] Ibid.

[126] Stargardt, *Witnesses of War: Children's Lives under the Nazis.*, 125.

[127] Michael Harris, *Unholy Orders: Tragedy at Mount Cashel* (Toronto: Penguin Books, 1990); Raftery and O'Sullivan, *Suffer the Little Children: The inside Story of Ireland's Industrial Schools*; Ann Thompson, *Say Sorry: A Harrowing Childhood in Catholic Orphanages* (Kindle, 2009); Canada's Human Rights History, "Duplessis Orphans," https://historyofrights.ca/encyclopaedia/main-events/duplessis-orphans/; Justice Ryan, "The Commission to Enquire into Child Abuse Report," (Ireland2009); Milotte, *Banished Babies: The Secret History of Ireland's Baby Export Business.*

[128] Mahlendorf, *The Shame of Survival; Working through a Nazi Childhood*, 121-3.

[129] Ibid., 123.

[130] Joanna Bourke, "Police Surgeons and Sexual Violence: A History," *The Lancet* 390, no. 10094 (2017).

[131] Hans Peter Bleuel, *Sex and Society in Nazi Germany* (Philadelphia: J.B.Lipincott Company, 1971), 241.

[132] Ibid.

[133] Flaschka, "Race, Rape and Gender in Nazi-Occupied Territories," 178.

[134] Ibid., 178, footnote 329.

[135] Ibid., 178.

[136] Ibid., 177-204.

[137] Ibid., 204-9.

[138] Erika Mann, *School for Barbarians* (New York: Dover Publications, 2014), 19-20.

[139] Ibid., 16.

[140] DW.Com, "Former Nazi Pedophile Nabbed in Argentina," DW.COM, http://m.dw,com/en/former-nazi-pedophile-nabbed-in-argentina/a-1515223.

[141] Nico Voigtländer and Hans-Joachim Voth, "Nazi Indoctrination and Anti-Semitic Beliefs in Germany," *Proceedings of the National Academy of Sciences of the United States of America* 112, no. 26 (2015 June).

[142] David Hogan and David Aretha, eds., *The Holocaust Chronicle* (Illinois: Publications International, 2001), 33.

[143] Ibid., 34.

[144] Ibid., 42.

[145] Hugues Theoret, *The Blue Shirts: Adrien Arcand and Fascist Anti-Semitism in Canada* (Ottawa: University of Ottawa Press, 2017), 127-9.

[146] Ibid., 132-9.

[147] Ibid., 137.

[148] Hogan and Aretha, *The Holocaust Chronicle*, 42.

[149] Elissa Mailander, *Female SS Guards and Workaday Violence: The Majdanek Concentration Camp, 1942-1944* (East Lansing, USA: Michigan State University Press, 2015), 25.

[150] Elvira Bauer, *Trau Keinem Fuchs Auf Grüner Heid Und Keinem Jud Auf Seinem Eid (Don't Trust a Fox in a Green Meadow or the Word of a Jew)* (Nuremberg: Stürmer Verlag, 1936).

[151] Hogan and Aretha, *The Holocaust Chronicle*, 42.

[152] Ibid., 71.

[153] Ibid., 55.

[154] Ibid.

[155] Ibid., 76.

[156] Ibid., 95.

[157] Ibid., 94.

[158] Ibid., 114.

[159] Ibid., 125.

[160] Ibid., 122.

[161] Ibid., 123, 41.

[162] Ibid., 132.

[163] Ibid., 149.

[164] Ibid.

[165] Beverley Chalmers, *Birth, Sex and Abuse: Women's Voices under Nazi Rule* (UK: Grosvenor House Publishers, 2015), 32.

[166] Hogan and Aretha, *The Holocaust Chronicle*, 151; Michael Burleigh, "Nazi "Euthanasia" Programs," in *Deadly Medicine: Creating the Master*

Race, ed. Dieter Kuntz (Washington: United States Holocaust Memorial Museum, 2008), 127-54.

[167] Henry Freidlander, "From "Euthanasia" to the "Final Solution"," in *Deadly Medicine*, ed. Dieter Kuntz (Washington: United States Holocaust Memorial Museum, 2008), 163; Hogan and Aretha, *The Holocaust Chronicle*, 169.

[168] Chalmers, *Birth, Sex and Abuse: Women's Voices under Nazi Rule*, 23-40; Hogan and Aretha, *The Holocaust Chronicle*, 169.

[169] Chalmers, *Birth, Sex and Abuse: Women's Voices under Nazi Rule*, 23-40, 177.

[170] Hogan and Aretha, *The Holocaust Chronicle*, 177.

[171] Stargardt, *Witnesses of War: Children's Lives under the Nazis*; Janina Bauman, *Winter in the Morning: A Young Girl's Life in the Warsaw Ghetto and Beyond.* (London, Great Britain: Virago Press, 1991); Beverley Chalmers, "What Should International Health Consultants Know?," *Bulletin of the World Health Organization* 77 (1999); Raul Hilberg, Stanislaw Staron, and Josef Kermisz, *The Warsaw Diary of Adam Czerniakow: Prelude to Doom* (New York: Stein and Day, 1982); Wolfgang W E Samuel, *The War of Our Childhood: Memories of World War II* (Jackson: University Press of Mississippi, 2002); Rywka Lipszye, *Rywka's Dairy: The Writings of a Jewish Girl from the Lodz Ghetto, Found at Auschwitz in 1945 and Published Seventy Years Later.* (San Fransisco, USA: Jewish family and Children's Services of San Fransisco, 2015); Alan Adelson and Robert Lapides, eds., *Lódź Ghetto: Inside a Community under Siege* (New York: Viking, 1989); Mary Berg, *The Diary of Mary Berg* (Oxford: Oneworld, 1945, 2007); Lynn H. Nicholas, *Cruel World: The Children of Europe in the Nazi Web* (New York: Vintage Books, 2006); Holliday, *Children's Wartime Diaries: Secret Writings from the Holocaust and World War II*; Heberer, *Children During the Holocaust*.

[172] Naomi Baumslag, *Murderous Medicine* (Washington DC: Baumslag, 2014), 35; Chalmers, *Birth, Sex and Abuse: Women's Voices under Nazi Rule*, 66-71.

[173] Boas, *We Are Witnesses: Five Diaries of Teenagers Who Died in the Holocaust*, 140.

[174] James M Glass, *Life Unworthy of Life: Racial Phobia and Mass Murder in Hitler's Germany* (New York: Basic Books, 1997), 173-4; Emanuel Ringelblum, *Ringelblumyoman Ve-Reshimot Mitkufat, Ha-Milhama [Diary and Notes from the Warsaw Ghetto: Sept 1939-December 1942]* (Jerusalem: Yad Vashem, September 1939-December 1942), 174.

[175] Yehuda Bauer, "Jewish Resistance and Passivity in the Face of the Holocaust," in *Unanswered Question*, ed. Francois Furet (New York: Schocken Books, 1989), 249.

[176] Zapruder, *Salvaged Papers: Young Writers' Diaries of the Holocaust*, 219.

[177] Marcel Tuchman, *Remember: My Stories of Survival and Beyond* (New York, Jerusalem: Yad Vashem and the Holocaust Survivors Memoirs Project, 2010), 30.

[178] Ibid., 40.

[179] Adelson and Lapides, *Lódź Ghetto: Inside a Community under Siege*, 328-31.

[180] Feigie Libman, Personal Communication, 16 May 2019.

[181] Ibid.

[182] Shelly Lore, *Criminal Experiments on Human Beings in Auschwitz and War Research Laboratories: Twenty Women Prisoners' Accounts* (San Fransisco: Mellen Research University Press, 1991), 78.

[183] Nechama Tec, *Defiance* (Oxford: Oxford University Press, 2013), 81-9.

[184] Bartley C Crum, *Behind the Silken Curtain: A Personal Account of Anglo-American Diplomacy in Palestine and the Middle East* (New York: Simon and Schuster, 1947), 94-6.

[185] Rosen, *Such Good Girls: The Journey of the Holocaust's Hidden Child Survivors*, 10.

[186] Desbois, *In Broad Daylight: The Secret Procedures Behind the Holocaust by Bullets*; *The Holocaust by Bullets:A Priest's Journey to Uncover the Truth Behind the Murder of 1.5 Million Jews* (New York: Palgrave, Macmillan, 2008).

[187] Anonymous (Aron*), "Testimony," (USA: Shoah Foundation Visual History Archive, 1997).

[188] Desbois, *In Broad Daylight: The Secret Procedures Behind the Holocaust by Bullets*, 64.

[189] *The Holocaust by Bullets:A Priest's Journey to Uncover the Truth Behind the Murder of 1.5 Million Jews*, 30.

[190] Ibid., 70, 90, 212-3.

[191] Michael J Bazyler and Frank M Tuerkheimer, *Forgotten Trials of the Holocaust* (New York: New York University Press, 2014), 168.

[192] Desbois, *The Holocaust by Bullets:A Priest's Journey to Uncover the Truth Behind the Murder of 1.5 Million Jews*, 109-10.

[193] Ibid., 125.

[194] Susan Zuccotti, *The Italians and the Holocaust: Persecution, Rescue, Survival* (New York: Basic Books, 1987), 185.

[195] Hogan and Aretha, *The Holocaust Chronicle*, 212.

[196] Ibid., 213.

[197] Ibid., 190.

[198] Ibid., 181.

[199] Bogner, *At the Mercy of Strangers: The Rescue of Jewish Children with Assumed Identities in Poland*, 32.

[200] Ibid., 35.

[201] Roger A. Ritvo and Diane M Plotkin, *Sisters in Sorrow: Voices of Care in the Holocaust* (College Station: Texas A & M University Press, 1998), 110.

[202] Erna Paris, *Unhealed Wounds: France and the Klaus Barbie Affair* (Toronto: Methuen, 1985), 69-71.

[203] Gisella Perl, *I Was a Doctor in Auschwitz*, Reprint edition 2007 ed. (North Stratford, NH: Ayer Company Publishers, 1948), 28.

[204] Lucie Adelsberger, *Auschwitz: A Doctor's Story* (Boston: Northeastern University Press, 1995), 85; Arthur Allen, *The Fantastic Laboratory of Dr Weigl: How Two Brave Scientists Battled Typhus and Sabotaged the Nazis* (New York: W W Norton and Co, 2014), 229.

[205] Azriel Eisenberg, *The Lost Generation: Children in the Holocaust* (New York: The Pilgrim Press, 1982), 138-9.

[206] Ibid.

[207] Alan Pakula, "Sophie's Choice," (USA: Universal Pictures, 1982).

[208] Yehudit Inbar, *Spots of Light: To Be a Woman in the Holocaust* (Jerusalem: Yad Vashem, 2007), 26.

[209] Dwork, *Children with a Star: Jewish Youth in Nazi Europe*, xviii-xix; Alexander Donat, *The Holocaust Kingdom: A Memoir* (New York: Holt, Rinehart and Winston, 1965), 91.

[210] Anonymous (Ursula*), "Testimony," (Israel: Ghetto Fighters House).

[211] Ritvo and Plotkin, *Sisters in Sorrow: Voices of Care in the Holocaust*, 45.

[212] Rita Gabis, *A Guest at the Shooter's Banquet: My Grandfather's SS Past, My Jewish Family, a Search for the Truth* (New York: Bloomsbury, 2015), 385.

[213] United States Holocaust Memorial Museum, "The Holocaust Encyclopedia," encyclopedia.ushmm.org/content/en/article/ravensbrueck..

[214] Rochelle G. Saidel, *The Jewish Women of Ravensbrück Concentration Camp* (Madison, Wisconsin: The University of Wisconsin Press, 2004), 78.

[215] Mailander, *Female SS Guards and Workaday Violence: The Majdanek Concentration Camp, 1942-1944*, 23.

[216] Tomi Reichental, *I Was a Boy in Belsen* (Dublin: The O'Brien Press, 2011); ibid.

[217] Thomas Buergenthal, *A Lucky Child: A Memoir of Surviving Auschwitz as a Young Boy* (New York: Basck Bay Books, 2007), 82.

[218] Ruth Elias, *Triumph of Hope: From Theresienstadt and Auschwitz to Israel*, trans. Margot Bettauer Dembo (New York: John Wiley and Sons, 1988), 115.

[219] Bill Niven, *The Buchenwald Child: Truth, Fiction and Propaganda* (New York: Camden House 2007), 20.

[220] Roberto Benigni, "Life Is Beautiful " (Italy: Miramax Films, 1997).

[221] Glass, *Life Unworthy of Life: Racial Phobia and Mass Murder in Hitler's Germany*, 173-4.

[222] Saidel, *The Jewish Women of Ravensbrück Concentration Camp*, 78.

223 Gunther Schwarberg, *The Murders at Bullenhuser Damm* (Bloomington, USA: Indiana University Press, 1984), 15.

224 Lila Perl and Marion Blumenthal Lazan, *Four Perfect Pebbles: A Holocaust Story* (New York: Scholastic Inc, 1996).

225 Crum, *Behind the Silken Curtain: A Personal Account of Anglo-American Diplomacy in Palestine and the Middle East*, 125.

226 Hannah Lévy-Haas, *Inside Belsen* (Sussex, UK: Harvester Press, 1982), 54-5.

227 Rena Kornreich Gelissen, *Rena's Promise: A Story of Two Sisters in Auschwitz* (London: Weidenfeld and Nicolson, 1996), 134-5.

228 Glass, *Life Unworthy of Life: Racial Phobia and Mass Murder in Hitler's Germany*, 123.

229 Anonymous, "The Story of the Children of Bullenhuser Damm," http://www.kinder-vom-bullenhuser-damm.de/_english/the_story.html

230 Daniel Jonah Goldhagen, *Hitler's Willing Executioners: Ordinary Germans and the Holocaust* (New York: Vintage Books, 1997), 308-9.

231 Mark Kurzem, *The Mascot: The Extraordinary Story of a Jewish Boy and an SS Extermination Squad* (London: Rider, 2007).

232 Eisenberg, *The Lost Generation: Children in the Holocaust*, 147.

233 Goldhagen, *Hitler's Willing Executioners: Ordinary Germans and the Holocaust*, 309.

234 Eichengreen, *Haunted Memories: Portraits of Women in the Holocaust*, 142.

235 Lucille Eichengreen and Harriet Hyman Chamberlain, *From Ashes to Life: My Memories of the Holocaust* (San Fransisco: Mercury House, 1994), 189.

236 Ibid.

237 Elaine Kalman Naves, *Shoshanna's Story: A Mother, a Daughter, and the Shadows of History* (Toronto: McClelland & Stewart, 2003), 73.

238 Ruvugiro, "Rwanda: The Gruesome Plight of Children During the Tutsi Genocide.".

239 Flaschka, "Race, Rape and Gender in Nazi-Occupied Territories," 178.

240 Ritvo and Plotkin, *Sisters in Sorrow: Voices of Care in the Holocaust*, 197.

241 Pnina Granirer, *Light within the Shadows: A Painter's Memoir* (Vancouver, Canada: Granville Island Publishing, 2017), 57.

242 Naves, *Shoshanna's Story: A Mother, a Daughter, and the Shadows of History*, 42.

243 Ibid., 46.

244 Behr, *Almost a Childhood: Growing up among the Nazis*, 39-40.

245 Granirer, *Light within the Shadows: A Painter's Memoir*, 57.

246 Anonymous (Erika*), "Testimony," (USA: Shoah Foundation Visual History Archive, 1997).

247 Ibid.

[248] Roland, *Life in the Third Reich: Daily Life in Nazi Germany 1933-1945*, 49-50.

[249] Ibid.

[250] Dwork, *Children with a Star: Jewish Youth in Nazi Europe*, 166.

[251] Nate Leipciger, *The Weight of Freedom* (Canada: Azrieli Foundation, 2015), 34-5.

[252] Bauman, *Winter in the Morning: A Young Girl's Life in the Warsaw Ghetto and Beyond.*, 60-1.

[253] Ibid., 63-4.

[254] Esther Katz and Joan Miriam Ringelheim, eds., *Proceedings of the Conference Women Surviving the Holocaust*, Occasional Papers (The Institute for Research in History, 1983), 38.

[255] Anonymous (Freda*), "Testimony," (USA: Shoah Foundation Visual History Archive, 1995).

[256] Berg, *The Diary of Mary Berg*, 13.

[257] Adelson and Lapides, *Lódź Ghetto: Inside a Community under Siege*, 135-6.

[258] Sala Pawlowicz, *I Will Survive* (New York: W W Norton and Company, Inc, 1962), 41.

[259] Chalmers, *Birth, Sex and Abuse: Women's Voices under Nazi Rule*.

[260] Pawlowicz, *I Will Survive*, 42.

[261] Ibid., 40-1.

[262] Mailander, *Female SS Guards and Workaday Violence: The Majdanek Concentration Camp, 1942-1944*, 264-5.

[263] Dana Lori Chalmers, "The Influence of Theatre and Paratheatre on the Holocaust" (Masters Thesis, Concordia University, 2008), 37.

[264] Boas, *We Are Witnesses: Five Diaries of Teenagers Who Died in the Holocaust*, 12-3.

[265] Stein, *Hidden Children: Forgotten Survivors of the Holocaust*, 39.

[266] (Two Sisters*) Anonymous, "Testimony," (Israel: Ghetto Fighters House Archive).

[267] Anonymous (Rita*), "Testimony," (Israel: Ghetto Figher's House Archive).

[268] Anonymous (Noam*), "Testimony," (Israel: Ghetto Fighters House Archive).

[269] Lev-Wiesel and Weinger, *Hell within Hell: Sexually Abused Child Holocaust Survivors*, 69-72.

[270] Ibid., 70.

[271] Ibid., 71.

[272] Ibid., 72.

[273] Liza Silbert, "Testimony," (USA: USC Shoah Foundation Institute for Visual History and Education).

[274] Marion Loew, "Testimony," (USA: USC Shoah Foundation Institute for Visual History and Education).

[275] Stargardt, *Witnesses of War: Children's Lives under the Nazis.*, 217.

[276] Ibid., 226.

[277] Ibid.

[278] Avigdor Shachan, *Burning Ice: The Ghettos of Transnistria*, East European Monographs, Boulder (New York: Columbia Unversity Press, 1996), 326.

[279] Ann Kirschner, *Sala's Gift: My Mother's Holocaust Story* (New York: Free Press, 2006), 146.

[280] Chalmers, *Birth, Sex and Abuse: Women's Voices under Nazi Rule.*

[281] Gelissen, *Rena's Promise: A Story of Two Sisters in Auschwitz*, 139.

[282] Ibid., 140.

[283] Eva Grinston, "Testimony," (USA: USC Shoah Foundation Institute for Visual History and Education Online Archive).

[284] Maria Scheffer, "Testimony," (USA: USC Shoah Foundation Institute for Visual History and Education On-Line Archive).

[285] Shari Braun, "Testimony," (USC Shoah Foundation Institute for Visual History and Education Online Archive.).

[286] Lev-Wiesel and Weinger, *Hell within Hell: Sexually Abused Child Holocaust Survivors*, 29-30.

[287] Lily Wolf, "Testimony," (USA: USC Shoah Foundation Institute for Visual History and Education Online Archive).

[288] G Erika, "Testimony," (Los Angeles: Survivors of the Shoah Visual History Foundation, 14 February 1997).

[289] George Reinitz and Richard King, *Wrestling with Life: From Hungary to Auschwitz to Montreal* (Montreal: McGill-Queen's University Press, 2017), 49.

[290] Mailander, *Female SS Guards and Workaday Violence: The Majdanek Concentration Camp, 1942-1944*, 264-5.

[291] Ibid.

[292] Ibid., 203.

[293] Yehuda Koren and Eilat Negev, *In Our Hearts We Were Giants: The Remarkable Story of the Lilliput Group - a Dwarf Family's Survival of the Holocaust* (New York: Carroll and Graf Publishers, 2004), 162.

[294] Ibid., 162-3.

[295] Gedaliah Shaik, "Biography: Abraham Cykiert (1926-2009)," Melbourne Chronicle, http://future.arts.monash.edu/yiddish-melbourne/biogrpahies-abraham-cykiert/.

[296] Chalmers, *Birth, Sex and Abuse: Women's Voices under Nazi Rule*, 210-32.

[297] Anonymous (Anna*), "Testimony " (USA: Shoah Foundation Visual History Archives 1997).

[298] Ibid.

[299] Ibid.

[300] Daniel Asa Rose, *Hiding Places* (New York: Simon and Schuster, 2000), 320-2.

[301] Bikont, *The Crime and the Silence: Confronting the Massacre of Jews in Wartime Jedwabne*, 456.

[302] Inbar, *Spots of Light: To Be a Woman in the Holocaust*, 77.

[303] Jacob Apenszlak, ed. *The Black Book of Polish Jewry: An Account of the Martyrdom of Polish Jewry* (New York: Roy Publishers, 1943), 29.

[304] Ibid., 9; Helene J Sinnreich, "The Rape of Jewish Women During the Holocaust," in *Sexual Violence against Jewish Women During the Holocaust*, ed. Sonja M Hedgepeth and Rochelle G Saidel (Waltham, Massachusetts: Brandeis University Press, 2010), 110.

[305] Hogan and Aretha, *The Holocaust Chronicle*, 95.

[306] Anonymous (Vivi*), "Testimony," (Israel: Ghetto Fighters House Archives, 1948 10 October).

[307] Hanna Krall, *Chasing the King of Hearts* (London: Peirene Press, 2013), 32-3.

[308] Joan Ringelheim, "Women and the Holocaust: A Reconsideration of Research.," in *Different Voices: Women and the Holocaust*, ed. Carol Rittner and John K Roth (New York: 1993), 377.

[309] Jonathan Friedman, *Speaking the Unspeakable: Essays on Sexuality, Gender, and Holocaust Survivor Memory* (Lanham: University Press of America, 2002), 53.

[310] Herzberg Sia (nee Izrailewitsch), "Testimony," (USA: USC Shoah Foundation Institute for Visual Histroy and Education On-Line Archive).

[311] Anonymous (Dalia*), "Testimony," (USA: Shoah Foundation Visual History Archive, 1996).

[312] Sinnreich, "The Rape of Jewish Women During the Holocaust," 112-4.

[313] Ibid.

[314] Bina W, "Testimony," (USC Shoah Foundation Institute for Visual History and Education Online Archive).

[315] David E Fishman, *The Book Smugglers* (USA: University Press of New England, 2017), 147.

[316] Aliza Barak- Ressler, *Cry Little Girl: A Tale of the Survival of a Family in Slovakia* (Jerusalem: Yad Vashem 2003), 189.

[317] Irene Binzer, "Testimony," (USA: USC Shoah Foundation Institute for Visual History and Education Online Archive).

[318] Sonia Palty, "Personal Testimony," Nizkor Project, www.nizkor.org/hweb/people/c/carmelly-felicia/palty-sonia.html.

[319] Ibid.

[320] Ibid.

[321] Ibid.

[322] Ibid.

[323] Chalmers, *Birth, Sex and Abuse: Women's Voices under Nazi Rule*, 223-6.

[324] Sinnreich, "The Rape of Jewish Women During the Holocaust," 113.

[325] Eliahu Rosenberg, "Testimony," (Israel: Ghetto Fighters House Archives).

[326] Anonymous (Tina*), "Testimony," (Israel: Ghetto Fighter's House Archives).

[327] Chalmers, *Birth, Sex and Abuse: Women's Voices under Nazi Rule*, 147-62.

[328] Reinitz and King, *Wrestling with Life: From Hungary to Auschwitz to Montreal*, 40.

[329] Desbois, *In Broad Daylight: The Secret Procedures Behind the Holocaust by Bullets*, 71.

[330] Ibid., 152-3.

[331] Ibid., 72.

[332] Ibid.

[333] Anatoly Podolsky, "The Tragic Fate of Ukrainian Jewish Women under Nazi Occupation, 1941-1944.," in *Sexual Violence against Jewish Women During the Holocaust*, ed. Sonja M Hedgepeth and Rochelle G Saidel (Waltham, Massachusetts: Brandeis University Press, 2010), 99.

[334] Anonymous (Carla*), "Testimony," (USA: Shoah Foundation Visual History Archive, 1998).

[335] Shachan, *Burning Ice: The Ghettos of Transnistria*, 58.

[336] Ibid., 60.

[337] Desbois, *The Holocaust by Bullets: A Priest's Journey to Uncover the Truth Behind the Murder of 1.5 Million Jews*, 83.

[338] Shachan, *Burning Ice: The Ghettos of Transnistria*, 54.

[339] Chalmers, *Birth, Sex and Abuse: Women's Voices under Nazi Rule*.

[340] Regina Mühlhäuser, "Between 'Racial Awareness' and Fantasies of Potencies: Nazi Sexual Politics in the Occupied Territories of the Soviet Union, 1942-1945," in *Brutality and Desire: War and Sexuality in Europe's Twentieth Century*, ed. Dagmar Herzog (Houndmills, Basingstoke, Hampshire: Pelgrave Macmillan, 2009), 199.

[341] Wendy Jo Gertjejanssen, "Victims, Heroes and Survivors: Sexual Violence on the Eastern Front During World War II" (University of Minnesota, 2004), 308.

[342] Nicholas, *Cruel World: The Children of Europe in the Nazi Web*, 430.

[343] B Beck, *Wehrmacht Und Sexuelle Gewalt: Sexualverbrechen Von Deutschen Militärgerichten 1939-1945* (Munich, Vienna and Zurich Paderborn, 2004), 234.

[344] Julian Eugeniusz Kulski, *Dying, We Live* (New York: Holt, Rinehart and Winston, 1979), 252.

[345] Stein, *Hidden Children: Forgotten Survivors of the Holocaust*, 241-2.

[346] Friedman, *Speaking the Unspeakable: Essays on Sexuality, Gender, and Holocaust Survivor Memory*, 59; Michael Nutkiewicz, "Shame, Guilt, and Anguish in Holocaust Survivor Testimony," *The Oral History Review* 30, no. 1 (2003): 1.

[347] "Shame, Guilt, and Anguish in Holocaust Survivor Testimony," 185-7; Friedman, *Speaking the Unspeakable: Essays on Sexuality, Gender, and Holocaust Survivor Memory*, 59.

348 US Government, "From Nazi Conspiracy and Aggression Volume VI," ed. Office of United States Chief counsel for Prosecution of Axis Criminality (USA: US Government Printing Office, 1946).

349 Ibid.

350 Anonymous (Leon*), "Testimony," (Israel: Beit Volim, Yad Vashem).

351 Julian Reuter, "Testimony," (USA: USC Shoah Foundation Institute for Visual History and Education).

352 Niven, *The Buchenwald Child: Truth, Fiction and Propaganda*, 19.

353 Ibid.

354 Eisenberg, *The Lost Generation: Children in the Holocaust*, 147.

355 Leipciger, *The Weight of Freedom*, 91-3.

356 Ibid., 100.

357 Ibid., 102.

358 Lyn Smith, *Remembering: Voices of the Holocaust* (New York: Carroll and Graf Publishers, 2005), 178.

359 Albert Haas, *The Doctor and the Damned* (New York: St Martin's Press, 1984), 97.

360 Ibid.

361 Heinz Heger, *The Men with the Pink Triangle* (New York: Alyson Books, 1980), 59.

362 Ibid.

363 Ibid., 44.

364 Anonymous (Frans*), "Testimony," (Israel: Beit Volim, Yad Vashem).

365 Anonymous (Gunter*), "Testimony," (Israel: Beit Volim, Yad Vashem).

366 Anonymous (Harry*), "Testimony," (Israel: Ghetto Fighters House Archives, 1948).

367 Branko Lustig, "Testimony," (USA: USC Shoah Foundation Institute for Visual History and Education Online Archive).

368 Kenneth Rowan, "Testimony," (USA: USC Shoah Foundation Institute for Visual History and Education Online Archive).

369 Sam Steinberg, "Testimony," (USA: USC Shoah Foundation Institute for Visual History and Education Online Archive).

370 Johannes-Dieter Steinert, *Holocaust Und Zwangsarbeit: Erinnnerungen Jüdische Kinder 1938-1945* (Essen: Klartext, 2018), 331-38.

371 Ibid., 335.

372 Wendy Holden, *Born Survivors* (London: Sphere, 2015), 340.

373 Steinert, *Holocaust Und Zwangsarbeit: Erinnnerungen Jüdische Kinder 1938-1945*, 336-7.

374 Wiesel, *Night*, 63-5.

375 Ka-Tzetnik, *Shivitti: A Vision*, 85.

376 *House of Dolls*.

377 *Piepel*.

378 Sivan, "Stoning the Messenger: Yehiel Dinur's House of Dolls and Piepel," 202.

242

379 Ibid., 203.
380 Ka-Tzetnik, *Atrocity*.
381 Ibid., 39.
382 Ibid., 115.
383 Wiesel, Night, 63-5; Smith, Remembering: Voices of the Holocaust, 178; Niven, The Buchenwald Child: Truth, Fiction and Propaganda, 19; Haas, The Doctor and the Damned, 97; Eisenberg, The Lost Generation: Children in the Holocaust, 147.
384 Wiesel, *Night*, 63-5.
385 Heger, *The Men with the Pink Triangle*, 59.
386 Chalmers, *Birth, Sex and Abuse: Women's Voices under Nazi Rule*, 208.
387 Boas, *We Are Witnesses: Five Diaries of Teenagers Who Died in the Holocaust*, 14; Sinnreich, "The Rape of Jewish Women During the Holocaust," 112-4.
388 Gabis, *A Guest at the Shooter's Banquet: My Grandfather's SS Past, My Jewish Family, a Search for the Truth*, 277.
389 Lucille Eichengreen and Rebecca Camhi Fromer, *Rumkowski and the Orphans of Lodz* (San Fransisco, : Mercury-House, 2000), 16-7, 31-5, 41-3, 58, 80-3.
390 Ibid., 14.
391 Ibid., 43.
392 Ibid., 31-35.
393 Ibid., 17.
394 Ibid., 43.
395 Ibid.
396 Ibid., 80-1.
397 Caroline Pukall, ed. *Human Sexuality: A Contemporary Introduction*, 2nd ed. (Don Mills, Ontario: Oxford University Press, 2017), 371-2.
398 Heifetz, *Too Young to Remember*, 83-4.
399 Ibid.
400 Ibid., 84.
401 Anonymous (Hannah*), "Testimony," (USA: Shoah Foundation Visual History Archive, 1998).
402 Ibid.
403 Lev-Wiesel and Weinger, *Hell within Hell: Sexually Abused Child Holocaust Survivors*, 69-72.
404 R. Lev-Wiesel and M. Amir, "Holocaust Child Survivors and Child Sexual Abuse," *Journal of Sexual Abuse* 14, no. 2 (2005): 69-83.
405 Chalmers, *Birth, Sex and Abuse: Women's Voices under Nazi Rule*, 121-4.
406 Baumslag, *Murderous Medicine*, 158.
407 Paul Weindling, *Victims and Survivors of Nazi Human Experiments: Science and Suffering in the Holocaust* (London: Bloomsbury Academic, 2015), 10-11.
408 Ibid., 11.

[409] Ibid.
[410] Ibid., 194.
[411] Ibid., 195.
[412] Ibid., 196.
[413] Ibid., 18-9; Tessa Chelouche, Geoffrey Brahmer, and Susan Benedict, *Casebook on Bioethics and the Holocaust* (Israel: Unesco Chair in Bioethics, 2013), 162.
[414] Weindling, *Victims and Survivors of Nazi Human Experiments: Science and Suffering in the Holocaust*, 29-30.
[415] Ibid.
[416] Chalmers, *Birth, Sex and Abuse: Women's Voices under Nazi Rule*, 29.
[417] Ibid., 33.
[418] Ibid., 36.
[419] Weindling, *Victims and Survivors of Nazi Human Experiments: Science and Suffering in the Holocaust*, 36-7.
[420] Ibid., 113.
[421] Ibid., 37.
[422] Ibid., 39.
[423] Ibid., 41.
[424] Ibid., 53.
[425] Ibid.
[426] Ibid., 113.
[427] Ibid., 114.
[428] Ibid., 113.
[429] Ibid., 116.
[430] Ibid., 128.
[431] Ibid., 159-60.
[432] Edwin Black, *Nazi Nexus: America's Corporate Connections to Hitler's Holocaust* (Washington D C: Dialog Press, 2009), 79.
[433] Richard J Evans, *The Third Reich at War* (New York: The Penguin Press, 2009), 609.
[434] Black, *Nazi Nexus: America's Corporate Connections to Hitler's Holocaust*, 83; Evans, *The Third Reich at War*, 611; Gerald L Posner and John Ware, *Mengele: The Complete Story* (New York: Cooper Square Press, 2000), 34.
[435] Evans, *The Third Reich at War*, 610.
[436] Efraim Reichenberg, "A Twin in Auschwitz," in *Yad Vashem International Holocaust Educators Seminar* (Jerusalem2009).
[437] Ibid.
[438] Ibid.
[439] Black, *Nazi Nexus: America's Corporate Connections to Hitler's Holocaust*, 79; Chalmers, *Birth, Sex and Abuse: Women's Voices under Nazi Rule*, 134.

440 Posner and Ware, *Mengele: The Complete Story*, 37.

441 Robert Jay Lifton, *The Nazi Doctors: Medical Killing and the Psychology of Genocide* (New York: Basic Books, Inc, 1986), 347-51.

442 Lucette Matalon Lagnado and Sheila Cohn Dekel, *Children of the Flames: Dr Josef Mengele and the Untold Story of the Twins of Auschwitz* (New York: William Morrow and Company, Inc, 1991), 70.

443 Eva Mozes Kor, *Echoes from Auschwitz: Dr Mengele's Twins: The Story of Eva and Miriam Mozes* (New York: CANDLES, 2002), 106-7.

444 Posner and Ware, *Mengele: The Complete Story*, 37.

445 Lifton, *The Nazi Doctors: Medical Killing and the Psychology of Genocide*, 357-9.

446 Lagnado and Dekel, *Children of the Flames: Dr Josef Mengele and the Untold Story of the Twins of Auschwitz*, 71.

447 Koren and Negev, *In Our Hearts We Were Giants: The Remarkable Story of the Lilliput Group - a Dwarf Family's Survival of the Holocaust*, 171-2.

448 Lagnado and Dekel, *Children of the Flames: Dr Josef Mengele and the Untold Story of the Twins of Auschwitz*, 71.

449 Koren and Negev, *In Our Hearts We Were Giants: The Remarkable Story of the Lilliput Group - a Dwarf Family's Survival of the Holocaust*, 171-2.

450 Ibid.

451 Lagnado and Dekel, *Children of the Flames: Dr Josef Mengele and the Untold Story of the Twins of Auschwitz*, 71.

452 Olga Lengyel, *Five Chimneys: A Woman Survivor's True Story of Auschwitz*, First Academy Chicago edition, 1995 ed. (Chicago: Ziff-Davis Publishing Company, 1947), 116.

453 Lifton, *The Nazi Doctors: Medical Killing and the Psychology of Genocide*, 372.

454 Koren and Negev, *In Our Hearts We Were Giants: The Remarkable Story of the Lilliput Group - a Dwarf Family's Survival of the Holocaust*, 171.

455 Ibid.

456 Ibid., 142.

457 Ibid., 136.

458 Ibid., 142.

459 Ibid., 140.

460 Ibid.

461 Sara Nomberg-Przytyk, *Auschwitz: True Tales from a Grotesque Land* (Chapel Hill: University of North Carolina Press, 1985), 90-1.

462 Ibid., 90-1, 170.

463 Lev-Wiesel and Weinger, *Hell within Hell: Sexually Abused Child Holocaust Survivors*, 22.

464 Ibid., 55.

465 Ibid.

466 Ibid., 53-57.

467 Anonymous (Isaac*), "Testimony," (Israel: Ghetto Fighters House Archives).

468 Allen, *The Fantastic Laboratory of Dr Weigl: How Two Brave Scientists Battled Typhus and Sabotaged the Nazis*, 201.

469 Baumslag, *Murderous Medicine*, 141. Allen, *The Fantastic Laboratory of Dr Weigl: How Two Brave Scientists Battled Typhus and Sabotaged the Nazis*, 209.

470 Weindling, *Victims and Survivors of Nazi Human Experiments: Science and Suffering in the Holocaust*, 62.

471 Baumslag, *Murderous Medicine*, 140-1.

472 Ibid., 159.

473 Anonymous, "Buchenwald Concentration Camp Atrocities "www. scrapbookpages.com/Buchenwald/Atrocities.html.

474 Baumslag, *Murderous Medicine*, 147; Eugen Kogon, *The Theory and Practice of Hell: The German Concentration Camps and the System Behind Them*, trans. Heinz Norden (New York: Berkeley Books, 1950), 149.

475 Baumslag, *Murderous Medicine*, 147; Kogon, *The Theory and Practice of Hell: The German Concentration Camps and the System Behind Them*.

476 Allen, *The Fantastic Laboratory of Dr Weigl: How Two Brave Scientists Battled Typhus and Sabotaged the Nazis*, 246.

477 Anonymous (Kai*), "Testimony," (Israel: Ghetto Fighter's House Archives).

478 Ibid.

479 Lengyel, *Five Chimneys: A Woman Survivor's True Story of Auschwitz*, 190.

480 John Cornwell, *Hitler's Scientists: Science, War and the Devil's Pact* (New York: Viking, 2003), 358.

481 Haas, *The Doctor and the Damned*; Brian Moser, "The Search for Mengele," (USA: First Run Features, 1985); Posner and Ware, *Mengele: The Complete Story*.

482 Perl, *I Was a Doctor in Auschwitz*; Joseph Sargent, "Out of the Ashes," (USA: Showtime Netwoks, 2004).

483 Shachan, *Burning Ice: The Ghettos of Transnistria*, 62.

484 Chalmers, *Birth, Sex and Abuse: Women's Voices under Nazi Rule*, 129.

485 Vivien Spitz, *Doctors from Hell: The Horrific Accounts of Nazi Experiments on Humans* (Boulder: Sentient Publications, 2005), 266.

486 Bruno Bettelheim, *Surviving the Holocaust* (London: Fontana Paperbacks, 1986), 131-2.

487 Stein, *Hidden Children: Forgotten Survivors of the Holocaust*, 268.

488 Lola Rein Kaufman, *The Hidden Girl: A True Story of the Holocaust* (New York: Scholastic Inc, 2008), 85; Maxine B Rosenberg, *Hiding to Survive:*

Stories of Jewish Children Rescued from the Holocaust (New York: Clarion Books, 1994), 5.

489 Kaufman, *The Hidden Girl: A True Story of the Holocaust*, 85.

490 Ibid.

491 Dwork, *Children with a Star: Jewish Youth in Nazi Europe*, 80.

492 Rosen, *Such Good Girls: The Journey of the Holocaust's Hidden Child Survivors*, 92.

493 Esther Hertzog, *Life, Death and Sacrifice: Women and Family in the Holocaust* (Jerusalem: Gefen Publishing House, 2008), 58.

494 Vromen, *Hidden Children of the Holocaust: Belgian Nuns and Their Daring Rescue of Young Jews from the Nazis*, 95.

495 Abrams and Blaikie, *Remember Us: A Collection of Memories Form Hungarian Hidden Children of the Holocaust*, 259.

496 Rosenberg, *Hiding to Survive: Stories of Jewish Children Rescued from the Holocaust.*

497 Janet Tobias, "No Place on Earth," (Magnolia Pictures, 2012).

498 Witold Medykowski, "Modes of Survival, Techniques of Hiding and Relations with the Local Population: The Polish Case," in *Hiding, Sheltering, and Borrowing Identities: Avenues of Rescue During the Holocaust*, ed. Dan Michman (Jerusalem: Yad Vashem, 2017), 45-56.

499 Kaufman, *The Hidden Girl: A True Story of the Holocaust*, 47.

500 Ibid., 91.

501 Ibid.

502 Kathy Kacer, *Hiding Edith: A True Story* (London: A & C Black, 2009), 7.

503 Walter Buchignani, *Tell No One Who You Are: The Hidden Childhood of Regine Miller* (Ontario, Canada: Tundra Books, 1994), 178.

504 United States Holocaust Memorial Museum, "Le Chambon-Sur-Lignon," USHMM, encyclopedia.ushmm.org/content/en/article/le-chambon-sur-lignon.

505 Yad Vashem, "Rescue of Children," Yad Vashem, www.yadvashem.org/odot_pdf/Microsoft%20Word%20-%205820.pdf

506 Reinitz and King, *Wrestling with Life: From Hungary to Auschwitz to Montreal*, 32-3.

507 Rosenberg, *Hiding to Survive: Stories of Jewish Children Rescued from the Holocaust*, 5-6.

508 Rosen, *Such Good Girls: The Journey of the Holocaust's Hidden Child Survivors*, 228; Erica Terry, "Sexual Abuse and the Hidden Children of the Holocaust," www.jspacenews.com/sexual-abuse-hidden-children-holocaust.

509 Paul Valent, "Early Abuse and Its Effects: Anne, a Holocaust and Sexual Abuse Survivor," in *Victoria Association of Psychotherapists Annual General Meeting* (Melbourne, Australia1995), 2.

[510] Rosen, *Such Good Girls: The Journey of the Holocaust's Hidden Child Survivors*, 226.

[511] Lev-Wiesel and Amir, "Holocaust Child Survivors and Child Sexual Abuse," 69-83.

[512] Holliday, *Children's Wartime Diaries: Secret Writings from the Holocaust and World War II*, 99-125.

[513] Ibid., 112.

[514] Ibid., 122.

[515] Ibid., 125.

[516] Diane Wolf, *Beyond Anne Frank: Hidden Children and Postwar Families in Holland* (Berkeley, California: University of California Press, 2007), 126-62.

[517] Anonymous (Boris*), "Testimony," (USA: Shoah Foundation Visual History Archive, 1998).

[518] Ibid.

[519] Ibid.

[520] Ibid.

[521] Stein, *Hidden Children: Forgotten Survivors of the Holocaust*, 26.

[522] Ibid., 33.

[523] Sabina Wagschal, (USC Shoah Foundation Institute for Visual History and Education Online Archive).

[524] Deborah Dwork and Robert Jan van Pelt, *Holocaust:A History* (New York: W.W. Norton and Company, 2003), 350.

[525] Lev-Wiesel and Weinger, *Hell within Hell: Sexually Abused Child Holocaust Survivors*, 45-6.

[526] Ibid.

[527] Ibid., 47.

[528] Ibid.

[529] Ibid., 41-7.

[530] Buchignani, *Tell No One Who You Are: The Hidden Childhood of Regine Miller*, 90.

[531] Lucy Lipiner, *Long Journey Home: A Young Girl's Memoir of Surviving the Holocaust* (New York: Usher Publishing, 2013), 102-3.

[532] Ibid.

[533] Ibid.

[534] Joan Ringelheim, "The Split between Gender and the Holocaust," in *Women and the Holocaust*, ed. Dalia Ofer and Lenore Weitzman (New Haven: Yale University Press, 1998), 342.

[535] van Es Bart, *The Cut out Girl* (USA: Penguin Books, 2019), 187-88, 95.

[536] Ibid., 187, 95.

[537] Ibid., 237.

[538] Lev-Wiesel and Weinger, *Hell within Hell: Sexually Abused Child Holocaust Survivors*, 33-9.

539 Paul Valent, *Child Survivors of the Holocaust* (New York and London: Bruner-Routledge, 2002), 253-4.
540 Ibid., 254-5.
541 Ibid., 256.
542 Ibid., 259.
543 Ibid., 260.
544 Rosen, *Such Good Girls: The Journey of the Holocaust's Hidden Child Survivors*, 228-9; Valent, "Early Abuse and Its Effects: Anne, a Holocaust and Sexual Abuse Survivor," 8; *Child Survivors of the Holocaust*, 256.
545 Calcasa, "Pedophiles and Child Molesters: The Differences," www.calcasa.org/wp-content/uploads/2007/11/pedophiles-and-child-molesters.doc.
546 Valent, *Child Survivors of the Holocaust*, 260.
547 "Early Abuse and Its Effects: Anne, a Holocaust and Sexual Abuse Survivor," 8; *Child Survivors of the Holocaust*, 260-1.
548 *Child Survivors of the Holocaust*, 264.
549 Dwork, *Children with a Star: Jewish Youth in Nazi Europe*, 80.
550 Marks, *The Hidden Children: The Secret Survivors of the Holocaust*, 219.
551 Lily Redner, "Testimony," (USA: USC Shoah Foundation Institute for Visual History and Education Online Archive).
552 Dwork, *Children with a Star: Jewish Youth in Nazi Europe*, 80.
553 Redner, "Testimony."
554 Lev-Wiesel and Amir, "Holocaust Child Survivors and Child Sexual Abuse," 69-83.
555 Carla Lessing, "Aging Child Holocaust Survivors of Sexual Abuse," in *Selfhelp Conference* (New York2012).
556 Bauman, *Winter in the Morning: A Young Girl's Life in the Warsaw Ghetto and Beyond.*, 128.
557 "Broken Silence," ed. James Moll (USA: Survivors of the Shoah Visual History Foundation, 2004).
558 Stein, *Hidden Children: Forgotten Survivors of the Holocaust*, 38.
559 Marks, *The Hidden Children: The Secret Survivors of the Holocaust*, 46.
560 Valent, *Child Survivors of the Holocaust*.106
561 Marks, *The Hidden Children: The Secret Survivors of the Holocaust*, 54.
562 Bauman, *Winter in the Morning: A Young Girl's Life in the Warsaw Ghetto and Beyond.*, 106-7.
563 Krall, *Chasing the King of Hearts*, 40.
564 Anonymous (Mona*), "Testimony," (Israel Beit Volim, Yad Vashem).
565 Sewek Okonowski, "Appointment in Samarra: The Diary of a Jew in Hiding in Warsaw," (Israel: Ghetto Fighter's House Archive, 2017).
566 Sara Avinum, *Rising from the Abyss* (Israel: Astrolog Publishing, 2005), 92-3.
567 Anonymous (Lula*), "Testimony," (Israel: Beit Volim, Yad Vashem).

568 Anonymous (Julia*), "Testimony," (USA: Shoah Foundation Visual History Archive, 1997).

569 Anonymous (Carl*), "Testimony," (USA: Shoah Foundation Visual History Archive, 1995).

570 Anonymous (Petra*), "Testimony," (Israel: Beit Volim, Yad Vashem).

571 Anonymous (Nona*), "Testimony," (Israel: Beit Volim, Yad Vashem).

572 Lev-Wiesel and Weinger, *Hell within Hell: Sexually Abused Child Holocaust Survivors*, 60.

573 Ibid., 61.

574 Ibid., 62-3.

575 Ibid., 63-4.

576 Ibid., 59-67.

577 Molly Applebaum, *Buried Words: The Diary of Molly Applebaum* (Canada: The Azrieli Foundation, 2017), xxv.

578 Ibid., xxvi-xxvii.

579 Ibid., 69.

580 Ibid., 21.

581 Ibid., 22.

582 Ibid.

583 Ibid., 23.

584 Ibid., 25.

585 Ibid., 25-7.

586 Ibid., 29-30.

587 Ibid., 30-1.

588 Ibid., xvi.

589 Ibid., xxix.

590 Ibid., xxviii.

591 Brigitte Medvin, "Testimony," (USA: USC Shoah Foundation Institute for Visual History and Education Online Archive).

592 Hanna Mishna, "Testimony," (USA: USC Shoah Foundation Institute for Visual History and Education Online Archive).

593 Ibid.

594 Irene Kempfner, "Testimony," (USA: USC Shoah Foundation Institute for Visual History and Education Online Archive).

595 Judy Abrams, *Tenuous Threads* (Canada: Azrieli Foundation 2012), 51.

596 Ibid., 52.

597 Ibid., 50-53.

598 Anonymous (Dovid*), "Testimony," (USA: Shoah Foundation Visual History Archive, 1997).

599 Crum, *Behind the Silken Curtain: A Personal Account of Anglo-American Diplomacy in Palestine and the Middle East*, 130.

600 Ibid., 131.

601 Ibid.

602 Robert Hilliard, *Surviving the Americans: The Continued Struggle of the Jews after Liberation* (New York: Seven Storied Press., 1997), 114-5.

603 Anonymous (Eric*), "Testimony," (USA: Shoah Foundation Visual History Archive, 1995).

604 Anonymous (Katrina*), "Testimony," (USA: Shoah Foundation Visual History Archive, 1998).

605 Hilliard, *Surviving the Americans: The Continued Struggle of the Jews after Liberation*, 3.

606 Norton, *The Kindertransport: Contesting Memory*, 64.

607 Ibid., 317-24.

608 Hogan and Aretha, *The Holocaust Chronicle*, 131.

609 Bob Moore, "The Structure of Rescue: Key Determinants in the Survival of Jews in Western Europe During the Holocaust," in *Hiding, Sheltering, and Borrowing Identities: Avenues of Rescue During the Holocaust*, ed. Dan Michman (Jerusalem: Yad Vashem, 2017), 27-43.

610 Yad Vashem, "Rescue of Children".

611 Crum, *Behind the Silken Curtain: A Personal Account of Anglo-American Diplomacy in Palestine and the Middle East*, 110.

612 Hogan and Aretha, *The Holocaust Chronicle*, 147.

613 Ibid., 157; Bettelheim, *Surviving the Holocaust*, 198.

614 Hogan and Aretha, *The Holocaust Chronicle*, 158.

615 Ibid.

616 Ibid., 178.

617 Irving Abella and Harold Troper, *None Is Too Many: Canada and the Jews of Europe 1933-1948* (Toronto: Key Porter Books 1983); Hogan and Aretha, *The Holocaust Chronicle*, 189.

618 Julie Summers, *When the Children Came Home: Stories of Wartime Evacuees* (London: Simon and Schuster, 2011), xi.

619 Ibid., 9.

620 Ibid., 31.

621 Ibid., 259.

622 Ibid., 248.

623 Ibid.

624 Ibid., 250.

625 Ibid., 263-4.

626 Ibid., 269.

627 Ibid., 274.

628 Ibid., 276.

629 Ibid., 276-79.

630 Ibid., 279.

631 Ibid., 266-7.

632 Ibid., 264-8.

633 Marks, *The Hidden Children: The Secret Survivors of the Holocaust*, 101; Rosen, *Such Good Girls: The Journey of the Holocaust's Hidden Child Survivors*, 140.

634 Eva Fogelman, "Sexual Abuse of Jewish Women During and after the Holocaust: A Psychological Perspective," in *Sexual Violence against Jewish Women During the Holocaust*, ed. Sonja M Hedgepeth and Rochelle G Saidel (Waltham, Massachusetts: Brandeis University Press, 2010), 271-2.

635 Stein, *Hidden Children: Forgotten Survivors of the Holocaust*, 188.

636 Ibid., 193.

637 Ibid., 196.

638 Ibid., 198.

639 Friedman, *Speaking the Unspeakable: Essays on Sexuality, Gender, and Holocaust Survivor Memory*, 63-4.

640 Anonymous (Stella*), "Testimony," (Israel: Beit Volim, Tel Aviv).

641 Mark Jonathan Harris and Deborah Oppenheimer, *Into the Arms of Strangers: Stories of the Kindertransport* (London: Bloomsbury Publishing, 2000), 210, 30; Norton, *The Kindertransport: Contesting Memory*, 104.

642 *The Kindertransport: Contesting Memory*, 321.

643 Jeremy Josephs and Susi Bechhöfer, *Rosa's Child: The True Story of One Woman's Quest for a Lost Mother and a Vanished Past* (London: I B Tauris Publishers, 1996), 43.

644 Ibid.

645 Ibid., 44.

646 Ibid., 49.

647 Ibid., 61.

648 Ibid., 66.

649 Ibid., 132.

650 Ibid., 139.

651 Ibid., 138-9.

652 Ibid., 144-5.

653 Irena Steinfeldt, "Rescuers-Rescued Relations - What Can and Cannot Be Found in the Files of the Righteous among Nations," in *Hiding, Sheltering, and Borrowing Identities: Avenues of Rescue During the Holocaust*, ed. Dan Michman (Jerusalem: Yad Vashem, 2017), 57-66.

654 Ibid., 57, note 2.

655 Rosenberg, *Hiding to Survive: Stories of Jewish Children Rescued from the Holocaust*, 7; "The Jewish Foundation for the Righteous ", https://jfr.org/rescuer-support-program/.

656 Miriam Gillis-Carlebach, *Each Child Is My Only One: Lotte Carlebach-Preuss, the Portrait of a Mother and Rabbi's Wife* (New York: Peter Lang, 2014), 160.

657 Noa Gidron, 9 May 2019 2019.

[658] Gelissen, *Rena's Promise: A Story of Two Sisters in Auschwitz*, 190.

[659] Jonathan Friedman, "Togetherness and Isolation: Holocaust Survivor Memories of Intimacy and Sexuality in the Ghettos," *The Oral History Review* 28, no. 1 (2001): 12.

[660] Nechama Tec, *Resilience and Courage: Women, Men and the Holocaust* (New Haven: Yale University Press, 2003), 311-3.

[661] Ibid., 311.

[662] Lev-Wiesel and Weinger, *Hell within Hell: Sexually Abused Child Holocaust Survivors*, 19.

[663] Lev-Wiesel and Amir, "Holocaust Child Survivors and Child Sexual Abuse," 78.

[664] Lessing, "Aging Child Holocaust Survivors of Sexual Abuse."

[665] Lev-Wiesel and Weinger, *Hell within Hell: Sexually Abused Child Holocaust Survivors*, 24.

[666] Ibid., 19-21.

[667] Ibid., 24-5.

[668] Ibid., 24.

[669] Shimon Cohen, 39 May 2017.

[670] Lev-Wiesel and Weinger, *Hell within Hell: Sexually Abused Child Holocaust Survivors*, 22.

[671] Lev-Wiesel and Amir, "Holocaust Child Survivors and Child Sexual Abuse," 69-83.

[672] Ibid., 78.

[673] Ibid., 49-52.

[674] Lev-Wiesel and Weinger, *Hell within Hell: Sexually Abused Child Holocaust Survivors*, 51.

[675] Ibid., 49-52.

[676] Lev-Wiesel and Amir, "Holocaust Child Survivors and Child Sexual Abuse," 78.

[677] Eisenberg, *The Lost Generation: Children in the Holocaust*, 292.

[678] Ibid.

[679] Stein, *Hidden Children: Forgotten Survivors of the Holocaust*, xi.

[680] Terry, "Sexual Abuse and the Hidden Children of the Holocaust".

[681] Steinfeldt, "Rescuers-Rescued Relations - What Can and Cannot Be Found in the Files of the Righteous among Nations," 65.

[682] Ibid.

[683] Anonymous (Irina*), "Testimony," (USA: Shoah Foundation Visual History Archive, 1998).

[684] Ibid.

[685] Adara Goldberg, *Holocaust Survivors in Canada: Exclusion, Inclusion, Transformation, 1947-1955* (Winnipeg: University of Manitoba, 2015), 237.

686 Heifetz, *Too Young to Remember*, 12,45; Marks, *The Hidden Children: The Secret Survivors of the Holocaust*, 302.

687 Stein, *Hidden Children: Forgotten Survivors of the Holocaust*, 182.

688 Sabina Heller, *Locked in the Darkness: Retrieving a Hidden Girl's Identity from the Holocaust* (New York, Jerusalem: Yad Vashem and the Holocaust Survivors' Memoirs Project, 2012), 163.

689 Marks, *The Hidden Children: The Secret Survivors of the Holocaust*, 146.

690 Holliday, *Children's Wartime Diaries: Secret Writings from the Holocaust and World War II*, 52.

691 Steinfeldt, "Rescuers-Rescued Relations - What Can and Cannot Be Found in the Files of the Righteous among Nations," 65; Reichental, *I Was a Boy in Belsen*, 198.

692 *I Was a Boy in Belsen*, 207.

693 Stein, *Hidden Children: Forgotten Survivors of the Holocaust*, 193; Chiger and Paisner, *The Girl in the Green Sweater*, 271; Kor, *Echoes from Auschwitz: Dr Mengele's Twins: The Story of Eva and Miriam Mozes*, xii; Mira Reym Binfold, "Diamonds in the Snow," (Brandeis University, USA: National Centre for Jewish Film, 1994).

694 Joseph Polak, *After the Holocaust the Bells Still Ring* (Jerusalem: Urim Publications, 2015), 12-3.

695 Ibid., 129.

696 Irene Gut Opdyke, *In My Hands: Memories of a Holocaust Rescuer* (New York: Dell Laurel Leaf, 1999), 261.

697 Mark Mazower, *Dark Continent: Europe's Twentieth Century* (New York: Vintage Books, 1998), 222.

698 Marks, *The Hidden Children: The Secret Survivors of the Holocaust*, 256.

699 Steinfeldt, "Rescuers-Rescued Relations - What Can and Cannot Be Found in the Files of the Righteous among Nations," 65.

700 Ibid.

701 United Nations, "Outcomes on Children," http://www.un.org/en/development/devagenda/children.shtml.

702 For example, in 1992, my then fifteen-year-old daughter was asked to speak at a conference on adolescent sexuality in St Petersburg, Russian Federation, which she willingly accepted to do. Ultimately, permission to do so was refused by the senior administration of WHO-Euro regardless of the Regional Advisor for Women's and Children's Health's wish and invitation. The more conservative members of WHO were unable to give credence to a 'real' adolescent's views on the subject.

703 Heberer, *Children During the Holocaust*, 129.

704 Bogner, *At the Mercy of Strangers: The Rescue of Jewish Children with Assumed Identities in Poland*, 223.

705 Wolf, *Beyond Anne Frank: Hidden Children and Postwar Families in Holland*, 4.

706 Ibid., 5.

707 Bogner, *At the Mercy of Strangers: The Rescue of Jewish Children with Assumed Identities in Poland,* 199, 261.

708 Ibid., 199.

709 Ibid., 262.

710 Ibid., 289.

711 Ibid., 268.

712 Avinum, *Rising from the Abyss,* 267.

713 Bogner, *At the Mercy of Strangers: The Rescue of Jewish Children with Assumed Identities in Poland,* 257-8.

714 Ibid., 262.

715 Ibid., 258.

716 Ibid., 279.

717 Ibid., 148.

718 Ibid., 285.

719 Ibid., 180.

720 Ibid.

721 Ibid.

722 Martin Sixsmith, *Philomena: A Mother, Her Son and a Fifty-Year Search* (London: Pan Books, 2010).

723 Norton, *The Kindertransport: Contesting Memory,* 246.

724 Bogner, *At the Mercy of Strangers: The Rescue of Jewish Children with Assumed Identities in Poland,* 178.

725 Ibid., 286.

726 Ibid., 278.

727 Ibid., 287.

728 Ibid., 163.

729 Ibid., 210-8.

730 Norton, *The Kindertransport: Contesting Memory,* 64,83.

731 Polak, *After the Holocaust the Bells Still Ring,* 102.

732 Bogner, *At the Mercy of Strangers: The Rescue of Jewish Children with Assumed Identities in Poland,* 223, 92.

733 Ibid., 293.

734 Sandra Rosenfeld, "The Difficulties Involved in the Rescue of Chlldren by Non-Jews - before and after Liberation," The International School for Holocaust Studies, Yad Vashem, www.yadvashem.org/yv/en/education/newsletter/33/difficulties_involved.asp; Bogner, *At the Mercy of Strangers: The Rescue of Jewish Children with Assumed Identities in Poland,* 293-4.

735 Rosenfeld, "The Difficulties Involved in the Rescue of Chlldren by Non-Jews - before and after Liberation" 9; Bogner, *At the Mercy of Strangers: The Rescue of Jewish Children with Assumed Identities in Poland,* 294.

736 *At the Mercy of Strangers: The Rescue of Jewish Children with Assumed Identities in Poland,* 298.

737 Norton, *The Kindertransport: Contesting Memory,* 317-24.

738 Ibid., 266.

739 Dana Solomon, Personal Communication, 1 December 2019.

740 Bogner, *At the Mercy of Strangers: The Rescue of Jewish Children with Assumed Identities in Poland*, 258, 337.

741 Steinfeldt, "Rescuers-Rescued Relations - What Can and Cannot Be Found in the Files of the Righteous among Nations," 64.

742 Rosen, *Such Good Girls: The Journey of the Holocaust's Hidden Child Survivors*, 204-5.

743 Yaakov Ariel, "Turning to Christianity: Hiding Jews and Conversions During the Holocaust," in *Hiding, Sheltering, and Borrowing Identities: Avenues of Rescue During the Holocaust*, ed. Dan Michman (Jerusalem: Yad Vashem, 2017), 331.

744 Rebecca Benhamon, "Jewish Children Hidden Twice over by the Church," Times of Israel, www.timesofisrael.com/jewish-children-hidden-twice-over-by-the-church.

745 Yael Hersonski, *A Film Unfinished* (Bell Films, 2010).

746 Hogan and Aretha, *The Holocaust Chronicle*.

747 Heberer, *Children During the Holocaust*; ibid.; ibid.; Israel Gutman, ed. *Encyclopedia of the Holocaust* (New York: Macmillan Publishing Company, 1990).

748 Valent, *Child Survivors of the Holocaust*; Lev-Wiesel and Weinger, *Hell within Hell: Sexually Abused Child Holocaust Survivors*.

749 Massuah Archivist, May 18 2017.

750 (Anna*), "Testimony ".

751 Gemma Del Duca, "The Vatican and the Shoah: Post-Holocaust Catholic Theology," in *International Seminar for Educators* (The International School for Holocaust Studies, Jerusalem, Israel: Yad Vashem, 2009).

752 Solomon.

753 Langer, *Holocaust Testimonies: The Ruins of Memory*, 36.

754 Desbois, *In Broad Daylight: The Secret Procedures Behind the Holocaust by Bullets*, 72.

755 Ibid.

756 Ibid., 73.

757 Ibid.

758 Ibid.

759 Ibid., 67, 73.

760 Ibid., 73.

761 Ibid.

762 BBC, "Larry Nassar Jailed for Another 40-125 Years.," BBC, www.bbc.com/news/world-us-canada-42950478.

763 Quebec Ombudsman, "The "Children of Duplessis" a Time for Solidarity," in *Assemblee Nationale Quebec* (QuebecJanauary 22, 1997); Truth and Reconciliation Commission, *Honouring the Truth, Reconciling for the*

Future (Canada: Government of Canada, 2015); Government of Canada, "Report of Royal Commission on Aboriginal Peoples," (Ottawa, ON: Government of Canada, 2006); Peter McClelland et al., "Royal Commission into Institutional Responses to Child Sexual Abuse," (Australia2017).

764 Bazyler and Tuerkheimer, *Forgotten Trials of the Holocaust*, 306-7.

765 Bettelheim, *Surviving the Holocaust*, 120.

766 Ibid.

767 Ibid.

768 Bazyler and Tuerkheimer, *Forgotten Trials of the Holocaust*, 306.

769 Ibid.

770 Bettelheim, *Surviving the Holocaust*, 199.

771 Ibid.

772 United States Holocaust Memorial Museum, http://www.ushmm.org/research/center/encyclopedia/.

773 Claims Conference, "New Survey by Claims Conference Finds Significant Lack of Holocaust Knowlege in the United States," Claims Conference, http://www.claimscon.org/study/.

774 Körber Foundation, "Germans Want to Learn from History," Körber Foundation, www.korberfoundation-stiftung/de.

775 BBC, "Holocaust Memorial Day: 'Shocking' Levels of Denial Remain," BBC, www.bbc.com/news/uk-47015184.

776 Claims Conference, "New Survey by the Azrieli Foundation and the Claims Conference Finds Critical Gaps in Holocaust Knowledge," Claims Conference, www.claimscon.org/study-canada; Karen Zraick, "Many Canadians Lack Basic Knowledge About the Holocaust, Study Finds.," New York Times, www.nytimes.com/2019/01/24/world/canada/canadians-holocaust.html.

777 Bazyler and Tuerkheimer, *Forgotten Trials of the Holocaust*, 41.

778 Hogan and Aretha, *The Holocaust Chronicle*, 699.

779 Ibid., 682.

780 Leipciger, *The Weight of Freedom*, 238.

781 Ibid., 238-41.

782 Bazyler and Tuerkheimer, *Forgotten Trials of the Holocaust*, 43.

783 Hogan and Aretha, *The Holocaust Chronicle*, 702.

784 Mailander, *Female SS Guards and Workaday Violence: The Majdanek Concentration Camp, 1942-1944*, 13.

785 Ibid., 21-2.

786 Ibid.

787 Hogan and Aretha, *The Holocaust Chronicle*, 677.

788 Jacob Dolinger, *The Case for Closing the UN: International Human Rights: A Study in Hypocracy* (Jerusalem, New York: Gefen, 2016), 98-9; Bazyler and Tuerkheimer, *Forgotten Trials of the Holocaust*, 45; Yad

Vashem, "The Holocaust in France," Yad Vashem, www.yadvashem.org/yv/en/holocaust/france/deportations.asp.- 11.000

789 Hogan and Arctha, *The Holocaust Chronicle*, 686.

790 BBC, "Holocaust: Dutch Pm Apologises over Failure to Protect Jews," BBC, www.bbc.com/news/world-europe-5128081; DW, "Netherlands Aplogizes for WWII Persecution of Jews for First Time," DW, www.dw.com/en/netherlands-apologizes-for-wwii-persecution-of-jews-for-first-time-52155867.

791 Boaz Cohen, "Setting the Agenda of Holocaust Research: Discord at Yad Vashem in the 1950's," in *Holocaust Historiography in Context: Emergence, Challenges, Polemics and Achievements*, ed. David Bankier and Dan Michman (Jerusalem: Yad Vashem and Berghahn Books, 2008), 270, note 4.

792 Mark Dworzecki, "To Ignore or to Tell the Truth," *Bein ha-betarim* (10 June 1945): 28-9.

793 Cohen, "Setting the Agenda of Holocaust Research: Discord at Yad Vashem in the 1950's," 270, note 4.

794 Ibid., 270.

795 Ibid.

796 Ibid., 270, 60 note 11.

797 Ibid., 270, note 44.

798 Lawrence Langer, *Admitting the Holocaust: Collected Essays* (Oxford: Oxford University Press, 1995), 5-6, 26-32.

799 Chalmers, *Birth, Sex and Abuse: Women's Voices under Nazi Rule*, 254-6; Shulamit Imber, "The Educational Philosophy of the International School for Holocaust Studies," in *International Seminar for Educators* (Jerusalem2009).

800 Bettelheim, *Surviving the Holocaust*, 137.

801 Sean Fein, "The Robin Camp Transcript: "... Keep Your Knees Together' and Other Key Passages," *The Globe and Mail* 2017.

802 Ibid.

803 US Review of Books, "Review: Birth, Sex and Abuse: Women's Voices under Nazi Rule," http://www.theusreview.com/USRhoffer.html#lnfic; M Grodin, "Review: Birth, Sex and Abuse: Women's Voices under Nazi Rule " *Modern Judaism* (2015); Open History, "Review of Birth, Sex and Abuse: Women's Voices under Nazi Rule by Beverley Chalmers ". www.openhistory.it/index.php/it/67-libri/shoah/677-beverley-chalmers-birth-sex-and-abuse-women-s-voices-under-nazi-rule-grosvenour-house-guilford-2015; M W Posner, "Review: Birth, Sex and Abuse: Women's Voices under Nazi Rule.," www.jewishbookcouncil.org/book/birth-sex-and-abuse-womens-voices-under-nazi-rule. ; R E Silverman, "Review: Birth, Sex and Abuse: Women's Voices under Nazi Rule " *Women in Judaism: A Multidisciplinary Journal* 12, no. 1 (2016); H Smith, 7th

August, 2017, https://wienerlibrary.co.uk/Blog?item=255&returnoff set=30; G Winston, "The Full Horror of the Nazis Treatment of Women Is Explored in This Important Book.," https://www.warhistoryonline.com/ featured/nazi-brutalization-womens-bodies-discovered-groundbreaking-study.html.

804 Beverley Chalmers, "Beverley Chalmers," www.bevchalmers.com.

805 Michelle Mouton, "Mouton on Chalmers: Birth, Sex and Abuse: Women's Voices under Nazi Rule," H-German, http://www.h-net.org/reviews/ showrev.php?id=46348.

806 Bazyler and Tuerkheimer, *Forgotten Trials of the Holocaust*, 211.

807 Ibid., 195.

808 Primo Levi, *The Drowned and the Saved* (New York: Vintage International, 1989), 42.

809 Lawrence Langer, *Versions of Survival: The Holocaust and the Human Spirit* (New York: State University of New York Press, 1982), 72.

810 Bazyler and Tuerkheimer, *Forgotten Trials of the Holocaust*, 195.

811 Ibid., 202.

812 Ibid., 206.

813 Ibid.

814 Ibid., 205.

815 Na'ama Shik, ed. *Sexual Abuse of Jewish Women in Auschwitz-Birkenau*, Brutality and Desire: War and Sexuality in Europe's Twentieth Century (Houndsmills, Basingstoke, Hampshire: Palgrave Macmillan, 2009), 237.

816 Anton Gill, *The Journey Back from Hell: Conversations with Concentration Camp Survivors* (London: Grafton Books, 1988), 419.

817 Yvonne Kozlovsky-Golan, ""Public Property": Sexual Abuse of Women and Girls in Cinematic Memory," in *Sexual Violence against Jewish Women During the Holocaust*, ed. Sonja M Hedgepeth and Rochelle G Saidel (Waltham, Massachusetts: Brandeis University Press, 2010), 244-5.

818 Ayala H Emmet, *Our Sister's Promised Land: Women, Politics and Israeli-Palestinian Co-Existence* (Michigan: University of Michigan Press, 2003), 147.

819 Dan Porat, *Bitter Reckoning* (Cambridge, Massachusetts: Belknap Press of Harvard University Press, 2019), 1; Bazyler and Tuerkheimer, *Forgotten Trials of the Holocaust*, 209.

820 *Forgotten Trials of the Holocaust*, 209.

821 Ibid., 215.

822 Ibid., 197; Giorgio Agamben, *Remnants of Auschwitz: The Witness and the Archives. 2002, 170* (New York: Zone Books, 2002), 170.

823 Levi, *The Drowned and the Saved*, 42; Bazyler and Tuerkheimer, *Forgotten Trials of the Holocaust*, 216.

824 *Forgotten Trials of the Holocaust*, 217; Agamben, *Remnants of Auschwitz: The Witness and the Archives. 2002, 170*, 170.

825 Chalmers, *Birth, Sex and Abuse: Women's Voices under Nazi Rule*, 277-79.
826 Imber, "The Educational Philosophy of the International School for Holocaust Studies."
827 Porat, *Bitter Reckoning*, 214.
828 Ibid.
829 Ibid.
830 Leipciger, *The Weight of Freedom*, 260.
831 Steinfeldt, "Rescuers-Rescued Relations - What Can and Cannot Be Found in the Files of the Righteous among Nations," 57.
832 Beate Müller, "Framing the Family: Visual Material in the Holocaust Diaries About, for and by Children.," in *Hiding, Sheltering, and Borrowing Identities: Avenues of Rescue During the Holocaust*, ed. Dan Michman (Jerusalem: Yad Vashem, 2017), 282.
833 Steinfeldt, "Rescuers-Rescued Relations - What Can and Cannot Be Found in the Files of the Righteous among Nations," 64.
834 Ariel, "Turning to Christianity: Hiding Jews and Conversions During the Holocaust," 338.
835 Pukall, *Human Sexuality: A Contemporary Introduction*, 371.
836 Ibid.
837 Ibid.
838 Calcasa, "Pedophiles and Child Molesters: The Differences".
839 Pukall, *Human Sexuality: A Contemporary Introduction*, 371.
840 Eichengreen and Fromer, *Rumkowski and the Orphans of Lodz*, 16-7, 31-5, 41-3, 58, 80-3.
841 Lev-Wiesel and Weinger, *Hell within Hell: Sexually Abused Child Holocaust Survivors*, 33-9.
842 Dwork, *Children with a Star: Jewish Youth in Nazi Europe*, 80.
843 Rosen, *Such Good Girls: The Journey of the Holocaust's Hidden Child Survivors*, 228-9; Valent, "Early Abuse and Its Effects: Anne, a Holocaust and Sexual Abuse Survivor," 8.
844 Marks, *The Hidden Children: The Secret Survivors of the Holocaust*, 219.
845 Redner, "Testimony."
846 Wagschal.
847 Dwork and Pelt, *Holocaust: A History*, 350.
848 Lev-Wiesel and Weinger, *Hell within Hell: Sexually Abused Child Holocaust Survivors*, 45-6.
849 Stein, *Hidden Children: Forgotten Survivors of the Holocaust*, 33.
850 Dwork and Pelt, *Holocaust: A History*, 350.
851 Wolf, *Beyond Anne Frank: Hidden Children and Postwar Families in Holland*, 126-62.
852 Applebaum, *Buried Words: The Diary of Molly Applebaum*.
853 Lev-Wiesel and Weinger, *Hell within Hell: Sexually Abused Child Holocaust Survivors*, 62-3.

[854] Nechama Tec, *Dry Tears* (Oxford, UK: Oxford University Press, 1982), 139.

[855] Krall, *Chasing the King of Hearts*, 40.

[856] Avinum, *Rising from the Abyss*, 92-3.

[857] Bauman, *Winter in the Morning: A Young Girl's Life in the Warsaw Ghetto and Beyond.*, 106-7.

[858] Lev-Wiesel and Weinger, *Hell within Hell: Sexually Abused Child Holocaust Survivors*, 69-72.

[859] Inbar, *Spots of Light: To Be a Woman in the Holocaust*, 77.

[860] Podolsky, "The Tragic Fate of Ukrainian Jewish Women under Nazi Occupation, 1941-1944.," 99.

[861] Lev-Wiesel and Weinger, *Hell within Hell: Sexually Abused Child Holocaust Survivors*, 33-9.

[862] Hogan and Aretha, *The Holocaust Chronicle*, 442.

[863] Lev-Wiesel and Weinger, *Hell within Hell: Sexually Abused Child Holocaust Survivors*, 33-9.

[864] Chalmers, *Birth, Sex and Abuse: Women's Voices under Nazi Rule*, 9-13.

[865] Ernst Hiemer, *The Poisonous Mushroom* (Germany: Julius Streicher, 1938).

[866] Veit Harlan, "Jud Süß," (Germany: Terra-Filmkunst GmbH, 1934).

[867] Beverley Chalmers, "Sexual Villainy in the Holocaust," ed. Burcu Genc and Corinna Lenhardt, *Villains* (UK: Inter-Disciplinary Press, UK, 2011), http://www.inter-disciplinary.net/wp-content/uploads/2011/04/vav2 ever1050311.pdf.

[868] Kathryn Farr, *Sex Trafficking: The Global Market in Women and Children* (New York: Worth Publishers, 2005), 167.

[869] Rose, *Hiding Places*, 320-2.

[870] Pawlowicz, *I Will Survive*, 42.

[871] Scott Ronis, "Sexual Assault and Harassment," in *Human Sexuality*, ed. Caroline Pukall (Canada: Oxford University Press, , 2107), 416.

[872] Mishna, "Testimony."

[873] Levi, *The Drowned and the Saved*, 47.

[874] Bettelheim, *Surviving the Holocaust*, 133.

[875] Ibid., 133-35.

[876] Ombudsman, "The "Children of Duplessis" a Time for Solidarity."; Commission, *Honouring the Truth, Reconciling for the Future*; Government of Canada, "Report of Royal Commission on Aboriginal Peoples."; McClelland et al., "Royal Commission into Institutional Responses to Child Sexual Abuse."

[877] The Stationary Office, "Lost in Care: Report of the Tribunal of Inquiry into the Abuse of Children in Care in the Former County Council Aras of Gwynedd and Clwyd since 1974.," (Department of Health, Wales1999); Peter Mullen, "The Magdalene Sisters," (Ireland: PEP Films, 2002).

878 Milloy, *A National Crime: The Canadian Government and the Residential School System 1879-1986.*

879 Ibid.; Farr, *Sex Trafficking: The Global Market in Women and Children.*

880 WHO, *Global and Regional Estimates of Violence against Women: Prevalence and Health Effects of Intimate Partner Violence and Non-Partner Sexual Violence* (Geneva: World Health Organization, 2013).

881 Courtney Brooks and Amina Umarova, "Despite Official Measures,Bride Kidnapping Endemic in Chechnya," Radio Free Europe/Radio Liberty, www.rferl.org/a/Despite_Official_Measures_Bride_Kidnapping_Endemic_In_Chechnya/2197575.html.

882 Kristy Kirkup, "Senator Yvonne Boyer: Forced Sterilization of Indigenous Women Is Still Happening," HuffPost Canada; Yvonne Boyer and Judith Bartlett, "External Review: Tubal Ligation in the Saskatoon Health Region: The Lived Experience of Aboriginal Women," ed. Health Region Saskatoon (Canada2017).

883 Lev-Wiesel and Weinger, *Hell within Hell: Sexually Abused Child Holocaust Survivors*, 23.

884 Charles River Editors, *The Rape of Nanking* (San Bernadino, California: Charles River Editors, 2016).

885 Lev-Wiesel and Weinger, *Hell within Hell: Sexually Abused Child Holocaust Survivors*, 23.

886 Ibid.

887 UNICEF, "Together for Girls: Sexual Violence Fact Sheet," UNICEF, www.unicef.org/protection/files/Together-for-Girls-Sexual-Violence-Fact-Sheet-July2012.pdf.

888 Flaschka, "Race, Rape and Gender in Nazi-Occupied Territories," 177-209.

889 Ronis, "Sexual Assault and Harassment," 416.

890 Dante Alighieri, *The Divine Comedy* (UK: Everyman's Library, 1320).

891 William Shakespeare, *Julius Caesar*, vol. Act III, Scene II, Line 182 (London: Oxford University Press, 1952).

892 Desbois, *The Holocaust by Bullets:A Priest's Journey to Uncover the Truth Behind the Murder of 1.5 Million Jews*, 67.

893 Bauman, *Winter in the Morning: A Young Girl's Life in the Warsaw Ghetto and Beyond.*, 60-1.

894 Granirer, *Light within the Shadows: A Painter's Memoir*, 57.

895 (Erika*), "Testimony."

896 Lore, *Criminal Experiments on Human Beings in Auschwitz and War Research Laboratories: Twenty Women Prisoners' Accounts*, 78.

897 Braun, "Testimony."

898 (Anna*), "Testimony ".

899 (Dalia*), "Testimony."

900 Buchignani, *Tell No One Who You Are: The Hidden Childhood of Regine Miller*, 90.

901 Roland, *Life in the Third Reich: Daily Life in Nazi Germany 1933-1945*, 49-50.

902 Granirer, *Light within the Shadows: A Painter's Memoir*, 57.

903 Loew, "Testimony."

904 Boas, *We Are Witnesses: Five Diaries of Teenagers Who Died in the Holocaust*, 12-3.

905 Scheffer, "Testimony."

906 Lev-Wiesel and Weinger, *Hell within Hell: Sexually Abused Child Holocaust Survivors*, 69-72.

907 Rose, *Hiding Places*, 320-2.

908 Bikont, *The Crime and the Silence: Confronting the Massacre of Jews in Wartime Jedwabne*, 456.

909 Inbar, *Spots of Light: To Be a Woman in the Holocaust*, 77.

910 Apenszlak, *The Black Book of Polish Jewry: An Account of the Martyrdom of Polish Jewry*, 9.

911 (Vivi*), "Testimony."

912 Ringelheim, "Women and the Holocaust: A Reconsideration of Research.," 377.

913 (Aron*), "Testimony."

914 (Carla*), "Testimony."

915 Desbois, *The Holocaust by Bullets: A Priest's Journey to Uncover the Truth Behind the Murder of 1.5 Million Jews*, 83.

916 Palty, "Personal Testimony".

917 Mühlhäuser, "Between 'Racial Awareness' and Fantasies of Potencies: Nazi Sexual Politics in the Occupied Territories of the Soviet Union, 1942-1945," 199.

918 Podolsky, "The Tragic Fate of Ukrainian Jewish Women under Nazi Occupation, 1941-1944.," 99.

919 Nicholas, *Cruel World: The Children of Europe in the Nazi Web*, 430.

920 Gertjejanssen, "Victims, Heroes and Survivors: Sexual Violence on the Eastern Front During World War II," 308.

921 Kulski, *Dying, We Live*, 252.

922 Friedman, *Speaking the Unspeakable: Essays on Sexuality, Gender, and Holocaust Survivor Memory*, 59; Nutkiewicz, "Shame, Guilt, and Anguish in Holocaust Survivor Testimony," 1.

923 Tec, *Dry Tears*, 139.

924 Desbois, *In Broad Daylight: The Secret Procedures Behind the Holocaust by Bullets*, 71.

925 Ibid., 72.

926 Ibid., 152-3.

927 Adelson and Lapides, *Łódź Ghetto: Inside a Community under Siege*, 135-6.

928 Chalmers, *Birth, Sex and Abuse: Women's Voices under Nazi Rule*, 222.

929 Anonymous (Jacob*), "Testimony," (Israel: Ghetto Fighter's House Archives).

930 Berg, *The Diary of Mary Berg*, 13.

931 (Noam*), "Testimony."

932 Anonymous, "Testimony."

933 (Rita*), "Testimony."

934 Pawlowicz, *I Will Survive*, 42.

935 Krall, *Chasing the King of Hearts*, 32-3.

936 Herzberg Sia (nee Izrailewitsch), "Testimony."

937 Sinnreich, "The Rape of Jewish Women During the Holocaust," 112-4.

938 Ibid.

939 Bina W, "Testimony."

940 Boas, *We Are Witnesses: Five Diaries of Teenagers Who Died in the Holocaust*, 14; Sinnreich, "The Rape of Jewish Women During the Holocaust," 112-4.

941 Gabis, *A Guest at the Shooter's Banquet: My Grandfather's SS Past, My Jewish Family, a Search for the Truth*, 277.

942 Stein, *Hidden Children: Forgotten Survivors of the Holocaust*, 241-2.

943 Eichengreen and Fromer, *Rumkowski and the Orphans of Lodz*, 80-1.

944 Ibid., 58.

945 Ibid., 16, 41-3.

946 Ibid., 17.

947 Ibid., 31-5.

948 Fishman, *The Book Smugglers*, 147.

949 Grinston, "Testimony."

950 Gabis, *A Guest at the Shooter's Banquet: My Grandfather's SS Past, My Jewish Family, a Search for the Truth*, 385.

951 (Freda*), "Testimony."

952 Rachel Hanan, "Testimony," (USA: USC Shoah Foundation Institute for Visual History and Education Online Archive).

953 Reinitz and King, *Wrestling with Life: From Hungary to Auschwitz to Montreal*, 49.

954 Dora Goldstein Roth, "Testimony," (USA: USC Shoah Foundation Institute for Visual History and Education Online Archive).

955 Ritvo and Plotkin, *Sisters in Sorrow: Voices of Care in the Holocaust*, 45.

956 Lev-Wiesel and Weinger, *Hell within Hell: Sexually Abused Child Holocaust Survivors*, 29-30.

957 Stargardt, *Witnesses of War: Children's Lives under the Nazis.*, 217.

958 Erica Gold, "Testimony," (USA: USC Shoah Foundation Institute for Visual History and Education Online Archive).

959 Friedman, *Speaking the Unspeakable: Essays on Sexuality, Gender, and Holocaust Survivor Memory*, 53.

960 Sinnreich, "The Rape of Jewish Women During the Holocaust," 113.

961 Rosenberg, "Testimony."

962 Ibid.

963 (Hannah*), "Testimony."

964 Lev-Wiesel and Weinger, *Hell within Hell: Sexually Abused Child Holocaust Survivors*, 51.

965 (Leon*), "Testimony."

966 Reuter, "Testimony."

967 Ibid.

968 Smith, *Remembering: Voices of the Holocaust*, 178.

969 Ibid., 44.

970 (Frans*), "Testimony."

971 (Gunter*), "Testimony."

972 (Harry*), "Testimony."

973 Lustig, "Testimony."

974 Rowan, "Testimony."

975 Steinberg, "Testimony."

976 Holden, *Born Survivors*, 340.

977 Steinert, *Holocaust Und Zwangsarbeit: Erinnnerungen Jüdische Kinder 1938-1945*, 331-38.

978 Ibid.

979 Ibid., 335.

980 Ibid., 336-7.

981 Leipciger, *The Weight of Freedom*, 91-3,100.

982 Ressler, *Cry Little Girl: A Tale of the Survival of a Family in Slovakia*, 189.

983 Binzer, "Testimony."

984 Lagnado and Dekel, *Children of the Flames: Dr Josef Mengele and the Untold Story of the Twins of Auschwitz*, 70.

985 (Isaac*), "Testimony."

986 Koren and Negev, *In Our Hearts We Were Giants: The Remarkable Story of the Lilliput Group - a Dwarf Family's Survival of the Holocaust*, 171-2.

987 Ibid.

988 Lagnado and Dekel, *Children of the Flames: Dr Josef Mengele and the Untold Story of the Twins of Auschwitz*, 71.

989 Nomberg-Przytyk, *Auschwitz: True Tales from a Grotesque Land*, 90-1; Koren and Negev, *In Our Hearts We Were Giants: The Remarkable Story of the Lilliput Group - a Dwarf Family's Survival of the Holocaust*.

[990] Lev-Wiesel and Weinger, *Hell within Hell: Sexually Abused Child Holocaust Survivors*, 55.

[991] Allen, *The Fantastic Laboratory of Dr Weigl: How Two Brave Scientists Battled Typhus and Sabotaged the Nazis*, 209.

[992] Stein, *Hidden Children: Forgotten Survivors of the Holocaust*, 39.

[993] Holliday, *Children's Wartime Diaries: Secret Writings from the Holocaust and World War II*, 99-125.

[994] Wolf, *Beyond Anne Frank: Hidden Children and Postwar Families in Holland*, 126-62.

[995] (Boris*), "Testimony."

[996] Stein, *Hidden Children: Forgotten Survivors of the Holocaust*, 33.

[997] Wagschal.

[998] Lipiner, *Long Journey Home: A Young Girl's Memoir of Surviving the Holocaust*, 102-3.

[999] Dwork and Pelt, *Holocaust:A History*, 350.

[1000] Lev-Wiesel and Weinger, *Hell within Hell: Sexually Abused Child Holocaust Survivors*, 45-6.

[1001] Ringelheim, "The Split between Gender and the Holocaust," 342.

[1002] Lev-Wiesel and Weinger, *Hell within Hell: Sexually Abused Child Holocaust Survivors*, 33-9.

[1003] Rosen, *Such Good Girls: The Journey of the Holocaust's Hidden Child Survivors*, 228-9; Valent, "Early Abuse and Its Effects: Anne, a Holocaust and Sexual Abuse Survivor," 8.

[1004] Dwork, *Children with a Star: Jewish Youth in Nazi Europe*, 80.

[1005] Marks, *The Hidden Children: The Secret Survivors of the Holocaust*, 219.

[1006] Redner, "Testimony."

[1007] Lev-Wiesel and Amir, "Holocaust Child Survivors and Child Sexual Abuse," 69-83.

[1008] "Broken Silence."

[1009] Lessing, "Aging Child Holocaust Survivors of Sexual Abuse."

[1010] Bauman, *Winter in the Morning: A Young Girl's Life in the Warsaw Ghetto and Beyond.*, 106-7.

[1011] (Julia*), "Testimony."

[1012] (Carl*), "Testimony."

[1013] (Lula*), "Testimony."

[1014] (Petra*), "Testimony."

[1015] (Nona*), "Testimony."

[1016] Lev-Wiesel and Weinger, *Hell within Hell: Sexually Abused Child Holocaust Survivors*, 60.

[1017] Applebaum, *Buried Words: The Diary of Molly Applebaum*, xxvi-xxvii.

[1018] Ibid.

[1019] (Ora*).

[1020] Bart, *The Cut out Girl*, 187-8, 95.

1021 Okonowski, "Appointment in Samarra: The Diary of a Jew in Hiding in Warsaw."

1022 Bauman, *Winter in the Morning: A Young Girl's Life in the Warsaw Ghetto and Beyond.*, 106-7.

1023 Krall, *Chasing the King of Hearts*, 40.

1024 (Mona*), "Testimony."

1025 Avinum, *Rising from the Abyss*, 92.

1026 Tec, *Defiance*, 81-9.

1027 Medvin, "Testimony."

1028 Mishna, "Testimony."

1029 Kempfner, "Testimony."

1030 Abrams, *Tenuous Threads*, 51.

1031 (Dovid*), "Testimony."

1032 (Eric*), "Testimony."

1033 (Katrina*), "Testimony."

1034 Wolf, *Beyond Anne Frank: Hidden Children and Postwar Families in Holland*, 4.

1035 Marks, *The Hidden Children: The Secret Survivors of the Holocaust*, 101; Rosen, *Such Good Girls: The Journey of the Holocaust's Hidden Child Survivors*, 140.

1036 Fogelman, "Sexual Abuse of Jewish Women During and after the Holocaust: A Psychological Perspective," 271-2.

1037 Stein, *Hidden Children: Forgotten Survivors of the Holocaust*, 196.

1038 Summers, *When the Children Came Home: Stories of Wartime Evacuees*, 266-7.

1039 Friedman, *Speaking the Unspeakable: Essays on Sexuality, Gender, and Holocaust Survivor Memory*, 63-4.

1040 (Stella*), "Testimony."

1041 Josephs and Bechhöfer, *Rosa's Child: The True Story of One Woman's Quest for a Lost Mother and a Vanished Past*, 43.

1042 Anonymous (Bella*), "Testimony," (USA: Shoah Foundation Visual History Archive, 1997).

1043 Harris and Oppenheimer, *Into the Arms of Strangers: Stories of the Kindertransport*, 210; Norton, *The Kindertransport: Contesting Memory*, 104.

1044 *The Kindertransport: Contesting Memory*, 321.

1045 Summers, *When the Children Came Home: Stories of Wartime Evacuees*, 250.

1046 Ibid., 269.

1047 Ibid., 274.

1048 Ibid., 276-79.

1049 Ibid.

1050 Ibid.

[1051] Ibid., 263-4.

[1052] Behr, *Almost a Childhood: Growing up among the Nazis*, 223.

[1053] Stargardt, *Witnesses of War: Children's Lives under the Nazis.*, 70-2.

[1054] Ibid., 125.

[1055] Bleuel, *Sex and Society in Nazi Germany*, 241.

[1056] Ibid.

BIBLIOGRAPHY

(Anna*), Anonymous. "Testimony ". USA: Shoah Foundation Visual History Archives 1997.

(Aron*), Anonymous. "Testimony." USA: Shoah Foundation Visual History Archive, 1997.

(Bella*), Anonymous. "Testimony." USA: Shoah Foundation Visual History Archive, 1997.

(Boris*), Anonymous. "Testimony." USA: Shoah Foundation Visual History Archive, 1998.

(Carl*), Anonymous. "Testimony." USA: Shoah Foundation Visual History Archive, 1995.

(Carla*), Anonymous. "Testimony." USA: Shoah Foundation Visual History Archive, 1998.

(Dalia*), Anonymous. "Testimony." USA: Shoah Foundation Visual History Archive, 1996.

(Dovid*), Anonymous. "Testimony." USA: Shoah Foundation Visual History Archive, 1997.

(Eric*), Anonymous. "Testimony." USA: Shoah Foundation Visual History Archive, 1995.

(Erika*), Anonymous. "Testimony." USA: Shoah Foundation Visual History Archive, 1997.

(Frans*), Anonymous. "Testimony." Israel: Beit Volim, Yad Vashem.

(Freda*), Anonymous. "Testimony." USA: Shoah Foundation Visual History Archive, 1995.

(Gunter*), Anonymous. "Testimony." Israel: Beit Volim, Yad Vashem.

(Hannah*), Anonymous. "Testimony." USA: Shoah Foundation Visual History Archive, 1998.

(Harry*), Anonymous. "Testimony." Israel: Ghetto Fighters House Archives, 1948.

(Irina*), Anonymous. "Testimony." USA: Shoah Foundation Visual History Archive, 1998.

(Isaac*), Anonymous. "Testimony." Israel: Ghetto Fighters House Archives.

(Jacob*), Anonymous. "Testimony." Israel: Ghetto Fighter's House Archives.

(Julia*), Anonymous. "Testimony." USA: Shoah Foundation Visual History Archive, 1997.

(Kai*), Anonymous. "Testimony." Israel: Ghetto Fighter's House Archives.

(Katrina*), Anonymous. "Testimony." USA: Shoah Foundation Visual History Archive, 1998.

(Leon*), Anonymous. "Testimony." Israel: Beit Volim, Yad Vashem.

(Lula*), Anonymous. "Testimony." Israel: Beit Volim, Yad Vashem.

(Mona*), Anonymous. "Testimony." Israel Beit Volim, Yad Vashem.

(Noam*), Anonymous. "Testimony." Israel: Ghetto Fighters House Archive.

(Nona*), Anonymous. "Testimony." Israel: Beit Volim, Yad Vashem.

(Ora*), Anonymous. 2017.

(Petra*), Anonymous. "Testimony." Israel: Beit Volim, Yad Vashem.

(Rita*), Anonymous. "Testimony." Israel: Ghetto Figher's House Archive.

(Stella*), Anonymous. "Testimony." Israel: Beit Volim, Tel Aviv.

(Tina*), Anonymous. "Testimony." Israel: Ghetto Fighter's House Archives.

(Ursula*), Anonymous. "Testimony." Israel: Ghetto Fighters House

(Vivi*), Anonymous. "Testimony." Israel: Ghetto Fighters House Archives, 1948 10 October.

Abella, Irving, and Harold Troper. *None Is Too Many: Canada and the Jews of Europe 1933-1948*. Toronto: Key Porter Books 1983.

Abrams, Judy. *Tenuous Threads*. Canada: Azrieli Foundation 2012.

Abrams, Judy, and Evi Blaikie. *Remember Us: A Collection of Memories Form Hungarian Hidden Children of the Holocaust*. Bloomington, Indiana: Authorhouse, 2010.

Adelsberger, Lucie. *Auschwitz: A Doctor's Story*. Boston: Northeastern University Press, 1995.

Adelson, Alan, and Robert Lapides, eds. *Lódź Ghetto: Inside a Community under Siege*. New York: Viking, 1989.

Agamben, Giorgio. *Remnants of Auschwitz: The Witness and the Archives. 2002, 170.* New York: Zone Books, 2002.

Alighieri, Dante. *The Divine Comedy.* UK: Everyman's Library, 1320.

Allen, Arthur. *The Fantastic Laboratory of Dr Weigl: How Two Brave Scientists Battled Typhus and Sabotaged the Nazis.* New York: W W Norton and Co, 2014.

Anonymous. "Buchenwald Concentration Camp Atrocities " www. scrapbookpages.com/Buchenwald/Atrocities.html.

———. "The Story of the Children of Bullenhuser Damm." http:// www.kinder-vom-bullenhuser-damm.de/_english/the_story. html

Anonymous, (Two Sisters*). "Testimony." Israel: Ghetto Fighters House Archive.

Apenszlak, Jacob, ed. *The Black Book of Polish Jewry: An Account of the Martyrdom of Polish Jewry.* New York: Roy Publishers, 1943.

Applebaum, Molly. *Buried Words: The Diary of Molly Applebaum.* Canada: The Azrieli Foundation, 2017.

Ariel, Yaakov. "Turning to Christianity: Hiding Jews and Conversions During the Holocaust." In *Hiding, Sheltering, and Borrowing Identities: Avenues of Rescue During the Holocaust,* edited by Dan Michman, 311-42. Jerusalem: Yad Vashem, 2017.

Avinum, Sara. *Rising from the Abyss.* Israel: Astrolog Publishing, 2005.

Bart, van Es. *The Cut out Girl.* USA: Penguin Books, 2019.

Bartov, Omer. *Anatomy of a Genocide: The Life and Death of a Town Called Buczacz.* New York: Simon and Schuster, 2018.

Bauer, Elvira. *Trau Keinem Fuchs Auf Grüner Heid Und Keinem Jud Auf Seinem Eid (Don't Trust a Fox in a Green Meadow or the Word of a Jew).* Nuremberg: Stürmer Verlag, 1936.

Bauer, Yehuda. "Jewish Resistance and Passivity in the Face of the Holocaust." In *Unanswered Question,* edited by Francois Furet. New York: Schocken Books, 1989.

Bauman, Janina. *Winter in the Morning: A Young Girl's Life in the Warsaw Ghetto and Beyond.* London, Great Britain: Virago Press, 1991.

Baumslag, Naomi. *Murderous Medicine.* Washington DC: Baumslag, 2014.

Bazyler, Michael J, and Frank M Tuerkheimer. *Forgotten Trials of the Holocaust.* New York: New York University Press, 2014.

BBC. "Holocaust Memorial Day: 'Shocking' Levels of Denial Remain." BBC, www.bbc.com/news/uk-47015184.

————. "Holocaust: Dutch Pm Apologises over Failure to Protect Jews." BBC, www.bbc.com/news/world-europe-5128081.

BBC. "Larry Nassar Jailed for Another 40-125 Years." BBC, www.bbc.com/news/world-us-canada-42950478.

Beck, B. *Wehrmacht Und Sexuelle Gewalt: Sexualverbrechen Von Deutschen Militärgerichten 1939-1945.* Munich, Vienna and Zurich Paderborn, 2004.

Behr, Hans-Georg. *Almost a Childhood: Growing up among the Nazis.* London: Granta Books, 2005.

Benhamon, Rebecca. "Jewish Children Hidden Twice over by the Church." Times of Israel, www.timesofisrael.com/jewish-children-hidden-twice-over-by-the-church.

Benigni, Roberto. "Life Is Beautiful ", 116 minutes. Italy: Miramax Films, 1997.

Berg, Mary. *The Diary of Mary Berg.* Oxford: Oneworld, 1945, 2007.

Bettelheim, Bruno. *Surviving the Holocaust.* London: Fontana Paperbacks, 1986.

Bikont, Anna. *The Crime and the Silence: Confronting the Massacre of Jews in Wartime Jedwabne.* New York: Farrar, Straus and giroux, 2004.

Bina W. "Testimony." USC Shoah Foundation Institute for Visual History and Education Online Archive.

Binfold, Mira Reym. "Diamonds in the Snow." 59 minutes. Brandeis University, USA: National Centre for Jewish Film, 1994.

Binzer, Irene. "Testimony." USA: USC Shoah Foundation Institute for Visual History and Education Online Archive.

Black, Edwin. *Nazi Nexus: America's Corporate Connections to Hitler's Holocaust.* Washington D C: Dialog Press, 2009.

Bleuel, Hans Peter. *Sex and Society in Nazi Germany.* Philadelphia: J.B.Lipincott Company, 1971.

Boas, Jacob. *We Are Witnesses: Five Diaries of Teenagers Who Died in the Holocaust.* New York: Scholastic Inc, 1996.

Bogner, Nahum. *At the Mercy of Strangers: The Rescue of Jewish Children with Assumed Identities in Poland.* Jerusalem: Yad Vashem, 2009.

Bourke, Joanna. "Police Surgeons and Sexual Violence: A History." *The Lancet* 390, no. 10094 (2017): 548-49.

Boyer, Yvonne, and Judith Bartlett. "External Review: Tubal Ligation in the Saskatoon Health Region: The Lived Experience of

Aboriginal Women." edited by Health Region Saskatoon. Canada, 2017.

Braun, Shari. "Testimony." USC Shoah Foundation Institute for Visual History and Education Online Archive.

"Broken Silence." edited by James Moll, 4hrs 43 mins. USA: Survivors of the Shoah Visual History Foundation, 2004.

Brooks, Courtney, and Amina Umarova. "Despite Official Measures, Bride Kidnapping Endemic in Chechnya." Radio Free Europe/ Radio Liberty, www.rferl.org/a/Despite_Official_Measures_ Bride_Kidnapping_Endemic_In_Chechnya/2197575.html.

Browning, Christopher. *Ordinary Men: Reserve Police Battalion 101 and the Final Solution in Poland.* New York: Harper Perennial, 1992.

Buchignani, Walter. *Tell No One Who You Are: The Hidden Childhood of Regine Miller.* Ontario, Canada: Tundra Books, 1994.

Buergenthal, Thomas. *A Lucky Child: A Memoir of Surviving Auschwitz as a Young Boy.* New York: Basck Bay Books, 2007.

Burleigh, Michael. "Nazi "Euthanasia" Programs." In *Deadly Medicine: Creating the Master Race,* edited by Dieter Kuntz, 127-53. Washington: United States Holocaust Memorial Museum, 2008.

Calcasa. "Pedophiles and Child Molesters: The Differences." www. calcasa.org/wp-content/uploads/2007/11/pedophiles-and-child-molesters.doc.

Canada's Human Rights History. "Duplessis Orphans." https:// historyofrights.ca/encyclopaedia/main-events/duplessis-orphans/.

Chalmers, Beverley. "Beverley Chalmers." www.bevchalmers.com.

———. *Birth, Sex and Abuse: Women's Voices under Nazi Rule.* UK: Grosvenor House Publishers, 2015.

———. "Sexual Villainy in the Holocaust." In *Villains,* edited by Burcu Genc and Corinna Lenhardt UK: Inter-Disciplinary Press, UK, 2011. http://www.inter-disciplinary.net/wp-content/ uploads/2011/04/vav2ever1050311.pdf.

———. "What Should International Health Consultants Know?". *Bulletin of the World Health Organization* 77 (1999): 97.

Chalmers, Dana Lori. "The Influence of Theatre and Paratheatre on the Holocaust." Masters Thesis, Concordia University, 2008.

Charles River Editors. *The Rape of Nanking.* San Bernadino, California: Charles River Editors, 2016.

Chelouche, Tessa, Geoffrey Brahmer, and Susan Benedict. *Casebook on Bioethics and the Holocaust.* Israel: Unesco Chair in Bioethics, 2013.

Chiger, Krystyna, and Daniel Paisner. *The Girl in the Green Sweater.* New York: St Martin's Griffin, 2008.

Claims Conference. "New Survey by Claims Conference Finds Significant Lack of Holocaust Knowlege in the United States." Claims Conference, http://www.claimscon.org/study/.

Cohen, Boaz. "The Children's Voice: Postwar Collection of Testimonies from Child Survivors of the Holocaust." *Holocaust and Genocide Studies* 21, no. 1 (2007): 73-95.

———. "Setting the Agenda of Holocaust Research: Discord at Yad Vashem in the 1950's." In *Holocaust Historiography in Context: Emergence, Challenges, Polemics and Achievements,* edited by David Bankier and Dan Michman, 255-92. Jerusalem: Yad Vashem and Berghahn Books, 2008.

Cohen, Shimon. 39 May 2017.

Commission, Truth and Reconciliation. *Honouring the Truth, Reconciling for the Future.* Canada: Government of Canada, 2015.

Conference, Claims. "New Survey by the Azrieli Foundation and the Claims Conference Finds Critical Gaps in Holocaust Knowledge." Claims Conference, www.claimscon.org/study-canada.

Cornwell, John. *Hitler's Scientists: Science, War and the Devil's Pact.* New York: Viking, 2003.

Crum, Bartley C. *Behind the Silken Curtain: A Personal Account of Anglo-American Diplomacy in Palestine and the Middle East.* New York: Simon and Schuster, 1947.

Dadrian, V. "Armenian Children Victims of Genocide." http://www.genocide-museum.am/eng/online_exhibition_3.php.

Del Duca, Gemma "The Vatican and the Shoah: Post-Holocaust Catholic Theology." In *International Seminar for Educators.* The International School for Holocaust Studies, Jerusalem, Israel: Yad Vashem, 2009.

deMuse, Lloyd. "The Childhood Origins of the Holocaust." Klagenfurth University, Austria, 2005.

Desbois, Father Patrick. *The Holocaust by Bullets:A Priest's Journey to Uncover the Truth Behind the Murder of 1.5 Million Jews.* New York: Palgrave, Macmillan, 2008.

Desbois, Father Patrick. *In Broad Daylight: The Secret Procedures Behind the Holocaust by Bullets.* New York: Arcade Publishing, 2015.

Dickens, Charles. *Dombey and Son.* UK: Wordsworth Classics, 1995.

Dobroszycki, Lucjan, ed. *The Chronicle of the Lodz Ghetto 1942-1943.* New Haven: Yale University Press 1984.

Dolinger, Jacob. *The Case for Closing the UN: International Human Rights: A Study in Hypocracy.* Jerusalem, New York: Gefen, 2016.

Donat, Alexander. *The Holocaust Kingdom: A Memoir.* New York: Holt, Rinehart and Winston, 1965.

DW. "Netherlands Aplogizes for WWII Persecution of Jews for First Time." DW, www.dw.com/en/netherlands-apologizes-for-wwii-persecution-of-jews-for-first-time-52155867.

DW.Com. "Former Nazi Pedophile Nabbed in Argentina." DW.COM, http://m.dw,com/en/former-nazi-pedophile-nabbed-in-argentina/a-1515223.

Dwork, Deborah. *Children with a Star: Jewish Youth in Nazi Europe.* New Haven: Yale University Press, 1991.

Dwork, Deborah, and Robert Jan van Pelt. *Holocaust:A History.* New York: W.W. Norton and Company, 2003.

Dworzecki, Mark. "To Ignore or to Tell the Truth." [In Hebrew]. *Bein ha-betarim* (10 June 1945): 28-29.

Eichengreen, Lucille. *Haunted Memories: Portraits of Women in the Holocaust.* Exeter, New Haven: Publishing Works Inc, 2011.

Eichengreen, Lucille, and Harriet Hyman Chamberlain. *From Ashes to Life: My Memories of the Holocaust.* San Fransisco: Mercury House, 1994.

Eichengreen, Lucille, and Rebecca Camhi Fromer. *Rumkowski and the Orphans of Lodz.* San Fransisco, : Mercury-House, 2000.

Eisenberg, Azriel. *The Lost Generation: Children in the Holocaust.* New York: The Pilgrim Press, 1982.

Elias, Ruth. *Triumph of Hope: From Theresienstadt and Auschwitz to Israel.* Translated by Margot Bettauer Dembo. New York: John Wiley and Sons, 1988.

Emmet, Ayala H. *Our Sister's Promised Land: Women, Politics and Israeli-Palestinian Co-Existence.* Michigan: University of Michigan Press, 2003.

Erika, G. "Testimony." Los Angeles: Survivors of the Shoah Visual History Foundation, 14 February 1997.

Evans, Richard J. *The Third Reich at War.* New York: The Penguin Press, 2009.

———. *The Third Reich in Power.* USA: Penguin Books, 2006.

Farr, Kathryn. *Sex Trafficking: The Global Market in Women and Children.* New York: Worth Publishers, 2005.

Fein, Sean. "The Robin Camp Transcript: "... Keep Your Knees Together' and Other Key Passages." *The Globe and Mail,* 2017.

Fishman, David E. *The Book Smugglers.* USA: University Press of New England, 2017.

Flaschka, Monika J. "Race, Rape and Gender in Nazi-Occupied Territories." Kent State University, USA, 2009.

Fogelman, Eva. "Sexual Abuse of Jewish Women During and after the Holocaust: A Psychological Perspective." In *Sexual Violence against Jewish Women During the Holocaust,* edited by Sonja M Hedgepeth and Rochelle G Saidel, 255-74. Waltham, Massachusetts: Brandeis University Press, 2010.

Freidlander, Henry. "From "Euthanasia" to the "Final Solution"." In *Deadly Medicine*, edited by Dieter Kuntz, 155-83. Washington: United States Holocaust Memorial Museum, 2008.

Friedman, Jonathan. *Speaking the Unspeakable: Essays on Sexuality, Gender, and Holocaust Survivor Memory.* Lanham: University Press of America, 2002.

———. "Togetherness and Isolation: Holocaust Survivor Memories of Intimacy and Sexuality in the Ghettos." *The Oral History Review* 28, no. 1 (2001): 1-16.

Gabis, Rita. *A Guest at the Shooter's Banquet: My Grandfather's SS Past, My Jewish Family, a Search for the Truth.* New York: Bloomsbury, 2015.

Gelissen, Rena Kornreich. *Rena's Promise: A Story of Two Sisters in Auschwitz.* London: Weidenfeld and Nicolson, 1996.

Gershoff, E T, and A Grogan-Kaylor. "Spanking and Child Outcomes: Old Controversies and New Meta-Analyses." *Journal of Family Psychology* 30 (2016): 453-69.

Gertjejanssen, Wendy Jo. "Victims, Heroes and Survivors: Sexual Violence on the Eastern Front During World War II." University of Minnesota, 2004.

Gidron, Noa. 9 May 2019.

Gill, Anton. *The Journey Back from Hell: Conversations with Concentration Camp Survivors.* London: Grafton Books, 1988.

Gillis-Carlebach, Miriam. *Each Child Is My Only One: Lotte Carlebach-Preuss, the Portrait of a Mother and Rabbi's Wife.* New York: Peter Lang, 2014.

Glass, James M. *Life Unworthy of Life: Racial Phobia and Mass Murder in Hitler's Germany.* New York: Basic Books, 1997.

Gold, Erica. "Testimony." USA: USC Shoah Foundation Institute for Visual History and Education Online Archive.

Goldberg, Adara. *Holocaust Survivors in Canada: Exclusion, Inclusion, Transformation, 1947-1955.* Winnipeg: University of Manitoba, 2015.

Goldhagen, Daniel Jonah. *Hitler's Willing Executioners: Ordinary Germans and the Holocaust.* New York: Vintage Books, 1997.

Government of Canada. "Report of Royal Commission on Aboriginal Peoples." Ottawa, ON: Government of Canada, 2006.

Granirer, Pnina. *Light within the Shadows: A Painter's Memoir.* Vancouver, Canada: Granville Island Publishing, 2017.

Grinston, Eva. "Testimony." USA: USC Shoah Foundation Institute for Visual History and Education Online Archive.

Grodin, M. "Review: Birth, Sex and Abuse: Women's Voices under Nazi Rule ". *Modern Judaism* (2015).

Gross, Jan T. *Neighbours: The Destruction of the Jewish Community in Jedwabne, Poland, 1941.* London: Random House, 2003.

Gutman, Israel, ed. *Encyclopedia of the Holocaust.* New York: Macmillan Publishing Company, 1990.

Haas, Albert. *The Doctor and the Damned.* New York: St Martin's Press, 1984.

Hanan, Rachel. "Testimony." USA: USC Shoah Foundation Institute for Visual History and Education Online Archive.

Hannah Lévy-Haas. *Inside Belsen.* Sussex, UK: Harvester Press, 1982.

Harlan, Veit. "Jud Süß." 197 minutes. Germany: Terra-Filmkunst GmbH, 1934.

Harris, Mark Jonathan, and Deborah Oppenheimer. *Into the Arms of Strangers: Stories of the Kindertransport.* London: Bloomsbury Publishing, 2000.

Harris, Michael. *Unholy Orders: Tragedy at Mount Cashel.* Toronto: Penguin Books, 1990.

Heberer, Patricia. *Children During the Holocaust.* Lanham, USA: Rowman and Littlefield, 2011.

Heger, Heinz. *The Men with the Pink Triangle.* New York: Alyson Books, 1980.

Heifetz, Julie. *Too Young to Remember.* Detroit: Wayne State University Press, 1989.

Heineman, Elizabeth. "Sexuality and Nazism: The Doubly Unspeakable?". *Journal of the History of Sexuality* 11, no. 1/2 (Jan-Apr 2002): 22-66.

Heller, Sabina. *Locked in the Darkness: Retrieving a Hidden Girl's Identity from the Holocaust.* New York, Jerusalem: Yad Vashem and the Holocaust Survivors' Memoirs Project, 2012.

Hersonski, Yael. *A Film Unfinished.* Bell Films, 2010.

Hertzog, Esther. *Life, Death and Sacrifice: Women and Family in the Holocaust.* Jerusalem: Gefen Publishing House, 2008.

Herzberg Sia (nee Izrailewitsch). "Testimony." USA: USC Shoah Foundation Institute for Visual Histroy and Education On-Line Archive.

Herzog, Dagmar. "Hubris and Hypocrisy, Incitement and Disavowal: Sexuality and German Fascism.". *Journal of the History of Sexuality* 11, no. 1/2 (2002): 3-21.

Hiemer, Ernst. *The Poisonous Mushroom.* Germany: Julius Streicher, 1938.

Hilberg, Raul, Stanislaw Staron, and Josef Kermisz. *The Warsaw Diary of Adam Czerniakow: Prelude to Doom.* New York: Stein and Day, 1982.

Hilliard, Robert. *Surviving the Americans: The Continued Struggle of the Jews after Liberation.* New York: Seven Storied Press., 1997.

Hochberg-Marianska, Maria, and Noe Gruss. *The Children Accuse.* London: Vallentine Mitchell, 1996.

Hogan, David, and David Aretha, eds. *The Holocaust Chronicle.* Illinois: Publications International, 2001.

Holden, Wendy. *Born Survivors.* London: Sphere, 2015.

Holliday, Laurel. *Children's Wartime Diaries: Secret Writings from the Holocaust and World War II.* London: BCA, 1995.

Imber, Shulamit. "The Educational Philosophy of the International School for Holocaust Studies." In *International Seminar for Educators.* Jerusalem, 2009.

Inbar, Yehudit. *Spots of Light: To Be a Woman in the Holocaust.* Jerusalem: Yad Vashem, 2007.

"The Jewish Foundation for the Righteous". https://jfr.org/rescuer-support-program/.

Josephs, Jeremy, and Susi Bechhöfer. *Rosa's Child: The True Story of One Woman's Quest for a Lost Mother and a Vanished Past.* London: I B Tauris Publishers, 1996.

Ka-Tzetnik, 135633. *Atrocity.* New York: Lyle Stuart, 1963.

———. *House of Dolls.* London: Granada, 1973.

———. *Phoenix over the Galilee.* New York: Harper and Rowe, 1966.

———. *Piepel.* London: The New English Library, 1961.

———. *Shivitti: A Vision.* Gateways, 1989.

Kacer, Kathy. *Hiding Edith: A True Story.* London: A & C Black, 2009.

Katz, Esther, and Joan Miriam Ringelheim, eds. *Proceedings of the Conference Women Surviving the Holocaust,* Occasional Papers: The Institute for Research in History, 1983.

Kaufman, Lola Rein. *The Hidden Girl: A True Story of the Holocaust.* New York: Scholastic Inc, 2008.

Kempfner, Irene. "Testimony." USA: USC Shoah Foundation Institute for Visual History and Education Online Archive.

Kirkup, Kristy. "Senator Yvonne Boyer: Forced Sterilization of Indigenous Women Is Still Happening." HuffPost Canada.

Kirschner, Ann. *Sala's Gift: My Mother's Holocaust Story.* New York: Free Press, 2006.

Klug, Etien G, Linda L Dahlberg, James A Merry, Anthony B Zwi, and Rafael Lozano. "Child Abuse and Neglect by Parents and Other Caregivers." Chap. 3 In *World Report on Violence and Health,* 57-86. Geneva: World Health Organization, 2002.

Kogon, Eugen. *The Theory and Practice of Hell: The German Concentration Camps and the System Behind Them.* Translated by Heinz Norden. New York: Berkeley Books, 1950.

Kor, Eva Mozes. *Echoes from Auschwitz: Dr Mengele's Twins: The Story of Eva and Miriam Mozes.* New York: CANDLES, 2002.

Körber Foundation. "Germans Want to Learn from History." Körber Foundation, www.korberfoundation-stiftung/de.

Koren, Yehuda, and Eilat Negev. *In Our Hearts We Were Giants: The Remarkable Story of the Lilliput Group - a Dwarf Family's Survival of the Holocaust.* New York: Carroll and Graf Publishers, 2004.

Kozlovsky-Golan, Yvonne. ""Public Property": Sexual Abuse of Women and Girls in Cinematic Memory." In *Sexual Violence against Jewish Women During the Holocaust,* edited by Sonja M Hedgepeth and Rochelle G Saidel, 234-51. Waltham, Massachusetts: Brandeis University Press, 2010.

Krall, Hanna. *Chasing the King of Hearts.* London: Peirene Press, 2013.

Krüger, A, F Krüger, and S Treptau. "Nudism in Nazi Germany: Indecent Behaviour or Physical Culture for the Well-Being of the Nation." *The International Journal of the History of Sport* 19, no. 4 (2002): 33-54.

Kulski, Julian Eugeniusz. *Dying , We Live.* New York: Holt, Rinehart and Winston, 1979.

Kurzem, Mark. *The Mascot: The Extraordinary Story of a Jewish Boy and an SS Extermination Squad.* London: Rider, 2007.

Lagnado, Lucette Matalon, and Sheila Cohn Dekel. *Children of the Flames: Dr Josef Mengele and the Untold Story of the Twins of Auschwitz.* New York: William Morrow and Company, Inc, 1991.

Langer, Lawrence. *Admitting the Holocaust: Collected Essays.* Oxford: Oxford University Press, 1995.

———. *Holocaust Testimonies: The Ruins of Memory.* New Haven and London: Yale University Press, 1991.

———. *Versions of Survival: The Holocaust and the Human Spirit* New York: State University of New York Press, 1982.

Leipciger, Nate. *The Weight of Freedom.* Canada: Azrieli Foundation, 2015.

Lengyel, Olga. *Five Chimneys: A Woman Survivor's True Story of Auschwitz.* First Academy Chicago edition, 1995 ed. Chicago: Ziff-Davis Publishing Company, 1947.

Lessing, Carla. "Aging Child Holocaust Survivors of Sexual Abuse." In *Selfhelp Conference.* New York, 2012.

Lev-Wiesel, R., and M. Amir. "Holocaust Child Survivors and Child Sexual Abuse." *Journal of Sexual Abuse* 14, no. 2 (2005): 69-83.

Lev-Wiesel, Rachel, and Susan Weinger. *Hell within Hell: Sexually Abused Child Holocaust Survivors.* Lanham, Maryland: University Press of America, 2011.

Levi, Primo. *The Drowned and the Saved.* New York: Vintage International, 1989.

Libman, Feigie. Personal Communication, 16 May 2019.

Lifton, Robert Jay. *The Nazi Doctors: Medical Killing and the Psychology of Genocide.* New York: Basic Books, Inc, 1986.

Lipiner, Lucy. *Long Journey Home: A Young Girl's Memoir of Surviving the Holocaust.* New York: Usher Publishing, 2013.

Lipstadt, Deborah. "Introduction." In *Auschwitz: A Doctor's Story,* edited by Lucie Adelsberger. Boston: Northeastern University Press, 1995.

Lipszye, Rywka. *Rywka's Dairy: The Writings of a Jewish Girl from the Lodz Ghetto, Found at Auschwitz in 1945 and Published Seventy Years Later.* San Fransisco, USA: Jewish family and Children's Services of San Fransisco, 2015.

Llewellyn, J, J Southey, and S Thompson. "Children in Nazi Germany." Alpha History, alphahistory.com/nazigermany/children-in-nazi-germany.

Loew, Marion. "Testimony." USA: USC Shoah Foundation Institute for Visual History and Education.

Longerich, Peter. *Goebbels: A Biography.* New York: Random house, 2015.

Lore, Shelly. *Criminal Experiments on Human Beings in Auschwitz and War Research Laboratories: Twenty Women Prisoners' Accounts.* San Fransisco: Mellen Research University Press, 1991.

Lustig, Branko. "Testimony." USA: USC Shoah Foundation Institute for Visual History and Education Online Archive

Mahlendorf, Ursula. *The Shame of Survival; Working through a Nazi Childhood.* Pennysylvania: The Pennsylvania State University Press, 2009.

Mailander, Elissa. *Female SS Guards and Workaday Violence: The Majdanek Concentration Camp, 1942-1944.* East Lansing, USA: Michigan State University Press, 2015.

Mann, Erika. *School for Barbarians.* New York: Dover Publications, 2014. 1938.

Marks, Jane. *The Hidden Children: The Secret Survivors of the Holocaust.* Great Britain: Bantam Books, 1995.

Massuah Archivist. May 18 2017.

Mazower, Mark. *Dark Continent: Europe's Twentieth Century.* New York: Vintage Books, 1998.

McClelland, Peter, Jennifer Coate, Bob Atkinson, Robert Fitzgerald, Helen Milroy, Andrew Murray, and Gail Furness. "Royal Commission into Institutional Responses to Child Sexual Abuse." Australia, 2017.

Medvin, Brigitte. "Testimony." USA: USC Shoah Foundation Institute for Visual History and Education Online Archive.

Medykowski, Witold. "Modes of Survival, Techniques of Hiding and Relations with the Local Population: The Polish Case." In *Hiding, Sheltering, and Borrowing Identities: Avenues of*

Rescue During the Holocaust, edited by Dan Michman, 45-56. Jerusalem: Yad Vashem, 2017.

Michlic, Joanna Beata. "The Aftermath and After: Memories of Child Survivors of the Holocaust." In *Lessons and Legacies X: Back to the Sources: Reexamining Perpetrators, Victims and Bystanders*, edited by Sara Horowitz, 141-89. Evanston, Illinois: Northwestern University Press, 2012.

Milloy, John S. *A National Crime: The Canadian Government and the Residential School System 1879-1986*. Manitoba: University of Manitoba Press, 1999.

Milotte, Mike. *Banished Babies: The Secret History of Ireland's Baby Export Business*. Dublin: New Island, 2012.

Mishna, Hanna. "Testimony." USA: USC Shoah Foundation Institute for Visual History and Education Online Archive.

Moore, Bob. "The Structure of Rescue: Key Determinants in the Survival of Jews in Western Europe During the Holocaust." In *Hiding, Sheltering, and Borrowing Identities: Avenues of Rescue During the Holocaust*, edited by Dan Michman, 27-43. Jerusalem: Yad Vashem, 2017.

Moser, Brian. "The Search for Mengele." 80 minutes. USA: First Run Features, 1985.

Mouton, Michelle. "Mouton on Chalmers: Birth, Sex and Abuse: Women's Voices under Nazi Rule." H-German, http://www.h-net.org/reviews/showrev.php?id=46348.

Mühlhäuser, Regina. "Between 'Racial Awareness' and Fantasies of Potencies: Nazi Sexual Politics in the Occupied Territories of the Soviet Union, 1942-1945." In *Brutality and Desire: War and Sexuality in Europe's Twentieth Century*, edited by Dagmar Herzog, 197-219. Houndmills, Basingstoke, Hampshire: Pelgrave Macmillan, 2009.

Mullen, Peter. "The Magdalene Sisters." 111 minutes. Ireland: PEP Films, 2002.

Müller, Beate. "Framing the Family: Visual Material in the Holocaust Diaries About, for and by Children.". In *Hiding, Sheltering, and Borrowing Identities: Avenues of Rescue During the Holocaust*, edited by Dan Michman, 271-91. Jerusalem: Yad Vashem, 2017.

Naves, Elaine Kalman. *Shoshanna's Story: A Mother, a Daughter, and the Shadows of History*. Toronto: McClelland & Stewart, 2003.

Nicholas, Lynn H. *Cruel World: The Children of Europe in the Nazi Web.* New York: Vintage Books, 2006.

Niven, Bill. *The Buchenwald Child: Truth, Fiction and Propaganda.* New York: Camden House 2007.

Nomberg-Przytyk, Sara. *Auschwitz: True Tales from a Grotesque Land.* Chapel Hill: University of North Carolina Press, 1985.

Norton, Jennifer Craig-. *The Kindertransport: Contesting Memory.* Bloomington, Indiana: Indiana University Press, 2019.

Nutkiewicz, Michael. "Shame, Guilt, and Anguish in Holocaust Survivor Testimony." *The Oral History Review* 30, no. 1 (2003): 1-22.

Okonowski, Sewek. "Appointment in Samarra: The Diary of a Jew in Hiding in Warsaw." Israel: Ghetto Fighter's House Archive, 2017.

Olaka, Musa Wakhungu. "Living a Genocide: Rape." USF Tampa Library, http://exhibits.lib.usf.edu/exhibits/show/darfur-genocide/modeofdestruction/rape.

Ombudsman, Quebec. "The "Children of Duplessis" a Time for Solidarity." In *Assemblee Nationale Quebec.* Quebec, Janauary 22, 1997.

Opdyke, Irene Gut. *In My Hands: Memories of a Holocaust Rescuer.* New York: Dell Laurel Leaf, 1999.

Open History. "Review of Birth, Sex and Abuse: Women's Voices under Nazi Rule by Beverley Chalmers ". www.openhistory.it/index.php/it/67-libri/shoah/677-beverley-chalmers-birth-sex-and-abuse-women-s-voices-under-nazi-rule-grosvenour-house-guilford-2015.

Owings, Alison. *Frauen: German Women Recall the Third Reich.* London: Penguin Books, 1993.

Pakula, Alan. "Sophie's Choice." 151 mins. USA: Universal Pictures, 1982.

Palty, Sonia. "Personal Testimony." Nizkor Project, www.nizkor.org/hweb/people/c/carmelly-felicia/palty-sonia.html.

Paris, Erna. *Unhealed Wounds: France and the Klaus Barbie Affair.* Toronto: Methuen, 1985.

Pawlowicz, Sala. *I Will Survive.* New York: W W Norton and Company, Inc, 1962.

Perl, Gisella. *I Was a Doctor in Auschwitz.* Reprint edition 2007 ed. North Stratford, NH: Ayer Company Publishers, 1948.

Perl, Lila, and Marion Blumenthal Lazan. *Four Perfect Pebbles: A Holocaust Story.* New York: Scholastic Inc, 1996.

Podolsky, Anatoly. "The Tragic Fate of Ukrainian Jewish Women under Nazi Occupation, 1941-1944.". In *Sexual Violence against Jewish Women During the Holocaust*, edited by Sonja M Hedgepeth and Rochelle G Saidel, 94-107. Waltham, Massachusetts: Brandeis University Press, 2010.

Polak, Joseph. *After the Holocaust the Bells Still Ring.* Jerusalem: Urim Publications, 2015.

Porat, Dan. *Bitter Reckoning.* Cambridge, Massachusetts: Belknap Press of Harvard University Press, 2019.

Posner, Gerald L, and John Ware. *Mengele: The Complete Story.* New York: Cooper Square Press, 2000.

Posner, M W. "Review: Birth, Sex and Abuse: Women's Voices under Nazi Rule. ." www.jewishbookcouncil.org/book/birth-sex-and-abuse-womens-voices-under-nazi-rule. .

Pukall, Caroline, ed. *Human Sexuality: A Contemporary Introduction.* 2nd ed. Don Mills, Ontario: Oxford University Press, 2017.

Pukall, Caroline, ed. *Human Sexuality: A Contemporary Introduction* Don Mills, Ontario, Canada: Oxford University Press, 2014.

Raftery, Mary, and Eoin O'Sullivan. *Suffer the Little Children: The inside Story of Ireland's Industrial Schools.* Dublin, Ireland: New Island Books, 1999.

Redner, Lily. "Testimony." USA: USC Shoah Foundation Institute for Visual History and Education Online Archive.

Reichenberg, Efraim. "A Twin in Auschwitz." In *Yad Vashem International Holocaust Educators Seminar.* Jerusalem, 2009.

Reichental, Tomi. *I Was a Boy in Belsen.* Dublin: The O'Brien Press, 2011.

Reinitz, George, and Richard King. *Wrestling with Life: From Hungary to Auschwitz to Montreal.* Montreal: McGill-Queen's University Press, 2017.

Ressler, Aliza Barak-. *Cry Little Girl: A Tale of the Survival of a Family in Slovakia.* Jerusalem: Yad Vashem 2003.

Reuter, Julian. "Testimony." USA: USC Shoah Foundation Institute for Visual History and Education.

Ringelblum, Emanuel. *Ringelblumyoman Ve-Reshimot Mitkufat, Ha-Milhama [Diary and Notes from the Warsaw Ghetto: Sept 1939-December 1942].* Jerusalem: Yad Vashem, September 1939-December 1942.

Ringelheim, Joan. "The Split between Gender and the Holocaust." In *Women and the Holocaust*, edited by Dalia Ofer and Lenore

Weitzman, 340-50. New Haven: Yale University Press, 1998.

———. "Women and the Holocaust: A Reconsideration of Research.". In *Different Voices: Women and the Holocaust*, edited by Carol Rittner and John K Roth, 373-418. New York, 1993.

Ritvo, Roger A., and Diane M Plotkin. *Sisters in Sorrow: Voices of Care in the Holocaust*. College Station: Texas A & M University Press, 1998.

Roland, Pauk. *Life in the Third Reich: Daily Life in Nazi Germany 1933-1945*. London: Arcturus, 2016.

Ronis, Scott. "Sexual Assault and Harassment." In *Human Sexuality*, edited by Caroline Pukall, 413-43. Canada: Oxford University Press, 2107.

Rose, Daniel Asa. *Hiding Places*. New York: Simon and Schuster, 2000.

Rosen, R D. *Such Good Girls: The Journey of the Holocaust's Hidden Child Survivors*. New York: Harper Perenial, 2014.

Rosenberg, Eliahu. "Testimony." Israel: Ghetto Fighters House Archives.

Rosenberg, Maxine B. *Hiding to Survive: Stories of Jewish Children Rescued from the Holocaust*. New York: Clarion Books, 1994.

Rosenfeld, Sandra. "The Difficulties Involved in the Rescue of Chlldren by Non-Jews - before and after Liberation." The International School for Holocaust Studies, Yad Vashem, www.yadvashem. org/yv/en/education/newsletter/33/difficulties_involved.asp.

Roth, Dora Goldstein. "Testimony." USA: USC Shoah Foundation Institute for Visual History and Education Online Archive.

Rowan, Kenneth. "Testimony." USA: USC Shoah Foundation Institute for Visual History and Education Online Archive.

Ruvugiro, Emmanuel Sehene. "Rwanda: The Gruesome Plight of Children During the Tutsi Genocide." Justiceinfo.net, www. justiceinfo.net/en/tribunals/ictr/34925-online-exhibition-pays-gruesome-tribute-to-child-suffering-in-rwandan-genocide. html.

Ryan, Justice. "The Commission to Enquire into Child Abuse Report." Ireland, 2009.

Saidel, Rochelle G. *The Jewish Women of Ravensbrück Concentration Camp*. Madison, Wisconsin: The University of Wisconsin Press, 2004.

Samuel, Wolfgang W E. *The War of Our Childhood: Memories of World War II*. Jackson: University Press of Mississippi, 2002.

Sargent, Joseph. "Out of the Ashes." USA: Showtime Netwoks, 2004.

Scheffer, Maria. "Testimony." USA: USC Shoah Foundation Institute for Visual History and Education On-Line Archive.

Schwarberg, Gunther. *The Murders at Bullenhuser Damm.* Bloomington, USA: Indiana University Press, 1984.

Shachan, Avigdor. *Burning Ice: The Ghettos of Transnistria.* East European Monographs, Boulder. New York: Columbia Unversity Press, 1996.

Shaik, Gedaliah. "Biography: Abraham Cykiert (1926-2009)." Melbourne Chronicle, http://future.arts.monash.edu/yiddish-melbourne/biogrpahies-abraham-cykiert/.

Shakespeare, William. *Julius Caesar.* Vol. Act III, Scene II, Line 182, London: Oxford University Press, 1952.

Shik, Na'ama, ed. *Sexual Abuse of Jewish Women in Auschwitz-Birkenau.* Edited by Dagmar Herzog, Brutality and Desire: War and Sexuality in Europe's Twentieth Century. Houndsmills, Basingstoke, Hampshire: Palgrave Macmillan, 2009.

Sichrovsky, Peter. *Born Guilty: Children of Nazi Families.* London: I.B.Tauris and Co Ltd, 1988.

Silbert, Liza. "Testimony." USA: USC Shoah Foundation Institute for Visual History and Education.

Silverman, R E. "Review: Birth, Sex and Abuse: Women's Voices under Nazi Rule ". *Women in Judaism: A Multidisciplinary Journal* 12, no. 1 (2016): 1-4.

Sinnreich, Helene J. "The Rape of Jewish Women During the Holocaust." In *Sexual Violence against Jewish Women During the Holocaust,* edited by Sonja M Hedgepeth and Rochelle G Saidel, 108-23. Waltham, Massachusetts: Brandeis University Press, 2010.

Sivan, Miryam. "Stoning the Messenger: Yehiel Dinur's House of Dolls and Piepel." In *Sexual Violence against Jewish Women During the Holocaust,* edited by Sonja M Hedgepeth and Rochelle G Saidel, 200-16. Waltham, Massachusetts: Brandeis University Press, 2010.

Sixsmith, Martin. *Philomena: A Mother, Her Son and a Fifty-Year Search.* London: Pan Books, 2010.

Smith, Bradley E, and Agnes F Peterson. *Heinrich Himmler: Geheimreden 1933 Bis 1945* Frankfort1974.

Smith, H. "Review Of: Birth, Sex and Abuse: Women's Voices under Nazi Rule." Wiener Library Blog, 7th August, 2017.

Smith, Lyn. *Remembering: Voices of the Holocaust.* New York: Carroll and Graf Publishers, 2005.

Solomon, Dana. Personal Communication, 1 December 2019.

Spitz, Vivien. *Doctors from Hell: The Horrific Accounts of Nazi Experiments on Humans.* Boulder: Sentient Publications, 2005.

Stargardt, Nicholas. *Witnesses of War: Children's Lives under the Nazis.* London: Jonathan Cape, 2005.

Stein, Andre. *Hidden Children: Forgotten Survivors of the Holocaust.* Canada: Penguin Books, 1993.

Steinberg, Sam. "Testimony." USA: USC Shoah Foundation Institute for Visual History and Education Online Archive.

Steinert, Johannes-Dieter. *Holocaust Und Zwangsarbeit: Erinnnerungen Jüdische Kinder 1938-1945.* Essen: Klartext, 2018.

Steinfeldt, Irena. "Rescuers-Rescued Relations - What Can and Cannot Be Found in the Files of the Righteous among Nations." In *Hiding, Sheltering, and Borrowing Identities: Avenues of Rescue During the Holocaust,* edited by Dan Michman, 57-66. Jerusalem: Yad Vashem, 2017.

Summers, Julie. *When the Children Came Home: Stories of Wartime Evacuees.* London: Simon and Schuster, 2011.

Tec, Nechama. *Defiance.* Oxford: Oxford University Press, 2013.

———. *Dry Tears.* Oxford, UK: Oxford University Press, 1982.

———. *Resilience and Courage: Women, Men and the Holocaust.* New Haven: Yale University Press, 2003.

Terry, Erica. "Sexual Abuse and the Hidden Children of the Holocaust." www.jspacenews.com/sexual-abuse-hidden-children-holocaust.

The History Place. "Hitler's Boy Soldiers." The History Place, www.historyplace.com/worldwar2/hitleryouth/hj-boy-soldiers.htm.

———. "Stalin's Forced Famine: 1932-9133: 7,000,000 Deaths." The History Place, http://www.historyplace.com/worldhistory/genocide/stalin.htm.

The Stationary Office. "Lost in Care: Report of the Tribunal of Inquiry into the Abuse of Children in Care in the Former County Council Aras of Gwynedd and Clwyd since 1974.". Department of Health, Wales, 1999.

Theoret, Hugues. *The Blue Shirts: Adrien Arcand and Fascist Anti-Semitism in Canada.* Ottawa: University of Ottawa Press, 2017.

Thompson, Ann. *Say Sorry: A Harrowing Childhood in Catholic Orphanages.* Kindle, 2009.

Timm, Uwe. *In My Brother's Shadow.* London: Bloomsbury, 2005.

Tobias, Janet. "No Place on Earth." 83mins: Magnolia Pictures, 2012.

Tuchman, Marcel. *Remember: My Stories of Survival and Beyond.* New York, Jerusalem: Yad Vashem and the Holocaust Survivors Memoirs Project, 2010.

UNICEF. "Together for Girls: Sexual Violence Fact Sheet." UNICEF, www.unicef.org/protection/files/Together-for-Girls-Sexual-Violence-Fact-Sheet-July2012.pdf.

United Nations. "Outcomes on Children." http://www.un.org/en/development/devagenda/children.shtml.

United States Holocaust Memorial Museum. http://www.ushmm.org/research/center/encyclopedia/.

———. "Children During the Holocaust." USHMM, https://encyclopedia.ushmm.org/content/en/article/children-during-the-holocaust.

———. "The Holocaust Encyclopedia." encyclopedia.ushmm.org/content/en/article/ravensbrueck.

———. "Le Chambon-Sur-Lignon." USHMM, encyclopedia.ushmm.org/content/en/article/le-chambon-sur-lignon.

United States Holocaust Memorial Museum. "Plight of Jewish Children." USHMM, www.ushmm.org/wic/en/article.php?ModuleId=10006124.

United to End Genocide. "The Cambodian Genocide." United to End Genocide, http://endgenocide.org/learn/past-genocides/the-cambodian-genocide/.

US Government. "From Nazi Conspiracy and Aggression Volume VI." edited by Office of United States Chief counsel for Prosecution of Axis Criminality, 1100-03. USA: US Government Printing Office, 1946.

US Review of Books. "Review: Birth, Sex and Abuse: Women's Voices under Nazi Rule." http://www.theusreview.com/USRhoffer.html#lnfic.

Valent, Paul. *Child Survivors of the Holocaust.* New York and London: Bruner-Routledge, 2002.

———. "Early Abuse and Its Effects: Anne, a Holocaust and Sexual Abuse Survivor." In *Victoria Association of Psychotherapists Annual General Meeting.* Melbourne, Australia, 1995.

Vitelli, Romeo. "Angel-Makers, Baby-Killers - Take Your Pick." *Quaill Bell Magazine* (9 October 2013 2013).

Voigtländer, Nico, and Hans-Joachim Voth. "Nazi Indoctrination and Anti-Semitic Beliefs in Germany." *Proceedings of the National Academy of Sciences of the United States of America* 112, no. 26 (2015 June): 7931-36.

Vromen, Susanne. *Hidden Children of the Holocaust: Belgian Nuns and Their Daring Rescue of Young Jews from the Nazis.* New York: Oxford University Press, 2008.

Wagschal, Sabina. USC Shoah Foundation Institute for Visual History and Education Online Archive.

Weindling, Paul. *Victims and Survivors of Nazi Human Experiments: Science and Suffering in the Holocaust.* London: Bloomsbury Academic, 2015.

WHO. *Global and Regional Estimates of Violence against Women: Prevalence and Health Effects of Intimate Partner Violence and Non-Partner Sexual Violence.* Geneva: World Health Organization, 2013.

Wiesel, Elie. *Night.* New York: Hill and Wang, 1958.

Winston, G. "The Full Horror of the Nazis Treatment of Women Is Explored in This Important Book. ." https://www.warhistoryonline.com/featured/nazi-brutalization-womens-bodies-discovered-groundbreaking-study.html.

Wolf, Diane. *Beyond Anne Frank: Hidden Children and Postwar Families in Holland.* Berkeley, California: University of California Press, 2007.

Wolf, Lily. "Testimony." USA: USC Shoah Foundation Institute for Visual History and Education Online Archive.

Woolf, Alex. *Children of the Holocaust.* London: Franklin Wwatts, 2014.

Yad Vashem. "The Holocaust in France." Yad Vashem, www.yadvashem.org/yv/en/holocaust/france/deportations.asp.

———. "Rescue of Children." Yad Vashem, www.yadvashem.org/odot_pdf/Microsoft%20Word%20-%205820.pdf

Zapruder, Alexandra. *Salvaged Papers: Young Writers' Diaries of the Holocaust.* USA: Yale University Press, 2002.

Zraick, Karen. "Many Canadians Lack Basic Knowledge About the Holocaust, Study Finds." New York Times, www.nytimes.com/2019/01/24/world/canada/canadians-holocaust.html.

Zuccotti, Susan. *The Italians and the Holocaust: Persecution, Rescue, Survival.* New York: Basic Books, 1987.